Body Parts

A Theological Anthropology

MICHELLE VOSS ROBERTS

FORTRESS PRESS
MINNEAPOLIS

BODY PARTS
A Theological Anthropology

Excerpts from *Meister Eckhart: The Essential Sermons, Commentaries, Treatises, and
Defense,* from The Classics of Western Spirituality, translated and introduced by
Edmund Colledge and Bernard McGinn, Copyright 1981 by the Missionary Society
of St. Paul the Apostle in the State of New York, Paulist Press, Inc. New York/
Mahwah, N.J. Used with permission of Paulist Press. www.paulistpress.com.

This research was undertaken with support of a Summer Stipend award from the
National Endowment for the Humanities. Any views, findings, conclusions, or
recommendations expressed in this publication do not necessarily reflect those of the
National Endowment for the Humanities.

Cover image: Eurydice 2014 by artist Freya Jobbins © 2017 Artists Rights Society
(ARS), New York / VISCOPY, Australia
Cover design: Rob Dewey

Print ISBN: 978-1-5064-1856-8
eBook ISBN: 978-1-5064-1857-5

For My Students

Contents

Abbreviations   ix

A Note on Diacritics   xi

Acknowledgments   xiii

Preface   xvii

Introduction   xxiii

1. The Conscious Body   1
2. The Limited Body (Part 1)   29
3. The Limited Body (Part 2)   53
4. The Subjective Body   77
5. The Engaged Body   101
6. The Elemental Body   125

Epilogue: The Eschatological Body   151

Bibliography   159

Index   173

Abbreviations

PTv *Paratrisika-Vivarana*—long commentary on *The Goddess of the Three* by Abhinavagupta

PTlv *Paratrisika-laghuvrtti*—short commentary on *The Goddess of the Three*, traditionally attributed to Abhinavagupta

References to the Bible follow the New Revised Standard Version, unless otherwise noted.

A Note on Diacritics

Sanskrit words have been transliterated without the use of diacritical marks. For readers unfamiliar with the script, it may be helpful to know that Sanskrit has three different *s* sounds. The *s* in Siva, Sakti, and Saivism is pronounced "sh."

Acknowledgments

My context—teaching theology at Wake Forest University School of Divinity in Winston-Salem, North Carolina—has shaped this inquiry into the Christian metaphor of the image of God in humanity. Conversations with students and colleagues about my comparative theological work have urged me to write for a general Christian audience; and so I have chosen my sources, questions, and the manner in which I engage them with these readers in mind. My research leave in the spring of 2016 is one of the many ways my dean, Gail O'Day, has supported me. Several classes made a special mark on this project, especially my very first Introduction to Christian Theology classes in 2011 and 2012, and the Theology and Disability course I co-taught with Jill Crainshaw in 2015. Working in spaces of deep inquiry and shared theological discovery is a joy.

This project also benefited from conversations at conferences. I presented the kernel of the idea at the Gensler Symposium at Middlebury College in 2013. The framework of the "body parts" developed further through presentations at the Comparative Theology Group of the American Academy of Religion in San Diego, and the "Methods and Criteria for Comparative Theology" conference at the University of Paderborn, Germany, in 2014. In 2015, a National Endowment for the Humanities Summer Stipend award supported the writing of several chapters. My 2016 research leave allowed me to write and refine additional chapters for the Southeastern Commission for the Study of Religion conference in Atlanta, the "God or the Divine" conference at the University of Münster, Germany, and the "Symposium on Divinity and the Body," organized by Lenart Škof in Ljubljana, Slovenia. An early working version of my study of the *tattva*s appears in the volume that emerged from the Paderborn conference, *How to Do Comparative Theology*, edited by Francis X. Clooney and Klaus von Stosch, and I am grateful to both of them for their constructive feedback.[1]

I was fortunate to receive my scholarly training in places where comparative theological discussion was welcomed by both Indologists and Christian theologians. I remain grateful for colleagues in the field, especially those in the Society for Hindu-Christian Studies, who remain willing to explore these intersections with me. Even as the constructive turn I take in this work has raised a few Indological eyebrows, there have been scholars willing to help me to refine my comparative framework for this project—not least Cat Prueitt and John Nemec, whose expertise in non-dual Saivism and Abhinavagupta's works far exceeds my own. They have steered me well in important ways and pointed out some of the growing edges that I consider part of the ongoing, back-and-forth nature of comparative inquiry.

This book's constructive proposal owes much to my theology colleagues. Elizabeth Gandolfo's beautiful thinking and writing about God's vulnerability informs the sections on the limited body. Jill Crainshaw urged me to keep liturgical practices in play and to work out the implications of limitation for the subjective body in chapter 4. That chapter also benefitted from the generous and perspicacious attention of Lacey Hudspeth. The analysis of the elemental body took shape in dialogue with many of my WFUSD colleagues, particularly Mark Jensen. Every stage of the process was fueled by coffee with my indefatigable writing partner, Katherine Shaner. Susan Robinson made my life easier with administrative support, as did Mark Batten with technical expertise. Michael Gibson, my editor at Fortress Press, has been an invaluable partner in shaping the manuscript.

I also owe a debt of gratitude to my research assistants. Lindsey Mullen designed the chart of the body parts that accompanies each chapter. Jungwoo Park's attention to detail is evident in the

1. Michelle Voss Roberts, "Embodiment, Anthropology, and Comparison: Thinking-Feeling with Abhinavagupta," in *How to Do Comparative Theology*, ed. Francis X. Clooney and Klaus von Stosch (New York: Fordham University Press, 2017).

bibliography and notes. Laurie Kenyon is to be commended for her indexing prowess. This book is for them, and for their classmates at Wake Forest University School of Divinity, who reflect the *imago Dei* and bear witness to it as agents of justice, reconciliation, and compassion in the world.

Preface

When Matthew Sanford was paralyzed from the chest down at age thirteen, he learned to "dislocate" his mind from his body. Watching him undergo excruciating treatments—the re-breaking of his back and wrists, suspension in inventive styles of traction, and violent surgeries—his mother suggested, "Matt, tomorrow, try leaving your body for a while." It worked. "A resource existed within me, a silent place into which I could retreat and find protection," he recalls. "What I didn't realize was the long-term cost of going there and becoming comfortable."[1]

Sanford's return to his body occurred many years later, when additional trauma gradually drew awareness to the memories he held therein. He began to practice yoga, which created an "opening to the fact that [his] body was conscious."[2] His physicians had dismissed his descriptions of feeling in his lower extremities as phantom pains, but he would later recognize them as an energetic presence that resides in the body. Today, he teaches yoga and helps people connect with a corporeal consciousness that modern medicine is only beginning to understand.

The mystery of how mind, body, and the powers of consciousness relate to one another is a central theme of this book. A view of the human person that centers upon and privileges a single power, the mind, has impoverished Christian theological anthropology. It has not always been this way in the Abrahamic religions. Many of the

---

1. Matthew Sanford, *Waking: A Memoir of Trauma and Transcendence* (Emmaus, PA: Rodale, 2006), 53–55.
2. Ibid., 184.

Hebrew Scriptures assume a holistic view of the human as "a living being" (*nefesh*). The term first occurs in the second creation narrative, when God breathes the breath of life into the dust creature and it becomes *nefesh*. As Joel Green explains, "*Nefesh* . . . in Genesis 2:7 does not refer to a part of the human being, nor to the human's possession of a metaphysically separate entity distinguishable from the human body such as a 'soul' or 'spirit.' Indeed, this text provides no basis at all for imagining that . . . some part of the human being is 'spiritual' as opposed to 'earthy' (or material)."[3] When the breath of life joins the soil, this compound becomes a unified, living being. In this ancient worldview, at death everyone, both good and bad, passes to Sheol, the shadowy underworld of the dead (see Ps 89:48).[4]

As new beliefs in an afterlife and the resurrection of the body developed, this holistic view was modified to account for a part of the human being that could survive death. Hellenic models came to predominate in the centuries when the later Hebrew Scriptures and the New Testament were written. The Greek Septuagint and New Testament translate *nefesh* as *psyche*, the word used in Platonist thought for the rational soul. Early Christian thinkers took over these connotations to cement the rational soul as "the seat of communion with God and Christian living, in contrast with the irrational element."[5] First- and second-century theologians exerted themselves to retain a place for the flesh (*sarx*) in the resurrected body, which would ensure the continuity and recognizability of the transformed individual in the afterlife.[6] However, the rational capacity of the soul, as the site of salvation, became the essential part of the human being and the part that survives death. As we will explore, the immaterial soul also became identified with the image of God in humanity.

This shift has carried social and ethical consequences. Even as further developments would move the image of God to other features,

---

3. Joel B. Green, "Why the *Imago Dei* Should Not Be Identified with the Soul," in *The Ashgate Research Companion to Theological Anthropology*, ed. Joshua R. Farris and Charles Taliaferro (Burlington, VT: Ashgate, 2015), 184.

4. In Hebrew Scriptures that reference necromancy, people residing in Sheol have a bodily form and are identifiable as individuals (see 1 Sam 28:14).

5. Green, "Why the *Imago Dei*," 187.

6. Taylor G. Petrey, *Resurrecting Parts: Early Christians on Desire, Reproduction, and Sexual Difference* (London and New York: Routledge, 2016), 3.

such as the will or moral capacity, the commonsense way of thinking about the nature, faculties, and destiny of the human being has been to search for the single superior capacity that makes us like God. In principle, of course, every human being would be endowed with such a capacity. In practice, Christian theologians have used this teaching to justify hierarchical social arrangements. The reasoning goes something like this: the adult male leaders of the church and society, who reflect the divine image most clearly by virtue of their superior understanding, should govern women, children, slaves, and others thought to be deficient in these capacities. The association of elite people with the intellect further cements social and economic distinctions. Such arguments creatively work around the affirmation that all human beings, Jew and Greek, slave and free, male and female, are one in Christ, the image of the invisible God (Gal 3:28, Col 1:15).

I write this theological anthropology within a particular context: the American South in the time of Black Lives Matter and Donald J. Trump's bid for the US presidency. The United States has been caught up in the *othering* that Christ was supposed to have overcome: black and white, gay and straight, men and women, Christians and Muslims, "real" Americans and immigrants. Of course, these tensions have always been present, but this season has brought out a renewed glee in saying "what everyone is already thinking," no matter how dehumanizing. A theological anthropology in the context of reified binaries must do more than identify the categories and mechanisms by which we *other* one another. It must also propose alternative ways of thinking about—and a spiritual practice of attending to—the multiplicity of ways of being human in the image of God.

The pluralism in which these tensions bubble is also one of theology's greatest resources. A plurality of methodologies has flooded Christian theology. Feminist, liberation, queer, and postcolonial perspectives are providing insights on doctrines previously dominated by white, European, male voices. Most recently, perspectives from disability studies have made incisive interventions in theological anthropology. These theologians challenge the doctrine with new questions about embodiment, normativity, and limitation. By privileging the critiques and contributions of these perspectives, I wager that this Christian theological anthropology can both reclaim and reimagine a just and compassionate model of the human being.

Religious pluralism, another context for this work, similarly represents a methodological opportunity. Matthew Sanford willfully disconnected his mind from his body after the accident that paralyzed him. He decided not to allow his consciousness full access to physical sensation. This move to "dislocate" from the body replicates a move made repeatedly in the Christian theological tradition, and as in Christian theology, although this strategy mitigated the pain, it led to further injury. His yoga practice enabled him to retie his awareness to the energy in his limbs. It led him back to an integrated sense of himself.

Christians, too, have forgotten how to do theology from the bodies we actually have. In our desire for an essence that cannot be touched by pain, we have wandered from the wisdom of the integrated *nefesh*. Comparison with Indian traditions can assist in dissolving the dualisms that devalue the body and elevate the mind beyond its limits, the hierarchies that devalue people whose rationality is judged inferior, and the human exceptionalism that makes us callous to the fate we subject upon nonhuman animals. As we recover the wisdom of some early, medieval, and contemporary Christian ways of thinking about the human person, our retrieval will be capacitated by a comparative conversation with one branch of the Hindu tradition: the non-dual Saivism of Kashmir.

The non-dual Saiva model shares some helpful features of the holistic view of *nefesh* in the Hebrew Scriptures that were attenuated in later Greek models. In both, the human being is united in a single vivifying energy: the breath of life, or for these Saivas, consciousness (*cit, caitanya, samvit*). This alternative model also bears resemblance to later Christian anthropologies, like that of Thomas Aquinas, that attempt to take stock of many human abilities and attributes, but it avoids his tendency to determine a single feature as the divine image and to rank the others in relation to it. The hope of this experiment in constructive theology is that, by shifting to an aggregate of faculties, theology might displace the outsized role reason has assumed in the Christian view and reopen the mystery of the embodied *imago Dei*.

Introduction

What is the image of God in humanity? This is one of the central questions of the domain of Christian theology known as *theological anthropology*. Treating topics such as human nature and purpose, freedom and sin, and difference and gender, this doctrine deals with what it means to be a human being in relation to our divine source. The phrase *image of God* first appears in the creation narrative, when God says, "Let us make humankind in our image, according to our likeness" (Gen 1:26). Despite its prominence at the very beginning of the Bible, no ecumenical council has ever hammered out the precise nature of the divine image in humanity. This gap has allowed a variety of theories to flourish.

When I ask my students how humanity images God, we collect our ideas on the board. First, they search for something in human experience that distinguishes humans from other species. To know, to discern, to think, to transcend the self—these seem like attributes possessed uniquely by humans, so the intellect or mind tops the list. Thomas Aquinas offers a concise statement of this prevalent Christian view: "Since man is said to be the image of God by reason of his intellectual nature, he is the most perfectly like God according to that in which he can best imitate God in his intellectual nature."[1]

Because the class has already read a bit of feminist and liberation theology, the association between "man" and intellect is not lost on them. Patriarchal logic associates women with the body, the Earth,

---

1. Thomas Aquinas, *Summa Theologiae*, trans. Fathers of the English Dominican Province, vol. 1 (New York: Benziger Brothers, 1948), 1.93.4.

and evil, in contrast with men's association with the superior spiritual faculties. On a similar logic, colonial racism concocted the view "that the Africans were too savage for Christianity; their 'opaque bodies' could not have been made in the *image* of God, rather they were created inferior, natural slaves."[2] This dualistic logic provides the rationale not only for debasing women and people of African descent but also for "subduing" the Earth in a disastrous manner. Body and materiality can be easily forgotten, if not denigrated, when we believe the most divine thing about us must be non-corporeal.

To many in the class, a disembodied view of the image of God feels like common sense, even though Christians have affirmed the goodness of creation and embodiment ever since the earliest theological and christological controversies. For example, when Marcion rejected the Hebrew Scriptures because he saw the creator of the material realm as an inferior deity, Tertullian and others affirmed the goodness of creation. When docetic Christologies, reluctant to associate divinity with the material body, claimed that Jesus only *appeared* to be human, the Council of Nicaea affirmed the goodness of the body with the teaching of Christ's two natures. Augustine, too, rejected the Manichaean dualism of spirit and matter, but he never fully overcame his suspicion of the body. Like Augustine, my students wrestle with the ethical implications of these historical struggles. Is it the case, as Karen Teel argues, that "unless we recognize that human *bodies* in all shapes, colors, and sizes are the image of God, we risk continuing to discriminate against one another on the basis of bodily differences"?[3] Should Christian theological anthropology not only acknowledge the goodness of materiality but also recognize bodies "as signaling the presence of the human and therefore also the image of God"?[4]

Of course, not every version of the nonmaterial image of God relies on a simple Platonic dualism between body and soul, or a gnostic dualism between matter and spirit. In fact, scholars are now

2. M. Shawn Copeland, *Enfleshing Freedom: Body, Race, and Being* (Minneapolis: Fortress Press, 2010), 27. Also see Derek S. Hicks, "The Debasement Campaign," in *Reclaiming Spirit in the Black Faith Tradition* (New York: Palgrave Macmillan, 2012), ch. 2.

3. Karen Teel, *Racism and the Image of God* (New York: Palgrave Macmillan, 2010), 163; my emphasis.

4. Ibid.

discovering that the "unorthodox" theories of the body in first- and second-century groups are not as anti-body as has been assumed.[5] Aquinas himself draws on Aristotle's survey of the human being, which differentiates the soul's powers as vegetative, sensitive, appetitive, locomotive, and intellectual. He further analyzes these into subcategories: nutrition, generation, common sense, imagination, estimation, memory, desire, free will, and so forth.[6] This approach both multiplies the parts of the human being and ameliorates the Platonic gulf between body and soul. It envisions the soul as the *form* of the body, thereby imbuing even the body with a trace of the intellectual image of God.[7]

And yet, despite the multiplicity of parts and a closer link between form and matter in his thought, for Aquinas the image of God remains in the mind, which together with the will comprises the soul.[8] On this basis, he makes a strong distinction between human beings as "rational creatures" and other creatures, in whom "we find a likeness [to God] by way of a trace" akin to the trace of the image found "in the other parts."[9] He uses the same logic to place the image of God in women on a lower tier than that of men: women share the ability to understand and love God, which resides in the mind, but "woman's bodily weakness, which represents a weakness of the soul and the mind," prevents her from developing and perfecting it.[10] Even in this more nuanced version of the doctrine, difficulties with materiality and embodied difference arise.

The class turns to other powers of the soul. Morality, will, or the ability to make ethical decisions becomes a top contender—and with greater scriptural warrant. In Genesis, the serpent tempts the woman

---

5. See Taylor G. Petrey, *Resurrecting Parts: Early Christians on Desire, Reproduction, and Sexual Difference* (London: Routledge, 2016), 1–2.

6. Aquinas, *Summa Theologiae*, 1.77–87.

7. For Aquinas, the human soul is an exception to form-matter unity insofar as it survives bodily death. Ordinarily, because form and matter belong together, when there is no body for the soul to inform, a creature passes out of existence. In the human case, however, the soul can exist temporarily without a body between earthly life and its reunion with it at the resurrection—a loophole that ensures the continuance of the individual human being. Aquinas, *Summa Theologiae*, 1.77.8, 1.89.

8. Ibid., 1.93–95.

9. Ibid., 1.93.6.

10. Michelle A. Gonzalez, *Created in God's Image: An Introduction to Feminist Theological Anthropology* (Maryknoll, NY: Orbis, 2007), 44, analyzing Aquinas, *Summa Theologiae*, 1.93.4.

with fruit that will make her "like God, knowing good and evil" (Gen 3:5), and indeed God is often envisaged as the author and judge of the moral realm.

We unpack the first few chapters of Genesis for further clues. The text makes an explicit connection between the human relationship with the world and the image of God:

> Let us make humankind in our image, according to our likeness; and let them have dominion over the fish of the sea, and over the birds of the air, and over the cattle, and all the wild animals of the earth, and over every creeping thing that creeps upon the earth. (Gen 1:26)

Perhaps the image entails "dominion": set apart from the other animals, humans are to rule over the other creatures, or be stewards in God's place. In the same passage, human purpose is also linked to creativity:

> God said to them, "Be fruitful and multiply, and fill the earth and subdue it; and have dominion over the fish of the sea and over the birds of the air and over every living thing that moves upon the earth." (Gen 1:28)

Humans have the ability, like other animals, to procreate, but we also develop this ability in creations of culture, art, and technology.

Taking another tack, a student proposes that we should look for the most concise statement of God's nature. He quotes, "Whoever does not love does not know God, for God is love" (1 John 4:8). The Christian affirmation of the Triune God—Lover, Beloved, and Love Itself—seems to support this proposal. Humans would image God, then, to the extent that we engage in loving relation with others.

By now we have collected quite a few options for the image of God in humanity. We begin to sort them. We determine that some of our suggestions are *substance anthropologies*: a substance such as the rational soul, the intellect, or the will is designated as the image of God. These mental capacities enable human beings to understand and love God and to choose what is good. Others are *functional anthropologies*, wherein the image is something we do: creativity, dominion over creation, or imitating the life, words, and actions of Jesus that manifest God's purpose in the world.[11] We also identify a *relational anthropology* in the proposal that, like the three-in-one God, people are not isolated monads but fulfill their purpose in life in community with God, other creatures, and the world.

I ask my class, "who is excluded from the image of God?" "No one!" the class answers. We probe a bit more to determine whether any of the models can avoid setting up a hierarchy that questions the inherent worth of some people on the basis of their ability to exercise the featured trait. One student provides a rationale for how people who are "mentally retarded" participate in rationality and, therefore, in the substance view of the image of God. Another student, an advocate for children with special needs in the school system, bristles at this outmoded label, and a third speaks up against idea that the image of God depends on mental abilities. Her infant granddaughter's seizures indicate many developmental difficulties, and by the definition we are considering, she would be less than fully human, deficient in her relationship to God. Who knows whether this child will be able to reason? For that matter, who knows whether she will be able to exercise "dominion" over creation, make moral choices, or exercise love in mutual relationship? The class supplies other examples—what about people suffering from Alzheimer's? People unable to procreate? People in a coma? This last scenario stumps the class. Rational thought, moral capacity, creativity, stewardship, mutual relationship—none seem possible here. Even if the coma patient is loved by others, can he love? My students trust God's gracious love for all people, but the implications of the doctrine now trouble them.

Theologians of disability have gravitated toward a relational understanding of the *imago Dei*. Human beings are interdependent. Each of us, at every moment, relies on God, other people, and the natural environment in profound ways. Our very identities are constituted by who we are to one another. When a baby enters the

---

11. The latter suggestion appears in the womanist theology of Delores Williams, who argues that God's image is revealed not in Jesus's bodily sex but in his life, words, and actions—in a word, his "ministerial vision." Delores S. Williams, *Sisters in the Wilderness: The Challenge of Womanist God-Talk* (Maryknoll, NY: Orbis, 1993), 167. Cf. Rosemary Radford Ruether, *Sexism and God-Talk: Toward a Feminist Theology* (Boston: Beacon, 1993), 134–38; and Elizabeth Johnson, *She Who Is: The Mystery of God in Feminist Theological Discourse* (New York: Crossroad, 1992), 72–73.

world, the parents are also born into new identity. Parents and children contribute different things to one another, and differences in ability can accentuate the vulnerability, hospitality, and joy of relation.[12] Rather than devaluing people because they cannot develop rational capacities to the same degree as others, or because they are not yet (or are no longer) "productive" or "contributing" members of society, their capacity to be in relation, to care for others and receive the care, becomes the locus of dignity and the *imago Dei*.

Certain difficulties continue to arise in relational anthropologies, however, insofar as the ability to relate to others becomes a capacity or function. Here, theological anthropology runs aground on the limit case of people with profound intellectual disabilities. Certainly, relationship occurs through the agency of parents, medical staff, and other caregivers, and these people can experience profound grace and insight in these relationships. But what about the coma patient or someone whose consciousness never develops past that of an infant? These persons can be loved by others, but can they reciprocate that love? As Molly Haslam observes, a relational emphasis still "betrays a bias toward a level of intellectual ability unavailable to individuals with profound intellectual disabilities."[13] The turn to the relational self implies that "participation in the *imago Dei* requires the intellectual capacity to conceive of the self as distinct from the world around us."[14] People with profound intellectual disabilities often cannot achieve this kind of self-other distinction.

We try relocating the teaching to another neighborhood of Christian theology. Perhaps it belongs under Christology. Early theologians viewed Christ as the one in whom we most clearly see humanity in God's image. The apostle Paul goes as far as to describe the first human being as "a type [image] of the one who was to come" (Rom 5:14). According to this reading, Adam and Eve are created in the image of Christ, who is the primary "image of the invisible God" (Col 1:15), and who later takes flesh so humanity can see the image clearly

---

12. See Thomas E. Reynolds, *Vulnerable Communion: A Theology of Disability and Hospitality* (Grand Rapids: Brazos, 2008); and Jean Vanier, *Becoming Human* (New York: Paulist, 1998).

13. Molly Claire Haslam, *A Constructive Theology of Intellectual Disability* (New York: Fordham University Press, 2012), 3.

14. Ibid., 4.

once again. This approach has definite strengths, but it continues to be used to exclude half of the human race from the fullness of the *imago Dei*, as illustrated by women's exclusion from ordination on the basis of Jesus's sex. Maleness has been taken as definitive of the divine reality; those whose gender or gender expression fails to meet current standards of masculinity bear the image of God in only a derivative or defective sense.

Perhaps we can find the answers we are looking for under the heading of eschatology, or ultimate destiny, since "what we will be has not yet been revealed" (1 John 3:2). We have never seen or experienced the *imago Dei* in its fullness, this argument goes. This, too, may be true, but pushing resolution to the end of time deprives the doctrine of its usefulness as guide for Christian life.

What about the idea of sin? This has potential for explaining why humanity does not live up to divine standards much of the time. "We cannot expect perfection in this fallen world," one student offers. "Imperfections result from sin." But whose ideal of the human should we consider to be perfect? This argument risks linking sin and disabilities, as when Jesus' disciples asked him whose sin caused someone's blindness, "this man's or his parents?'" (John 9:2). Another student chimes in, reminding the class that Jesus rejected this way of thinking. Perhaps, then, rather than blaming disability on sin, the sin lies in how society responds to people with disabilities, with moral judgments, pity, patronizing attitudes, and general discomfort.

We pause. We are still left without an answer, and some students then wonder whether, because of its inevitable exclusions, the notion of the *imago Dei* should be expunged from the Christian doctrinal vocabulary. If this Christian doctrine makes idols out of various human abilities, then perhaps this very claim causes more trouble than it is worth.

I want to suggest that there is still room within the *imago Dei* to expand and include, but this will not come from finding the lowest common denominator, the single thing that will unite the coma patient with the physics professor. The professor could leave class and be in a coma twenty minutes later. Theologically, this fact demands a more fluid view of the human: one does not possess the image of God at one minute and lose it the next. The doctrine must also expand to include the multiplicity of ways of being human so that is does not reduce the *imago Dei* to a single cognitive faculty but can fan out to embrace a range of modes of embodiment.

To this end, rather than attempting to justify or fix a particular interpretation of the *imago Dei*, Christian theologians might try on other models. This book interrogates the meaning of the biblical metaphor through another set of categories. By trying on an unfamiliar worldview, perhaps we might momentarily halt the incessant circling of the customary categories—mind, brain, soul, self—as well as the usual assumptions about how these categories relate to one another.[15]

A NEW CONVERSATION PARTNER

As I continue to puzzle through Christian views of the *imago Dei*, then, I introduce a new conversation partner. The strand of Hindu traditions known as non-dual Saivism, specifically Abhinavagupta's Trika interpretation of it, also views the human being as a reflection of the divine. Its nuanced and full-bodied exploration of this metaphor might spark new possibilities—or revive the memory of forgotten parts of the Christian heritage—for Christian theologians grappling with questions of diversity, embodiment, and inclusion.

The idea of doing theology in North America by thinking about Hindu ideas might seem strange to Christian readers. However, there has never been a time when Christian communities did *not* develop their ideas about God, humanity, and the world in conversation with other religious and philosophical systems. The New Testament shows ample evidence of the earliest Christians negotiating their relationship with Jewish and Gentile communities and figuring out how best to talk about Jesus by using the resources at hand. As they did so, they collected a plurality of titles drawn from Judaism (Christ,

---

15. For a critical overview of contemporary options in analytic philosophy, see William Hasker, *The Emergent Self* (Ithaca, NY: Cornell University Press, 1999). A range of Christian theological versions of these models can be found in Joshua R. Farris and Charles Taliaferro, eds., *The Ashgate Research Companion to Theological Anthropology* (Burlington, VT: Ashgate, 2015).

Messiah), Greek philosophy and Gnosticism (Logos), and Roman religion and imperial ideology (Savior, Lord).[16] The same kind of interplay has occurred in relation to the nature of the human being. Christians have incorporated a holistic model of the human being from ancient Hebrew thought, a body-soul-spirit anthropology from classical Greek thought, and a mind-body schema from the modern West. Our context today offers a variety of worldviews that make sense of what it means to be human. Each of these developed in a similarly dialogical way; for example, portions of the schema examined in this book were first staples of Buddhist philosophy and earlier dualistic Śaiva scriptures before being taken up by the anthropology of the non-dual Kashmiri schools.

It can be freeing to recall that all theology engages in metaphorical thinking, and that metaphors are pictures, not doctrines. We name toward divine and human mysteries that language can never fully capture. Pictures are powerful, however, and the hierarchical model of the human person as mind and body has become so firmly ensconced that it has become Christian common sense. However, this common sense should not exert the authority accorded to revelation, which itself plays with several models. Although the Christian councils have never determined a definitive philosophical view of the human person, we can also be guided by what they have ruled out, including views of Christ and creation that denigrate the body. Although ambivalence about embodiment persists in theological treatments of the *imago Dei*, new models open up new possibilities of thought. If a new model can help Christians to harmonize thought, intent, and action, a thought experiment such as this one may bear fruit.[17]

Interreligious exchange is nothing new, but what *is* new is how theologians are describing their relation to religious diversity. Apologetic works for Christianity have often pitted Christian truth against a polemical caricature of the "error" of others. Missionaries have

16. Bede Benjamin Bidlack, "What Child Is This? Jesus, Lord Lao, and Divine Identity," in *Comparing Faithfully: Insights for Systematic Theological Reflection*, ed. Michelle Voss Roberts (New York: Fordham University Press, 2016), 195–215.

17. This argument has been advanced by Sallie McFague, whose works are a major conversation partner in the present project. See, for example, Sallie McFague, *Models of God: Theology for an Ecological, Nuclear Age* (Philadelphia: Fortress Press, 1987).

sometimes studied other faiths in order to refute them or to show how Christianity fulfills their partial truths. Since the sixteenth century, with the expansion of travel, trade, and colonies, these endeavors have also gone hand in hand with European imperial aspirations. Foreign lands and their religions were often treated as "resources" for Westerners—including scholars of religion—to exploit and appropriate for themselves.

Awareness of the history of Christian engagement with other traditions might lead people to avoid studying them altogether. However, neglect of religious neighbors is another way to denigrate them, implying that their history, ideas, and contemporary contributions are not worth considering. The postcolonial (or, arguably neocolonial) moment calls for a different theological approach. The discipline of comparative theology provides one such option: comparative theologians aspire to represent other traditions accurately and responsibly, make well-informed comparisons, and remain open to learning from religious neighbors.[18] Like all deep and prolonged theological work, comparative theology can contribute new ways to understand the doctrines of the church. As interreligious learning inspires new thought about the questions of one's own faith tradition, constructive theology may emerge.[19]

The present work of comparative theology contends that, in light of the roadblocks encountered in recent Christian theological anthropology, a comparative look at Christian and non-dual Saiva uses of *image*, *mirror*, and *reflection* language can offer new routes into a life-giving and inclusive view of the human person. Postcolonial critics may worry that this project is yet another example of Western appropriation of other cultures. There is also the risk that how I construe this tradition will miss the mark or, worse, contribute to the marginalization or stigmatization of other religious groups. After all, my own religious formation and ordination is in Christianity, not Hinduism.

It would be an isolating world indeed if everyone were restricted to

18. For an accessible introduction to comparative theology, see Francis X. Clooney, *Comparative Theology: Deep Learning Across Religious Borders* (Chichester: Wiley-Blackwell, 2010).

19. For essays that share this constructive trajectory and contribute to a range of doctrines, see Voss Roberts, *Comparing Faithfully*.

learning and discussing only the things that were already part of their identity. I do not identify as a person with a disability, at least for the time being, but it would be irresponsible to imagine that theologies of disability have nothing to do with me. I am also a white, overeducated, middle-class, heterosexual woman who benefits from US economic and political influence in the world. Yet, I can try to tell a story that is about more than these things, learning from thinkers who embody different perspectives in the world. Telling a larger story is one helpful way to reframe the question of appropriation. For example, Nancy Pineda-Madrid suggests that "the search for more valid appropriations is not an attempt to reduce [a topic of reflection] to a 'common' experience but rather is an attempt to recognize the complexity of the distinctive ways [it] is understood."[20] To tell a theological story involves being responsive and responsible to people and points of view otherwise excluded.

In our case, "appropriating" Abhinavagupta's categories is a way of telling the story of what it means to be human in fuller awareness of other ways of telling the story. The interests involved in telling this story in our accustomed, hierarchical ways will become clear as we proceed. We need other perspectives—from inside and outside the Christian tradition—to tell a more inclusive story. To think with a model of the human person developed in another part of the world (India) does not mean that a Christian needs to become a Hindu or adopt "Hindu beliefs." As always, the task of the theologian is to reflect faithfully upon revelation and inherited traditions within a shifting context.

ABHINAVAGUPTA'S TRADITION

This book does not attempt to survey all Hindu views of the human person. Every great religious tradition is internally complex. Historical movements, regional differences, arguments with neighboring sects, and the occasional flare of a brilliant theological synthesis make it just as impossible to make statements about what "all Hindus" or

---

20. Nancy Pineda-Madrid, *Suffering and Salvation in Ciudad Juárez* (Minneapolis: Fortress Press, 2011), 21.

"all Muslims" believe as it is to make such statements about all Christians. It is often more appropriate to talk about *Hinduisms* and *Christianities* in the plural.

We focus on a particular tradition that world religions textbooks place under the broad umbrella of Hinduism: the non-dual Saivism that originated in Kashmir. Naming this tradition presents some difficulty. The non-dual Saivism of Kashmir is not a single tradition but a family of historical sects and schools of thought that includes Kaula, Krama, Mata, Pratyabhijña, and Trika sub-traditions.[21] Although many refer to this group of traditions with the shorthand *Kashmir Saivism*, the name is misleading—first of all because these philosophies expanded outside India's northern region of Kashmir, and second because other Saiva traditions, such as the dualistic Saiva Siddhanta, were also represented in Kashmir. In sum, "This term is a misnomer, being both overly specific geographically and overly general doctrinally."[22] However, it is useful to note that *Kashmiri Saivism* or *Kashmir Saivism* has been claimed by contemporary descendants in the spiritual lineage of Swami Lakshman Joo.[23]

By the term *non-dual Saivism*, I indicate a lineage that begins with Somananda and includes the great teachers Utpaladeva, Laksmanagupta, and Abhinavagupta. The tradition is called *Saivism* because it names ultimate reality as Siva, the Goddess Sakti, or both together. In view of this interplay, I will ordinarily refer to its deity as *Siva-Sakti*. The tradition can be called *non-dual* because, on the one hand, it affirms the reality of the world of difference (i.e., not monism), and on the other hand, it recognizes the non-difference between Siva and

21. Interested readers can learn more about these non-dual Saiva traditions by following the references in the footnotes. For an overview of the various schools, see Alexis Sanderson, "Saivism and the Tantric Traditions," in *The World's Religions: The Religions of Asia*, ed. Friedhelm Hardy (London: Routledge, 1988), 128–72.

22. John Nemec, *The Ubiquitous Siva: Somananda's Sivadrsti and His Tantric Interlocutors* (Oxford: Oxford University Press, 2011), 2n5. Cf. Mark Dyczkowski, *The Doctrine of Vibration: An Analysis of the Doctrines and Practices of Kashmir Shaivism* (Albany: State University of New York Press, 1987), 222–23n12.

23. See Mark Dyczkowski, The Trika Shaivism of Kashmir: Lectures, Writings, Music by Mark Dyczkowski, http://www.anuttaratrikakula.org/; and Bettina Bäumer, Bettina Sharada Bäumer, http://tinyurl.com/y722fzjx. Certain "Hindu-based traditions" such as Siddha Yoga and the Nityananda Institute in the West also trace their authority back to this tradition. Gavin Flood, *The Tantric Body: The Secret Tradition of Hindu Religion* (London: I. B. Taurus, 2005), 186.

Sakti and the corresponding non-difference between them and creation (i.e., not dualism). What unites the non-dual Saiva schools is their tantric orientation. *Tantric* means that, unlike the Indian traditions that take the Vedas as their textual foundation, they treat texts called Tantras as authoritative. As we shall see, a notable difference is that these texts reject Vedic distinctions between purity and pollution.

My main interlocutors within this milieu will be two texts that enumerate categories that reflect divine consciousness in the human being. Each is a commentary on *The Goddess of the Three (Paratrisika)*, a Tantra from the Trika school.[24] Both commentaries are traditionally attributed to one of India's great synthetic thinkers, Abhinavagupta (ca. 950–1025), a polymath conversant with all of the non-dual Saiva texts and traditions of his day (and more). Abhinavagupta is "credited with making the metaphor of reflection into a favored trope" of his branch of Saivism.[25] Current scholarship accepts him as the author of the long commentary, *Paratrisika-Vivarana* (PTv), whereas the short commentary traditionally attributed to him, *Paratrisika-laghu-vrtti* (PTlv), is more likely a later South Indian text.[26] The commentaries function as a catalyst for my constructive theological work: their analysis of the reflection of the divine in humanity in five sets of categories provides the present book's structure. These categories spur a search within the Christian theological tradition for analogues. They prompt me to investigate whether the dimensions of human life they describe can (or should) be considered part of the *imago Dei*; in each case, we find openings within Christianity that can be widened,

24. The words *Trika* and *Paratrisika* share a reference to the basic triad of Siva, Sakti, and *nara* (lit., man). The third point (*nara*) stands for phenomenal reality as a microcosm of the whole (PTv, 4).

25. David Peter Lawrence, "Remarks on Abhinavagupta's Use of the Analogy of Reflection," *Journal of Indian Philosophy* 33, no. 5–6 (2005): 586.

26. On authorship of the commentaries, see Bettina Bäumer, *Abhinavagupta's Hermeneutics of the Absolute Anuttaraprakriya: An Interpretation of His Paratrisika Vivarana* (Shimla: Indian Institute of Advanced Study, 2011), 33–35. Citations of these texts come from the English translations available to me at the time of writing: Abhinavagupta, *Para-trisika-Vivarana: The Secret of Tantric Mysticism*, ed. Bettina Bäumer, trans. Jaideva Singh (Delhi: Motilal Banarsidass, 1988), hereafter PTv; and Abhinavagupta, *Paratrisikalaghuvrttih*, in *The Triadic Heart of Siva: Kaula Tantricism of Abhinavagupta in the Non-Dual Shaivism of Kashmir*, ed. Paul Eduardo Muller-Ortega (Albany: State University of New York Press, 1989), 203–32, hereafter PTlv.

retrieved, and developed into a holistic and inclusive anthropology. This comparative encounter expands the *imago Dei* from the single flat surface of a mirror into a brilliant jewel, reflecting light from many facets.

Although the reflection metaphor sparks recognition of a similarity, we should hesitate to equate the two divine image traditions. Each is shaped by distinct liturgical contexts, cosmologies, and meditation techniques. Furthermore, the phrase *image of God* is a particularly Christian construal of the metaphor. Christianity is clearly theistic: talk of *God* is prominent. The non-dual Saiva tradition tends toward both more and less in its treatment of divinity. Beyond the divine Siva-Sakti, this tradition identifies innumerable principles in the universe and in the human body as goddesses. At the same time, the tradition views consciousness as the primary reality, and everything that exists—including these many deities—as modifications of consciousness. The personal, theistic forms of the deity often take a backseat within this philosophical view of consciousness that has variously been categorized as idealism, monism, non-dualism, pantheism, or panentheism. As we will learn, rather than "image of God," language of the *body of consciousness* features prominently in non-dual Saiva texts. This comparative matchup therefore facilitates a rare connection between "image" and "body," so that the *imago Dei* might begin to manifest with *body parts*.

This project uncovers only the tip of an iceberg for its Christian audience. One reason is that, although I have identified a variety of openings within the Christian tradition for this constructive work to take root, other openings will occur to other readers. This is part of the idiosyncrasy—and richness—of a comparative project.[27] Similarly, Abhinavagupta's tradition holds much more within it to spark recognition and constructive reflection. For instance, readers familiar with Indic traditions may be surprised at the marginal role played by

---

27. My faculty colleagues suggested a number of new connections with their particular disciplines and areas of expertise. My astute editor, Michael Gibson, identified perhaps the most fruitful opening for further thought: the work of the sixth–seventh-century theologian Maximus the Confessor contains numerous parallels to Abhinavagupta, including his notion of the human being as microcosm. See Lars Thunberg, *Microcosm and Mediator: The Theological Anthropology of Maximus the Confessor*, 2nd ed. (Chicago: Open Court, 1995).

the subtle body (*suksmasarira*) in what follows. Abhinavagupta shares with other tantric and yogic systems an understanding of the flow of breath (*prana*) through channels (*nadis*) that intersect in energy centers (*cakras*) ascending from the base of the spine to the crown of the head. These concepts of the body are better known in the West than the "body parts" (*tattvas*) discussed here. The subtle body plays an important role in the tradition's meditation practices. However, because the reflection metaphor applies not to the subtle body but to the system of thirty-six body parts, we will pursue the latter path.[28]

MANY FACETS

How, then, does the metaphor of reflection work in these texts? How does the image of divinity come to be reflected not from a single mirrored surface but from many jewel-like facets?

Abhinavagupta's long commentary, the *Paratrisika-Vivarana*, is structured around the conceit of a mirror. The first half of the text concerns the original (*bimba*), and the second deals with the reflection (*pratibimba*) (PTv, 83).[29] This is no unitary reflection. Reflection is another way to describe creation, which is the "manifestation or expansion" of divine consciousness (PTv, 85). In one vivid metaphor to which we will return several times, when the deity Siva opens his eyes, creation unfolds in thirty-six parts (*tattvas*), and when he closes his eyes, these parts fold back into pure consciousness. The opening and closing of the eyes correspond with the creation and dissolution of the world or, returning to the mirror analogy, the manifestation and disappearance of the image. Furthermore, divine consciousness manifests twice: in the macrocosm of the world and in the microcosm

28. For an introduction to the Indian subtle body traditions, see Geoffrey Samuel, "The Subtle Body in India and Beyond," in *Religion and the Subtle Body in Asia and the West: Between Mind and Body*, ed. Geoffrey Samuel and Jay Johnston (London: Routledge, 2013). For more detail, see Flood, *Tantric Body*; and Lilian Silburn, *Kundalini: Energy of the Depths* (Albany: State University of New York Press, 1988).

29. Abhinavagupta writes at the transition between the two parts, "In the previous portion, it is the nature . . . of [the unsurpassable] that has been described. From now it is its external manifestation or expansion that is going to be described. On the analogy of a mirror, the divine source of light is known as *bimba* (in its process of . . . withdrawal) and its reflection in its own mirror is known as . . . manifestation or expansion" (PTv, 85).

of individual beings. One commentator has translated *tattva*s as "cosmotheandric realities" to emphasize these repetitions among divinity, cosmos, and humanity.[30]

Despite the diversity of creation, divine consciousness remains unified. Abhinavagupta again appeals to the nature of mirrors to explain this: just as the reflection in a mirror inverts the image of the original, with left appearing as right, so too the first category to emerge within divine consciousness (Sakti) appears in the world as the last (the earth principle), and vice versa. The subtle and the manifest are not different, in the sense that a face and its reflection are not different from one another. Both the original and the reflection are consciousness.

At the same time, the original and its reflection are not identical. Even though they are not two, they are also not one. The Sanskrit term meaning *non-dual* (*advaita*) expresses this well. Abhinavagupta describes the relationship as "non-difference in difference according to the principle of reflection" (PTv, 120). As a face and its reflection are not identical but appear in reverse order, the world and the human being reflect the divine original in such a way that they can still be distinguished from it.

Abhinavagupta compounds the visual metaphor of reflection in his understanding of revelation. John Dupuche explains, "The pair of terms 'splendor' (*prakasa*) and 'reflection' (*vimarsa*) are used to express the ineffable consciousness. . . . If consciousness is splendor then *vimarsa* is the awareness of the splendor. . . . Reflection (*vimarsa*) is simply the self-revelation of consciousness and so is the primary act of revelation."[31] Analogous terms pile upon one another. If the pair *bimba-pratibimba* expresses a cosmology (how the world is made to appear), the parallel construction, *prakasa-vimarsa*, works out its implications for epistemology (how beings can come to know this reality) and soteriology (how knowledge can liberate). *Vimarsa* connotes "reflecting upon," realizing, or becoming aware of the divine light (*prakasa*). Each pairing is rooted in the original divine pair, Siva and his active manifestation, Sakti.

---

30. Bäumer, *Abhinavagupta's Hermeneutics*, 142.

31. John R. Dupuche, *Abhinavagupta: The Kula Ritual, as Elaborated in Chapter 29 of the Tantraloka* (Delhi: Motilal Banarsidass, 2003), 36–37.

Unlike the creation story in Genesis, which leaves the content of the image open to interpretation, the non-dual Saiva tradition is quite specific. The image consists of the thirty-six categories (*tattvas*), and it is described in terms of a body, "the body of consciousness" or "body of light."[32] Gavin Flood designates this framework an "extensible" body because the pattern of emanation and return is recapitulated in the individual body, the body of the cosmos, and the body of the Absolute.[33]

Abhinavagupta's tradition thus holds together image and embodiment—two things that I suggest Christians should consider in relation to the teaching that humanity is created *imago Dei*. Bringing this scheme into a comparative theological framework has the potential to expand Christian ways of conceiving of the human person as the image of God. It includes the body, which is often ignored in the relational and functional versions of the *imago Dei*. It is multiple, avoiding the temptations and exclusions of choosing a single substance or faculty as the divine image in humanity. It resists a hierarchy of image-bearing by affirming that divine consciousness permeates each part, even when this is difficult to perceive.

The following chart of the thirty-six parts will accompany our exploration of this metaphor.[34] The five groups that Abhinavagupta describes range from the subtlest degrees of subject-object distinction (as Siva begins to emerge from absorption in meditation) to the most concrete levels of manifestation (when his eyes are fully open). In order to focus this constructive reading of the body parts, I limit my exposition of them in certain ways. For instance, although some of Abhinavagupta's texts underline this system's non-dualism by referring to the Ultimate as the thirty-seventh category (or beyond the thirty-seventh),[35] I restrict my analysis to the thirty-six principles

32. Gavin Flood's analysis of these terms tracks the terms *vijnanadeha* and *cidvapus* (body of consciousness), *prakasavapus* (body of light), and *paravyomavapus* (body of absolute space), among others. Gavin Flood, *Body and Cosmology in Kashmir Saivism* (San Francisco: Mellen Research University Press, 1993), 94.

33. Flood, *Body and Cosmology*, 3.

34. This image was designed for *Body Parts* by Lindsey Mullen and modified by Mark Batten.

35. E.g., Abhinavagupta, *Malinislokavarttika* I, 99ab, in *Abhinavagupta's Philosophy of Revelation: An Edition and Annotated Translation of* Malinislokavarttika I, 1–399, trans. Jürgen Hanneder (Groningen: Egbert Forsten, 1998), 75, cf. 171.

described in the two commentaries. Abhinavagupta also expends a great deal of energy in these texts correlating the parts to the phonemes of the Sanskrit alphabet.[36] Because this esoteric convention is more bewildering than illuminating for the intended audience of this book, I refer to the groups of *tattva*s more descriptively, as the conscious body, the limited body, the subjective body, the engaged body, and the elemental body. Each group prompts a search for openings within Christian interpretations of the image of God in humanity that might be more fully expanded and affirmed.

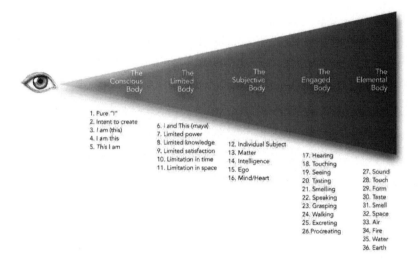

Fig. 1.

OVERVIEW

The ensuing chapters follow these aggregates in order of appearance. Each polishes a facet of the jewel of embodied existence that reflects divinity. Chapter 1, "The Conscious Body," picks up where the class discussion recounted in this introduction leaves off: the case of the coma patient. It expands upon current theologies of disability by articulating the movement of consciousness between the unity of the

36. For an explication of this phoneme mysticism, see Bäumer, *Abhinavagupta's Hermeneutics*, 141–89.

subject and awareness of an object. Psychological analogies for the Trinity, Logos Christologies, apophatic themes, and non-dual teachings from the Christian contemplative tradition all provide openings to consider these degrees of consciousness as imaging God, particularly in people with profound intellectual disabilities.

Chapters 2 and 3 take up the limited body. These body parts are this project's most challenging—and, for that reason, perhaps most significant—contributions to a Christian theological anthropology. Claiming these aspects of existence as *imago Dei* eliminates lingering suggestions by Christian thinkers that limitation or disability diminishes the *imago Dei*. Because of the intractability of this legacy, chapter 2 disentangles limitation from sin and suggests, with Christian ethicist Reinhold Niebuhr, that sin often comes in the form of denial of limitation. Abhinavagupta's tradition draws attention to six particular limitations: limits in individuality, power, knowledge, satisfaction, time, and place (or contingency). I develop Deborah Creamer's limits model of humanity through this framework and, in chapter 3, argue that each of these limits can faithfully be understood as part of the image of God. If a community can recognize that limitations in time, place, knowledge, ability, and individuality are not aberrations but part of an existence that images the incarnate deity, it will refuse to dehumanize anyone unable to develop any particular faculty.

Chapter 4 treats the subjective body, a set of capacities that both contains the rational mind and exceeds it. It encompasses the individual center of consciousness, materiality, intelligence, ego-sense, and the mind/heart. The mind's positioning in the *middle* of this thirty-six-part schema, rather than at the apex of the image of God, has the potential to shift its privileged place within the Christian view. These faculties are multiple, unexceptional (shared by other species), and limited. Along with similar claims in emerging Christian theological work on mental illness, these comparative insights can help to intervene in church environments that still stigmatize not only mental illness but also intellectual and developmental disabilities.

Chapter 5, "The Engaged Body," enters the territory most commonly associated with the phrase *body parts*: the organs of sensation and action. Irenaeus of Lyons offers an intriguing precedent for viewing the physical body as *imago Dei*. We consider how the senses and the organs of action image the relational God as humans engage with others in embodied and intentional ways, including as sexual beings. Disabilities are not exceptions to this rule but sites for understanding the diverse manners of engagement with others and the world that reflect divinity.

In chapter 6, "The Elemental Body," we consider parallels between the Indian schema, earlier Christian procession-return cosmologies, and the dynamism of contemporary views of the origin of the universe. The comparison surfaces tensions between affirmation of the divine presence in all of creation and hierarchical views that devalue the material realm. Non-dual Saiva cosmology and soteriology offer helpful clues that might inspire Christians to retrieve the elements as foundational to the *imago Dei*. These insights join the work of Sallie McFague and others to choose metaphors for God's relation to the world that support just ecological and economic habits.

One of the virtues of this robust and holistic anthropology is that it introduces multiplicity into the notion of the *imago Dei*. The image is no longer a flat surface, which either reflects the divine image or does not, or which reflects the singular image more or less clearly. If the *imago Dei* is more like a jewel with many facets, it can affirm the strengths of earlier anthropologies. Like Christian substantialist accounts, the proposed view includes mental attributes, but the image-bearing attributes multiply to include other things like physical organs and the elements. The model retains strengths of a functional model, since it includes capacities to engage the world. However, it also presupposes limitation, preventing any particular disability or limited function from disqualifying a person from the dignity of being recognized as *imago Dei*. The relational model, which highlights a person's relation to God and others, is rolled into this view as well. The strengths of the Christian inheritance are affirmed, but in view of contemporary critiques, this comparison can make more room for multiplicity and diversity.

PRACTICES OF ATTENTION

This book proposes a cognitive shift in what it means to be a human being. Similar cognitive shifts have been proposed in other contemporary theologies, including disability, feminist, and liberation theologies. Theological anthropology is an important dimension of this work because it pertains to everything that humanity touches. Because theological anthropology runs so deep, however, it has also not been as malleable as these promising fields had hoped. For example, although feminist theology has instilled a genuine desire for just and egalitarian communities in generations of seminary students, patriarchal language for God still predominates in Christian hymnody, liturgy, and preaching. Christian worship remains dominated by androcentric language that reinforces the maleness of God and the secondary humanity of women. People with disabilities continue to find themselves shut out of worship spaces because of able-bodied and able-minded norms. Christian congregations remain segregated by race and social class.

Why? Sometimes clergy cite the fear that people in the pew will reject changes to the status quo, but there is also evidence that obstacles reside at a deeper psychological level within otherwise-willing clergy members themselves. Jennie Knight's research finds, for instance, that women with longtime practices of praying to God using feminine names and images from nature still admit that the "old, white man in the sky" has a hold on their imaginations—*he* shows up, unbidden, when they pray.[37] Their emotional and intuitive religious responses do not match up with their intellectual beliefs because the theology has not penetrated to an experiential level. These newer beliefs have not been allowed to destabilize formative experiences of gender, race, and spirituality. In other words, the theology accepted in the head has not migrated to the heart.

As it turns out, it is not enough to *think* differently about being human in order to be better humans. These beliefs touch and shape us almost at the cellular level. "Embodiment," as educational theorist Beth Berila defines it, "refers to the imprints and manifestations of

---

37. Jennie S. Knight, *Feminist Mysticism and Images of God* (St. Louis: Chalice, 2011), 10.

power, ideology, and socialization on our very bodies."[38] Power operates through them, making us men and women, Northerners and Southerners, black, white, and Latinx, Republicans and Democrats, in the image of those who have come before. Even when we resist these inherited scripts, they set the tone for the conversation. Such categories can be deeply internalized before the work of uprooting them begins.[39]

If we are to move forward with our project of reimagining the *imago Dei* in humanity, we will do well to learn from this cautionary tale and attend not only to ideas about God and humanity but also to the practices that create and reinforce them at the embodied and intuitive level. If disciplinary practices inscribe ideologies upon us, then we will need practices to help us unlearn them. As a religious educator, Knight recommends a spirit of play and experimentation with alternative images. It is not enough to think about and critique images of God; people must both pray with them and play with them. By expanding the spiritual repertoire experientially, the theological shifts begin to become commonsense ways of relating to God and the world.

Similarly, it is one thing to appreciate the diverse body parts as integral to the *imago Dei* intellectually, but it is another to understand *in one's bones* that people with differing abilities and formation fully and truly embody it. With Berila and Knight, I recommend contemplative disciplines to foster this shift. "It is no accident that virtually all mindfulness practices guide practitioners to meet their experiences with curiosity and compassion," Berila writes. "We have to first become aware of our responses and learn to understand them before we can hope to change them."[40] Contemplation leads to awareness, which capacitates action.

At the end of each chapter, therefore, I suggest practices of attention relevant to the set of body parts it considers.[41] Together,

---

38. Beth Berila, *Integrating Mindfulness into Anti-Oppression Pedagogy* (London: Routledge, 2016), 36.

39. Ibid., 47.

40. Ibid., 52.

41. A version of these practices for group or individual exploration can be found at https://www.michellevossroberts.com/practices.html.

these practices contribute to what McFague calls an attention epistemology:

> An attention epistemology is central to embodied knowing and doing, for it takes with utmost seriousness the differences that separate all beings. . . . [We] can learn this lesson best perhaps when we gauge our response to a being very unlike ourselves. . . . If we were to give such a being our attention, we would most probably act differently than we presently do toward it—for from this kind of knowing—attention to the other in its own, other, different embodiment—follows a doing appropriate to what and who that being is.[42]

This epistemology resonates with the Saiva system we are considering here. The central metaphor of consciousness entails practices of attending to the interplay between subject and object, between divine awareness and the world it creates.

The non-dual Saiva tradition has theorized a variety of ways to reach the liberating awareness of the divine presence in everything. These range from external practices (individual means), through interior concentration (empowered means) and liberation through the grace of a guru (divine means), to instantaneous liberation obtained without practices (no means). This book's practical approach resembles the *individual* or *empowered means* insofar as it employs the body parts to develop a habitual awareness of the image of God in all things. Of course, the immediate awareness of the "no means" would be a preferable, and easier, way to this rather elusive goal. Given that no easy societal solutions have presented themselves, and no collective flashes of insight have eliminated deeply ingrained senses of difference and division, the slow practice of attentiveness may be the most realistic means of developing habits of perceiving the image of God. This is a path not for the saint or enlightened being but for ordinary Christians on the way to sanctification.[43]

Each facet of the *imago Dei* can serve as an object for practices of attention. The practices in chapter 1 hone in on

---

42. Sallie McFague, *The Body of God: An Ecological Theology* (Minneapolis: Fortress Press, 1993), 50–51.

43. One contemporary practitioner comments on the difficulty of the goal before us, "Only the *yogi* whose awareness is already merged with Siva . . . can perceive the world as a reflection (*pratibimba*) of the Divine (*bimba*)." Bäumer, *Abhinavagupta's Hermeneutics*, 190.

the subtle movements of consciousness that precede all thought and action in order to counteract habitual perceptions that divinity is external to the self. Chapter 2 considers how a practice of embracing limits might helpfully attune a person to the gifts of interdependence and finitude. Chapter 3 employs practices of the imagination to disrupt the normative assumptions that racialized and other types of power imprint upon us. For example, attending to the historical memories and literary works of others can expand one's awareness of other perspectives and one's own limited formation. Chapter 4 contests the mind's alleged infallibility and proposes introspective practices that observe the operation of human subjectivity, attend to the inner life, and grieve the recognition that one's own story is not the only true story. Chapter 5 leverages a distinction between the *imago Dei* and the *imago Christi* in order to attend to vulnerable bodies in the practice of the Eucharist. Chapter 6 then directs sacramental attention to the physical elements through practices of the breath.

Running like a red thread through each of these practices is the intent to discover the divine presence in the moment at hand. If divine consciousness pervades (at least) thirty-six dimensions of existence, then human beings can employ these dimensions to recognize the divine image in them. "True religion is not something which affects the mind or the spirit alone," writes Jyoti Sahi. "The body, and all that the body implies in the sense of physical awareness and the use of the senses, also constitutes an essential aspect of being human and fully alive."[44] My hope is that Christians might employ these practices and cultivate a holistic and fully embodied knowledge that each part reflects the divine image.

My emphasis differs from some of the Christian theologians who are renewing interest in bodily practices, for whom the senses point away from themselves to a transcendent reality. T. J. Gorringe, for instance, calls upon physical sight to behold the "sheer gracious beauty of the world which mirrors the gracious beauty of God," and he recalls Karl Barth's praise of Mozart's music for causing people to

44. Jyoti Sahi, *Holy Ground: A New Approach to the Mission of the Church in India* (Auckland, NZL: Pace, 1998), 15. Sahi is one in a chorus of voices singing this tune. See Thomas Ryan, ed., *Reclaiming the Body in Christian Spirituality* (New York: Paulist, 2004); and Stephanie Paulsell, *Honoring the Body: Meditations on a Christian Practice* (San Francisco: Jossey-Bass, 2002).

hear the peace that passes understanding. In both cases, the senses mediate a sublime truth beyond the terrestrial realm.[45] As with some forms of asceticism that deprive the senses, for them the spiritual purpose of attending to the senses is to point to something higher so that the practitioner can become focused on God rather than the world.

Without a doubt, physicality can be a site of transcendence, as I have explored elsewhere.[46] This comparative framework, however, recognizes that even in the mundane operation of body parts, even in ordinary time, human beings image and encounter the incarnate God. Most of the practices I lift up for consideration neither transport the practitioner into ecstasy nor deprive the senses. Rather, a mysticism of daily life attends to ordinary activities and sensitizes a person to God's presence in them.

Prayer is, at root, a practice of attention, Simone Weil observes.[47] The beauty of attention to the ordinary—to routine actions such as showering or making dinner—is that it draws out the quiet and persistent divine presence in each and every sensory encounter. One might marvel at the complex workings of the body parts, or one might direct them outward by "people watching" or noticing part of God's creation.[48] Simple activities—listening and being heard, tasting and relishing a new food, or exploring how the skin's sensitivity varies in different body parts—can uncover the basic grammar of the perceiving body. Similarly, in the expansive definition of body parts considered here, each can become the site for practices of attention that may contribute to wise and compassionate ways of being in the world.

45. Timothy Gorringe, *The Education of Desire* (Harrisburg, PA: Trinity International, 2002), 19, 16. Don Saliers similarly views the physical senses as "crucial" but ancillary to the recovery of the "senses" of "awe, delight, truthfulness, and hope" in worship. See Don E. Saliers, *Worship Come to Its Senses* (Nashville: Abingdon, 1996), 14.

46. Michelle Voss Roberts, *Tastes of the Divine: Hindu and Christian Theologies of Emotion* (New York: Fordham University Press, 2014), especially the introduction and ch. 8.

47. Simone Weil, *Waiting for God*, trans. Emma Craufurd (New York: Putnam, 1951), 105.

48. Carl Koch and Joyce Heil, *Created in God's Image: Meditating on Our Body* (Winona, MN: Saint Mary's Press, 1991), 91.

1.

The Conscious Body

In search of the *imago Dei*, the class discussion recounted in the introduction faltered at the limit case of the coma patient. Beginning there might shed new light on theological anthropology. What is the experience of such a person?

Medical models for classifying traumatic brain injury offer clues. They delineate a spectrum of levels of consciousness that can be measured through observable factors. For instance, the Glasgow Coma Scale assigns a score based on three factors: eye opening, motor response, and verbal response. Does a person open her eyes spontaneously? In response to speech? To pain? Not at all? Does a person move his body in response to commands? To localized stimuli? To general stimuli? By withdrawing? By extending or flexing one set of muscles but not others? Not at all? By assigning points for eye opening, "best motor response," and verbal response, medical professionals can plot indicators of consciousness on a scale of three to fifteen.[1] Another measure, the Ranchos Los Amigos scale, organizes the severity of brain injury by response to environmental stimuli. Here, consciousness is measured through types of response to stimuli. In level 1, "No Response," visual, auditory, tactile, and painful stimuli cause no change in a person's behavior. In level 2, "Generalized Response,"

---

1. Patricia A. Winkler, "Traumatic Brain Injury," *Umphred's Neurological Rehabilitation*, ed. Darcy A. Umphred, Rolando T. Lazaro, Margaret L. Roller, and Gordon Burton, 6th ed. (St. Louis: Mosby, 2013), 753–90, box 24-4.

a person responds reflexively to pain and makes generalized, non-purposeful bodily movements or vocalizations in response to auditory and other external factors, sometimes after a delay. Level 3, "Localized Response," includes turning toward a sound, blinking in response to light, withdrawing from painful stimuli, or indicating awareness of the presence of other people. At level 4, "Confused-Agitated," a person will be cognitively alert, but purposeful movements, such as sitting up, walking, or attempting to remove tubes are sporadic and do not correspond to the environment or promptings of others. In level 5, "Confused-Inappropriate," a patient exhibits impaired memory, lacks goal-directed behavior, and can respond to simple commands only if consistent structures and cues are present. In level 6, "Confused-Appropriate," a person's verbal and motor responses to self, familiar others, and basic needs become more regular. Familiar tasks can be completed with moderate assistance. A person whose cognitive ability is at level 7, "Automatic-Appropriate," is "consistently oriented to person and place," needs some assistance in relation to time, and is able to learn new tasks. Awareness of appropriate social behavior, abilities, and consequences are markers of level 8, "Purposeful-Appropriate." With each level, the person's responsiveness—to others, to one's abilities and goals, and to the future—increases.[2]

These scales are helpful in describing degrees of traumatic brain injury and impairment. They illuminate a range of states of consciousness that take multiple factors into account. They also place these states of consciousness along a spectrum of development. Consciousness and responsiveness are not either-or qualities. They emerge, develop, and exhibit a variety of physical indicators. For these reasons, they shed light on the consciousness not only of the coma patient but also of people with a range of intellectual abilities.

AN EMERGENTIST RESPONSE

In his work, *Theology and Down Syndrome*, theologian Amos Yong takes up conversation with cognitive neurosciences in order to pro-

---

2. Chris Hagen, "Rancho Los Amigos—Revised," Centre for Neuro Skills, 1997, http://tinyurl.com/ybwqhlmu.

pose an emergentist view of the human person.[3] This view starts with the body as the basic human reality. From this basis, including the physical properties of the brain, emerge "mental (cognitional) properties—including morality, consciousness and self-consciousness, and aesthetic creativity—[that] are dependent on but not fully explicable by physical (brain) properties."[4] Many scientists attribute these factors solely to physical properties such as hormones or brain activity and exclude religious concepts such as the soul. Yong's view differs in that it allows for a spiritual dimension, the soul, "as an emergent set of distinctive features and capabilities constituted by but irreducible to the sum of the body's biological parts."[5] Consciousness depends on, but is not reduced to, the human body and brain.

Yong advises theologians to approach disability in a holistic and interdisciplinary manner. By attending to biology, ecology, politics, and other factors, emergentism embeds the value of a person in "webs of significance" that "[resist] positivistic quantification."[6] It is here that Yong locates a basis for talking about "the human spirit, which manifests itself unmistakably in the experience of disability."[7] Persons can "transcend our bodily experiences of disability even if such transcendence neither ignores nor wishes away the demands of the body."[8]

An emergentist typology has a number of strengths to recommend itself for a holistic and inclusive Christian anthropology. It begins with the body as constitutive of a human person. Yong writes, "the human person must be understood to be *at least embodied*, even if one's spiritual capacities are less manifest phenomenologically."[9] This view affirms the Christian emphasis on the created goodness of the body and the resurrection hope of an embodied future. It is relational, acknowledging the influence of environmental, social, and other factors. It includes all people.

3. For an overview of varieties of emergentism, see William Hasker, "Why Emergence?" in Farris and Taliaferro, *Ashgate Research Companion*, 151–61.

4. Amos Yong, *Theology and Down Syndrome: Reimagining Disability in Late Modernity* (Waco, TX: Baylor University Press, 2007), 170.

5. Ibid.

6. Ibid., 172.

7. Ibid.

8. Ibid.

9. Ibid., 171; my emphasis.

Yong's emergentist anthropology locates the soul within the matrix of subject-object awareness. He writes, "human beings are never merely either (knowing) subjects or (material) objects, but are rather simultaneously subjective objects (bodies who know themselves as such) and objective subjects (thinkers or feelers who are nevertheless constituted by their bodies). Human persons are souls or spiritual beings in at least this sense."[10] The soul is not some essence separate from the body but emerges as subjectivity develops within a body. Expanding this insight relationally, one might say that the human spirit does not descend, pure and fully formed, from some heavenly realm but emerges as the subject relates to its embodied self and to embodied others.

Yong's view resembles the Glasgow and Rancho Los Amigos scales, which similarly orient themselves to embodiment by marking degrees of awareness, from the opening of the eyes, to recognition of sensory stimuli and other people, to various degrees of coherence and communication. Such nuanced approaches vastly improve upon models of the human that fixate on a single substance, function, or relation as the source of a uniquely human dignity.

THE CHALLENGE OF PROFOUND INTELLECTUAL DISABILITY

But there is a problem. If a theology emphasizes consciousness, whether of self or other, does it exclude those of us with profound intellectual disabilities? And if human ability emerges, what is to prevent the assumption that people in whom abilities have not emerged are less perfect, less the image of God?

To explore these questions, theologian Molly Haslam introduces the reader to Chan, a composite figure that she sketches from her experience as a physical therapist. Chan was born with cerebral palsy. His IQ is below 25, and he is developmentally similar to an infant who has not learned to roll, hold its head upright, or sit unsupported. "In terms of his level of communication, Chan's behavior does not indicate the ability to comprehend words or sentences; neither is

10. Ibid., 183.

he able to produce them. He does not demonstrate an ability to use gestures or sounds with the intent to communicate his needs or wants."[11] Chan's caregiver Philip feeds, bathes, and moves Chan from his bed to his chair. He brings him to a day treatment center for people with intellectual disabilities. Chan responds to his environment. Philip notices that Chan exhibits "awake behavior" when Philip arrives in the morning, but when other caregivers are present, he exhibits more "sleep behavior." At physical therapy, when the therapist aligns Chan's body left or right of center, the movement of his neck and leg indicates that he is trying to right his posture. When others at the center play with a bright yellow balloon, his vocalization and motor activity increases, so Philip moves his chair to be near to the game.[12]

Chan's behavior can be described as responsive but not intentional. He responds to the presence of certain objects and people, and he exhibits awareness of the position of his body. However, he does not show the intent to communicate, for example, by moving his eyes between a person and the desired object. He does not exhibit intent to accomplish goals, for example, by trying a new behavior when another does not work. This is significant for Haslam in relation to influential theologians like Gordon Kaufman or George Lindbeck, whose view of the human is tied up with self-reflection, intentionality, and language use. "Chan does not possess the capacity to employ concepts of self and other required for intentional agency . . . [nor] an ability to express himself symbolically using public gestures, words, or actions with the intent to give meaning to experience."[13]

Haslam pushes theological anthropology into new territory. Although intellectual disability has recently become the subject of a number of theological works, it remains undertheorized. This emerging scholarship includes Amos Yong's important work on Down syndrome and Thomas Reynolds's theology from the

11. Haslam, *Constructive Theology*, 57.
12. Ibid., 57–63.
13. Ibid., 53–54. Kaufman treats intentional agency as the marker of the human, whereas Lindbeck points to the ability to use symbolic communication. Gordon D. Kaufman, *In Face of Mystery* (Cambridge, MA: Harvard University Press, 1993), 103. George A. Lindbeck, *The Nature of Doctrine: Religion and Theology in a Postliberal Age* (Philadelphia: Westminster, 1984), 38.

experience of raising a child whose diagnoses include Asperger's and Tourette's syndromes. Both theologians reject a substance anthropology (i.e., the image of God as the mind or some other such entity) in favor of a relational notion of the human. "Created in God's image, we are beings with the capacity to respect, be faithful to, and show compassionate regard for others," Reynolds writes.[14] Despite their intent to the contrary, Haslam observes, this relational emphasis still "betrays a bias toward a level of intellectual ability unavailable to individuals with profound intellectual disabilities."[15] Their turn to the relational self implies that "participation in the *imago Dei* requires the intellectual capacity to conceive of the self as distinct from the world around us."[16] In other words, it requires that a person be self-conscious.

Although Haslam emphasizes responsiveness as a marker of the image of God and as a shared feature of being human that is embodied in diverse ways,[17] our comparative frame might allow us to reconsider consciousness, of which responsiveness is one indicator, as a metaphor for the *imago Dei*. Is it possible to employ this metaphor in a way that includes people with profound intellectual disabilities? Is it possible to imagine the emergence of consciousness without diminishing those in whom it does not develop to the point of self- or self-other awareness? And if this emergence is part of the *imago Dei*, in what sense can God be imagined as one who also emerges? Interreligious comparison can help us to imagine possibilities that Christian theologians have forgotten or left undeveloped.

CONSCIOUSNESS AND THE DIVINE BODY

Here, we turn to our Hindu conversation partners to spark the Christian theological imagination. Like the Christian tradition, non-dual Saivism uses the language of "reflection" to describe how humans

14. Reynolds, *Vulnerable Communion*, 185. "Relation to others" thus defined is one of "three dimensions" of the *imago Dei*, which require self-awareness and self-transcendence; the others are "creativity with others" and "availability for others" (ibid., 177). Cf. Yong, *Theology and Down Syndrome*, 184–88.

15. Haslam, *Constructive Theology*, 3.

16. Ibid., 4.

17. Ibid., 104–6.

mirror the divine. The coherence of this Saiva model derives from the ocular metaphor. The body parts can be viewed as thirty-six degrees of focus for divine consciousness. In this chapter, we focus on the first five degrees of consciousness. Although each one of the thirty-six parts is the body of consciousness (*vijnanadeha, cidvapus*), we might uniquely call these five "the conscious body" because they designate the movement of consciousness as it moves in and out of focus, wakening, emerging, and returning to an indistinct void.

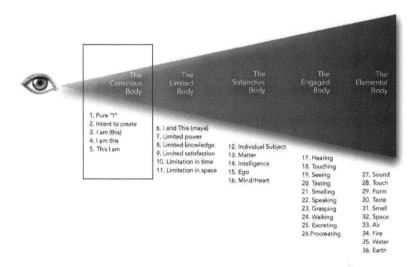

Fig. 2.

The non-dual Saiva framework resembles the emergentist scheme outlined by Yong, but with some differences. Rather than beginning from the body as the site from which various capacities emerge, this framework begins with divine consciousness. Like the Glasgow Coma Scale, the first indicator of consciousness is that Siva opens his eyes. A blurry differentiation begins to take place in the divine subject, as the possibility of perceiving an object arises. From the hazy, generalized responses of stages 2 and 3 of the Rancho Los Amigos Scale gradually emerges a more coherent and localized recognition.

The first five degrees of focus (*tattva*s, principles) can be described as a gradual perception of an object distinct from the subject.[18]

1. Siva   Pure "I"

2. Sakti   Intent to perceive/create

3. Sadasiva   *I am* (this)

4. Isvara   I am this

5. Suddhavidya   *This* I am

The first principle is Siva, which denotes the complete oneness of the divine subject with itself. It is pure "I." The second principle is called Sakti, which signifies the first glimmer of the divine intent to create or perceive. The functions of creation and perception are identical (Western philosophies have a corollary: *esse est percipi*, "to be is to be perceived"). In the third degree, a sense of the subject in relation to an object begins to come into view: *I am* (this). The emphasis is on the subject, with the object barely beginning to emerge. In the fourth degree, subject and object are equally present: I am this. And in the fifth, the emphasis tilts toward the object: *This* I am. Amid these fine differentiations of subject from object, a strong sense of unity remains.[19]

These subtleties might seem rather airy and disembodied, but examples are close at hand. An infant begins life in total, blissful union with the mother in the womb. Consciousness of others gradually emerges in typical people in the first few months of life. Infants perceive the world as an extension of themselves, existing in symbiosis with their primary caregivers. Initially, the world feels like an extension of the self: *I am* (this). Only the starkest of light-dark contrasts

18. Jaideva Singh, introduction to *Pratyabhijñahrdayam: The Secret of Self-Recognition*, trans. Jaideva Singh, 4th rev. ed. (Delhi: Motilal Banarsidass, 2003), 8–12. Abhinavagupta acknowledges alternative enumerations of this set of body parts in PTv, 101–2.

19. The names for the next three degrees of focus are *sadasiva* and *isvara*, which are additional names of Siva-Sakti, and *suddhavidya*, which names the purity (*suddha*) of knowledge (*vidya*) in these initial five movements of consciousness. For Abhinavagupta's articulation of the balance between "I" and "this" in these body parts, see Abhinavagupta, *An Introduction to Tantric Philosophy: The Paramarthasara of Abhinavagupta and Its Commentary of Yogaraja*, trans. Lyne Bansat-Boudon and Kamalesha Datta Tripathi (London: Routledge, 2011), 117–26.

register in the visual field. Awareness revolves entirely around sensations of one's own pleasure and pain. Gradually, it becomes evident that the presence or absence of various objects are related to the sensations. The breast or bottle, warm touches, familiar smells, and wet or dry clothing contribute to the awareness of *I am this*. Soon, the caregiver's face, a favorite lovey, a pacifier—though still extensions of the self—come into focus as specific objects: *This* I am. Only gradually does an individual emerge as a distinct being, and other objects gradually come into view as distinct as well.

This pattern parallels the unfolding of Siva-Sakti's consciousness from unity to differentiation of self and other. Sleep is another useful analogy. In deep sleep, we return to a state of undifferentiated unity. When we dream, we perceive objects that are not external to ourselves. When we wake, the objects we perceive are genuinely outside ourselves. Although we usually do not catch hold of the transitions between one state and another, these are obvious places where consciousness fades in and out of focus toward self and others.

All of these degrees of consciousness occur in bodies, as in the emergentist paradigm, but non-dual Saiva theology goes further by viewing them as body parts. The thirty-six *tattva*s are called the body of consciousness. Here, the emergence of various faculties from one another is not only visible in human development but is also the principle of creation and the nature of divine self-awareness. According to the logic that "to be is to be perceived," nothing comes into existence until it is thought or perceived into being by God. The universe is God's embodiment, and the human being is the microcosm of this process. Humans mirror God in their various degrees of perception, whether the total unity of the subject in deep sleep or the awareness of others in the world.

Significant for our inquiry in relation to the *imago Dei* of people with profound intellectual disability is that the blurry realms of consciousness between pure subject and awareness of objects are recognized as reflections of the divine.[20] The remainder of this chapter

20. The most thorough treatment of how difference and non-difference are equally valid modes of perception in the philosophy of Abhinavagupta can be found in chapters 7 and 8 of Isabelle Ratié, *Le Soi et l'Autre: Identité, Différence et Altérité dans la Philosophie de la Pratyabhijñā* (Leiden: Brill, 2011).

discerns a variety of openings for such an affirmation within the Christian theological tradition.

OPENING 1: PSYCHOLOGICAL ANALOGIES
FOR THE TRINITY

Thinking with these categories first of all suggests consciousness, rather than the rational mind, as the orienting metaphor. Augustine considers this metaphor amid others as he searches for images of the Trinity within human experiences. These have been called psychological analogies because they locate faculties and processes within human subjectivity.

Augustine begins his search for images of the Trinity with external perceptions, such as "the body which is seen and the form which is impressed from it on the attention of the observer and the intention of the will which couples the two together." He continues searching, however, because they are inadequate to the divine three-in-one: "these three are not equal to each other nor of one substance." He finds a better analogy in "consciousness itself," where three things—memory, understanding, and will—are contained within the single subject. Here, "the same three are of one substance, namely the image of the body which is in the memory, and the form derived from it when the thinking attention turns to it, and the intention of the will joining the two together." Memory, understanding, and will can be distinguished from one another but are of the same mental "substance." He improves upon the analogy once again by diminishing the role of the external world and making the object, wisdom from God, something that is entirely within the mind to be remembered, understood, and willed.[21]

Self-consciousness has been a favorite metaphor for the Trinity in the Western (Latin) Christian tradition because it mirrors a mystery that defies definition: divine oneness and threeness. The one divine being is known to Christians in three ways. In Trinitarian theology, the first person of the Trinity, often called "the Father," or simply

---

21. His own summary of this progression can be found in Augustine, *The Trinity*, ed. John E. Rotelle, trans. Edmund Hill (Brooklyn, NY: New City, 1991), 398 (15.1).

"God," eternally begets or generates the second person, "the Son," or "the Word." The prologue to the gospel of John states,

> In the beginning was the Word, and the Word was with God, and the Word was God. He was in the beginning with God. All things came into being through him, and without him not one thing came into being. What has come into being in him was life, and the life was the light of all people. (John 1:1–4)

Notable in this theology of the Word (Logos) is that this second principle is both identified as God and somehow different from (with) God. It is eternal, and it is the principle of creation, life, and light in the world. This principle was important in early Christian councils that articulated the divinity of Christ. Later councils in the Western church extended the rationale of divine union-in-differentiation to a third "person," the Holy Spirit, who proceeds, or is breathed, from the first two persons.

This way of viewing the relationship between God and God's creative principle has intriguing parallels to Siva and Sakti, the first two principles in the non-dual Saiva view. Sakti is the feminine counterpart to the masculine Siva. Although she emerges as distinct from him in the movement of divine consciousness, they are actually not different from one another. Siva is often depicted as half-male, half-female (*ardhanarisvara*) to express this unity. The word Sakti means "power." Hindus have a saying: "Siva is *sava* (a corpse) without Sakti." Without her creative power, no external reality can arise from the void of pure consciousness.

When Christian theologians connect the Logos of the Christian Testament with the feminine principle of Sophia or Lady Wisdom in the Hebrew Bible, the parallels run even deeper. In Proverbs, Wisdom proclaims, "The Lord created me at the beginning of his work, the first of his acts of long ago . . . when he marked out the foundations of the earth, then I was beside him, like a master worker" (Prov 8:22, 29–30). She leaves a divine trace on the world so that "the heavens are telling the glory of God; and the firmament proclaims [God's] handiwork" (Ps 19:1). Although the Sophia principle is often subsumed into the masculine Logos-Christ in Christian doctrines of creation, it places an active, feminine, divine principle of creativity at the beginning of creation.[22]

Christian theologians disagree about the extent to which nature itself reveals God's existence and attributes. Nevertheless, a persistent thread of Logos theology weaves itself throughout the tradition in the principle that the creation reveals the creator and that reason (*logos*) and other faculties can impart knowledge of God.[23]

The Logos/Sophia tradition is fertile ground for comparison with non-dual Saivism. Working with the Logos theology of the twentieth-century Catholic theologian Bernard Lonergan, who worked out a theological and philosophical method based in the workings of consciousness, David Lawrence notes similarities between these theories of knowledge:

> It is of special interest that God's creative logos is frequently conceived as something like His *self-recognition*. This may be understood in that God is existentially prior to His creation, whether this is conceived as *ex nihilo* or through emanation. Accordingly, His understanding of the rationality by which He constitutes the world must primordially be an understanding of something within Himself, which we may call a kind of self-recognition. In this way, according to the traditional Christian doctrine as well as the Pratyabhijña [branch of non-dual Saivism], it is God's self-recognition that provides the necessary grounds for all other recognitive interpretations of the world.[24]

In other words, for both traditions, divine consciousness/Word/Wisdom permeates the creation that it brings into being. As God perceives the world, God recognizes Godself in it. This principle of consciousness/Word/Wisdom also facilitates human knowledge of God

22. The Trinitarian implications for divine Sophia are worked out most fully by Elizabeth A. Johnson, *She Who Is*, part 3.

23. I return to these tensions regarding the possibility of a natural theology in chapter 6. In natural theology, because the Logos is God's ordering principle and brings creation into being, the divine Logos is present within creatures, which participate in its existence and design. Creatures can follow this natural connection toward knowledge of God and union with the creator. God is thus present in the world as well as in Scripture, the divine commandments, and the incarnate Word. By contrast, theologies that emphasize sin and separation from God deny the efficacy of the testimony of the natural world.

24. David Peter Lawrence, *Rediscovering God with Transcendental Argument: A Contemporary Interpretation of Monistic Kashmiri Saiva Philosophy* (Albany: State University of New York Press, 1999), 21.

and the world. By participating in the divine Logos in themselves and in the world, humans can come into communion with God.[25]

Again, this principle of divine self-recognition implicates more than the rational capacities. Shallow versions of this theology stop at arguing for the compatibility of theology and philosophy, as if the truths of reason are enough—or nearly enough—for knowledge of God. The principles of Logos or Sophia, however, cannot be reduced to logic. They are the very ontological framework for creation, the possibility of cognition and relation, and the meaning and truth that permeate reality. God creates reflections of Godself. All knowledge participates in the knowledge of God by Godself. When we perceive, we tap into divine self-perception. When we know, it is part of God's self-knowledge. When we love, we participate in the dynamic divine self-relation. Every creature is held in the divine image by the divine desire to perceive it.

Christian theologians and philosophers have tended to focus on the movement between the first two body parts in the non-dual Saiva model, Siva and Sakti, as analogous to the relationship between the persons of the Trinity. This important comparative opening does not quite answer our concerns with the exclusory nature of the *imago Dei*, however, because the Christian association between Logos and knowledge, and between the divine Word and language use, still privileges cognitive activity as the image of God. In the non-dual Saiva paradigm, consciousness cannot be reduced to the intellect or mind. These emerge only later, in the subjective body, and so our comparative perspective urges us further.[26] Let us push onward beyond the first two principles.

25. Nicholas Bamford, a Byzantine Orthodox comparative theologian, correlates Sakti's transformative power (*kriya*) with the divinizing work usually associated with the Holy Spirit. Nicholas Bamford, *Converging Theologies: Comparing and Converging Terms within the Byzantine and Pratyabhijña (Kashmir Saivite) Traditions within a Space for Convergence* (Delhi: ISPCK, 2011), 76, cf. 61.

26. As discussed in chapter 4, the mental faculty (*manas*) develops only after considerable further unfolding of consciousness. It is neither the apex nor the telos of human becoming.

OPENING 2: APOPHASIS

In the next three body parts, the unified divine subject gradually shifts its attention toward an object. Each degree of focus marks a place along the continuum of perception, with distinctions so subtle that they ordinarily go unnoticed in human consciousness. For most people, who experience objects in the world as external from them, it takes considerable discipline to experience these fine degrees of unity amid the world's diversity. Some Hindu practitioners take these subtle states of awareness as the goal of meditation. With practice, a person can learn to observe the transitions in consciousness at the first inkling of a thought, the first glimmer of desire, or the first movement of the intent to act. In these transitions, the thinking, desiring, intending subject and the object thought, desired, or intended have barely begun to differentiate. This is the relation between Siva and the world at the inception of creation, when Siva has only begun, through Sakti's stirring, to open his eyes. This state recurs at the end of a cosmic cycle, when Siva closes his eyes and the world folds back into pure consciousness.

These degrees of consciousness in the Saiva typology have eluded formal Christian doctrines of the human person, but we do find parallels in the Christian tradition. Done properly, theology includes the awareness that all human affirmations ultimately fall short of describing God. Divinity transcends human language and thought constructs. For this reason, Thomas Aquinas insists that affirmative (or kataphatic) theology must be accompanied both by analogical thinking, which recognizes that human metaphors describe God in certain respects but not others, and by the negative or apophatic mode.[27] According to the latter, we come closest to naming God when we say what God is not: God is not a thing, not a creature, not a human being. God is no thing, and therefore theology must un-say (*apophasis*) every declaration about God.

One common apophatic strategy is to deny that God can be equated with anything in creation, beginning with its "lower"

---

27. Aquinas develops this argument in *Summa Theologiae* 1.12–13. Elizabeth Johnson (*She Who Is*, ch. 6) explores these three classic methodological approaches.

dimensions: God is not really a rock, an eagle, or a human being. Contemplation then continues through the "higher" principles and mental constructs to deny that these can contain God as well. Meister Eckhart blasts through theological truisms, likening even the noblest statements to lies. Though fitting as the language of prayer and praise, God cannot be contained by any concept our minds can think: not *truth*, not *being*, not even *goodness*.[28]

In this theological opening, the gradual dissolution of the distinctions required by language use in Christian theology finds a parallel articulation in the gradual dissolution of the conscious body. Through this unraveling of concepts, the theologian can only name God or Siva as "I am" or, better yet, must fall silent.

OPENING 3: CONTEMPLATIVE NON-DUALISM

In addition to unsaying theological language, some Christian thinkers also venture to dissolve the subject-object distinction upon which language relies. The basic perception of "you" and "me" as separate identities is added to the list of inadequate ways of thinking about God. God is no thing, and therefore God is not a thing external to other things. Throughout the ages, a variety of contemplative practices have fostered this counterintuitive awareness of creation's fundamental union with God.

The period of the contemplative tradition that Bernard McGinn calls "the flowering of mysticism" is especially rich for imagining union with the divine. In the twelfth and thirteenth centuries, with the founding of the mendicant orders and the flourishing of the beguine movement, vernacular languages were increasingly used for theology.[29] This was a highly inventive time for European languages, with an outpouring of new vocabulary and literature that would shape regional and linguistic identities for centuries. Women, many

28. Meister Eckhart, "Sermon 83," in *Meister Eckhart: The Essential Sermons, Commentaries, Treatises, and Defense*, trans. Edmund Colledge and Bernard McGinn (New York: Paulist, 1981), 206–7. This insight reflects the influence of Pseudo-Dionysius, "The Mystical Theology," in *The Complete Works*, trans. Colm Luibheid (New York: Paulist, 1987), 141.

29. Bernard McGinn, *The Flowering of Mysticism: Men and Women in the New Mysticism—1200–1350* (New York: Crossroad, 1998).

of whom were excluded from education in Latin, took up the poetic forms and conventions of their own languages to express their love for God. Hadewijch of Antwerp, for example, imagines God as Lady Love and herself as a knight errant bound to her service. She and other beguines speak of union with God in erotic terms, drawing on the metaphor of sexual union to express the mystery of simultaneous union with and distinction from the divine Beloved. Mechthild of Magdeburg speaks of God and the soul as "melting . . . in [their] union."[30] Marguerite Porete goes farther and describes union with God in terms of the "annihilation" of the self that allows a person to unite with God in the nothingness from which she was created.[31]

Church officials have consistently viewed such statements with suspicion, despite their congruence with apophatic themes. The facts that Mechthild was told that her book might be burned and that Porete herself was burned as a relapsed heretic in 1310 suggest that the difficulty of understanding their wisdom might stem from the inadequacy of official theological categories. Influenced by his relationship with beguine communities, Meister Eckhart employed both Latin and the German vernacular to explore these themes.[32] As with the beguines, his apophatic writing is full of paradoxes that his enemies seized upon as heresies, and a number of his statements, removed from their apophatic context, were condemned in the papal bull *In Agro Domenico* in 1329.[33]

Eckhart explores the boundary of subject and object in relation to the Trinity and God's relationship with the individual soul. For him, the Trinitarian dynamic preserves the mystery of *one* that is at the same time *multiple*. Trinity enjoys a kind of non-dual existence—non-different, and yet not reduced to one—for which ordinary language fails. He associates this apophatic modality with the

30. Mechthild of Magdeburg, *The Flowing Light of the Godhead*, trans. Frank Tobin (New York: Paulist, 1998), 1.17, cf. 6.13.

31. Marguerite Porete, *The Mirror of Simple Souls*, trans. Ellen Babinsky (New York: Paulist, 1993), esp. the fifth stage of the soul in ch. 118.

32. See Bernard McGinn, ed., *Meister Eckhart and the Beguine Mystics: Hadewijch of Brabant, Mechthild of Magdeburg, and Marguerite Porete* (New York: Continuum, 1994).

33. Bernard McGinn, "Theological Summary," in *Meister Eckhart: The Essential Sermons, Commentaries, Treatises, and Defense*, trans. Edmund Colledge and Bernard McGinn (New York: Paulist, 1981), 31.

fundamental union of God with the soul. Many of the signature themes in his sermons—detachment, breaking through, becoming nothing, going out and remaining within, the little spark, and the birth of the Son in the soul—stand for this union. Each of these themes pushes the mind toward the place where all concepts fail, where the subject-object duality that cognition imposes must be overcome in contemplation.

Eckhart's scholarly defenders advise that his vernacular sermons should be read alongside his Latin works, which reify distinctions that the sermons loosen.[34] Rather than dismissing his rhetoric, we might understand the vernacular sermons as both showing the mind its limits and nuancing the firmer dualities of the Latin commentaries. The first five degrees of consciousness proposed in comparative perspective can help us see a degree of detail that is usually missing in Christian analyses of consciousness.

Consider this short and controversial passage from sermon 6, which depicts the double motion of procession (creation) and return (salvation). First, Eckhart evokes the origins of Trinitarian union-in-difference and the birth of the soul.

> The Father gives birth to his Son in eternity, equal to himself. "The Word was with God, and God was the Word" (John 1:1); it was the same in the same nature. Yet I say more: He has given birth to him in my soul. Not only is the soul with him, and he equal with it, but he is in it, and the Father gives his Son birth in the soul in the same way as he gives him birth in eternity, and not otherwise. He must do it whether he likes it or not. The Father gives birth to his Son without ceasing; and I say more: He gives me birth, me, his Son and the same Son. I say more: He gives birth not only to me, his Son, but he gives birth to me as himself and himself as me and to me as his being and nature. In the innermost source, there I spring out in the Holy Spirit, where there is one life and one being and one work. Everything God performs is one; therefore he gives me, his Son, birth without any distinction.[35]

Later, he describes the reverse dynamic that occurs in salvation: "I am so changed into him that he produces his being in me as one, not just

---

34. Cf. ibid., 26.
35. Eckhart, *Meister Eckhart*, 187–88.

similar. By the living God, this is true! There is no distinction."[36] This is less an ontological change than a soul's awakening to the union with God that has been the case since the moment of creation.

These are radical statements. Perhaps, some commentators suggest, they are not intended as technical theological maps of the soul's relation to God but are meant to encourage Christians toward contemplation and piety. The poiesis of Eckhart's sermons is part of their apophasis, however. Their shock value drives the mind beyond customary dualities, to "explore those 'limit-situations' in which God becomes present to us in a more conscious way."[37] Eckhart's theopoetics make gradations between God and the soul possible that the orthodoxy of his time could not.

Meister Eckhart, Sermon 6	The Conscious Body
	Maya
The Father gives birth to his Son from eternity, equal to himself. "The Word was with God, and God was the Word" (John 1:1); it was the same in the same nature.	*This* I am
Yet I say more: He has given birth to him in my soul. Not only is the soul with him, and he equal with it, but he is in it, and the Father gives his Son birth in the soul in the same way as he gives him birth from eternity, and not otherwise. He must do it whether he likes it or not. The Father gives birth to his Son without ceasing;	
and I say more: He gives me birth, me, his Son and the same Son.	I am this
I say more: He gives birth not only to me, his Son, but he gives birth to me as himself and himself as me and to me as his being and nature.	*I am* (this)
In the innermost source, there I spring out in the Holy Spirit, where there is one life and one being and one work.	Intent to create
Everything God performs is one; therefore he gives me, his Son, birth without any distinction.	Pure "I"

Via comparison, can a Christian theologian dare to say what these "unsayings" express? If we place the first passage side-by-side with the parts of the conscious body, new distinctions might arise in

---

36. Ibid., 188.
37. McGinn, "Theological Summary," 31.

the Christian theological imagination. Such a juxtaposition does not equate Eckhart's statements with the non-dual Saiva categories, as they arise from distinct religious contexts, but next to one another they creatively generate possibilities for reflection.

Alongside these categories, Eckhart's progression from distinction to union can be seen as expressing something more than an utter, and potentially unorthodox, monism. He marks several of these degrees with transitions such as "I say more." At the beginning of the passage, the Father gives birth to his Son in eternity, equal to himself. With the emphasis on the Son or the Word, this equality resembles the fifth degree of consciousness: *This* I am. He then adds the soul to this intra-Trinitarian dynamic so that the birth of the Son occurs within the soul. With the soul as the *locus* of the divine birthing, Eckhart preserves a degree of difference between God and the soul.

He now adds greater subtlety: "and I say more: He gives me birth, me, his Son and the same Son." In this twist, the soul is born in the same way as the Son so that they are the same. The soul can say, "I am this." There is still "this" Son, but the emphasis lies on the soul's identification with it in their origins.

Next comes an even stronger intuition of union: "I say more: . . . he gives birth to me as himself and himself as me and to me as his being and nature." As the distinctions dissolve, the awareness moves toward pure being: *I am* (this).

Then, with the introduction of the Holy Spirit, there is another subtle distinction—divine agency in creation: "In the innermost source, there I spring out in the Holy Spirit, where there is one life and one being and one work." Could the Holy Spirit here be functioning like Sakti, providing the impetus and intent to create?

Finally, Eckhart concludes with a radical statement of divine unity, pure "I," without distinction: "Everything God performs is one; therefore he gives me, his Son, birth without any distinction." It is from this non-dual place, in which the soul is established, that Eckhart can advise, "So therefore let us pray to God that we may be free of God."[38]

Here, Eckhart expresses through language a mode of consciousness

---

38. Eckhart, "Sermon 52," in *Meister Eckhart*, 200.

that defies language. The distinctions that language requires only enter with the firm realization of "I *and* this," which the non-dual Saiva system names as the sixth body part: *maya*, the principle that veils union from ordinary awareness. Eckhart's Latin works preserve a sharper divide between creator and creation than his vernacular sermons.[39] Beside this system, one might say that the Latin works reflect ordinary consciousness veiled by *maya*, which places God and the soul in completely different categories. Eckhart's two sets of work necessarily unsettle one another because of tensions within the Christian tradition between apophasis and kataphasis and between divine transcendence and immanence. How can one say in words what Scriptures and contemplative practices hint about the possibility of union with God? By building these subtleties into its system, Saiva metaphysics is able to hold in tension both the explanation for the seeming solidity of the divide and the religious wisdom of the saints who point beyond it. Such distinctions might prove useful in Christian theological anthropology as well.

OPENING 4: THE VOID

The dissolution of the self is not all sweetness and consolation. As Eckhart acknowledges, "If God were to withdraw what is [God's], all creatures would turn into nothing."[40] This awareness contributes to a non-dual understanding of one's relationship to divinity, but neither Eckhart nor Abhinavagupta quite acknowledges what the world came to witness in the twentieth and twenty-first centuries: a void in which God not only transcends categories but is conspicuously absent.

The dissolution cuts two ways: "I" and "this." On one side, the disorientation of trauma, the ghastly hallucinations of mental illness, or the violation of rape can unravel a person's sense of self much more rapidly than the contemplative disciplines. The categories of the contemplative body might be expanded to describe the unbearable

39. See, for example, Eckhart, "Selections from the Commentaries on Genesis" and "Commentary on John" in *Meister Eckhart*, 83, 131–34.

40. Meister Eckhart, "Sermon 83," in *Meister Eckhart: Teacher and Preacher*, ed. Bernard McGinn (New York: Paulist Press, 1986), 342.

stripping of the self into which human beings unwillingly can be thrown.

On the other side, personal and collective traumas, such as those wrought by genocide, can experientially dismantle God's existence. When Elie Wiesel witnesses a child struggling on the gallows of Auschwitz, a voice rises up in him proclaiming that God is "hanging here from this gallows." He comments, "The human creature, humiliated and offended in ways that are inconceivable to the mind or the heart, defies the blind and deaf divinity."[41] Perhaps human beings, in our inhumanity, are capable of executing the trace of divinity in our midst. Perhaps, because such horrors are possible, there is no divinity worthy of the name. An impulse to be free of God, and of the concepts and projections that have stood in for God, now arises from horror and disgust at the apparent absence of goodness at the heart of historical reality. To invoke "God" as underlying all this is blasphemy—not an offense to the deity but to the dignity of the human race. Better not to say "God" at all.

When philosophers of the twentieth century name the *death of God*, they identify, among other things, an experience of a void in which there is no solace, no divinizing presence, no assurance of divine attention and care that might lead to equanimity. Such experiences relativize all metaphysical speculations. The emanation/return structures I am examining in this book have especially come under attack, insofar as they have been used to erect a hierarchy of being. In such hierarchies, beings form a ladder of lesser to greater resemblance to (divine) Being. Such ladders have proven supremely useful for propping up human projects of domination, including those of reason and the state, in the name of God.[42]

The validity of these critiques demonstrates the importance of apophatic contemplative discipline. When trauma and evil rip a hole in the meaning-making structures, the most appropriate response is not always to rush in and fill it with words, or with a divine Being who omnipotently patches the holes, but rather to bear witness to

41. Elie Wiesel, *Night*, trans. Marion Wiesel (New York: Macmillan, 2012).
42. This arc of critique, running from Hegel and Nietzsche through Thomas Altizer and John Caputo, has been assisted by the critiques of ontotheology (equating God with Being) from Martin Heidegger and Jacques Derrida.

the void. Metaphysics—detached from contemplative practice—tends toward domination. It is all too easy for priests and kings to lay claim to the Absolute, to equate it with contingent human values, and then to defend those values with all the zeal and might of an empire. Practice is the key. The contemplative wisdom of the void does not find God sitting atop the hierarchy of Being to justify whatever *is*. Instead, it discerns divinity within the silent heart that has been stripped of the assertion of "I" against "it."

"The ladder urges us beyond ourselves. Hence its importance," the Jewish poet Edmond Jabès writes. "But in a void, where do we place it?"[43] Hierarchy finds no support there.

CONSCIOUSNESS AS *IMAGO DEI*

Through these openings within the theological tradition, we have glimpsed how the subtle degrees of the conscious body might find resonance in a Christian theological anthropology. The classical Augustinian tradition takes human self-relation as an enormously helpful metaphor for the Trinity, hinting that the structure of human consciousness derives from our creation in God's image. We experience, in microcosm, something of God's fundamental apprehension of difference-in-unity. Beyond this, an apophatic impulse hovers around the work of theology, reminding its practitioners that words are creations of human language, inadequate to the divine mystery. Practices of prayer and experiences of contemplation also point beyond customary distinctions. Some brave souls, such as Meister Eckhart, have used language in novel ways in order to express something of the subtle degrees of relation between God and the soul. And finally, intuitions of a divine void or absence evoke another mode of consciousness, at turns pacifying and terrifying.

Having explored some of Christian theology's openings into nondual consciousness, we may return to the challenge profound intellectual disability has posed to theological anthropology in order to articulate with greater clarity how Chan manifests the image of God.

---

43. Edmond Jabès, *From the Book to the Book: An Edmond Jabès Reader*, trans. Rosmarie Waldrop (Hanover, NH: University Press of New England, 1991), 65.

THE CONSCIOUS BODY   23

Molly Haslam places Chan's modes of consciousness within the framework of Martin Buber's anthropology. Buber locates genuine humanity in the immediacy of an *I-Thou* relation, which differs from an external, instrumental *I-It* relationship: "There is no reflecting, categorizing or ordering of the Thou on the part of the I here, and there are no concepts or ideas that mediate the relation between them."[44] By contrast, in I-It relations, the subject and object no longer stand in the unmediated presence of one another. Ideas, categories, and desires come between them. Reflective activity interrupts and distances.

Persons with profound intellectual disabilities embody the immediacy of the I-Thou relation, which "establishes itself naturally in such individuals," as Buber himself observes.[45] Because of his disability, Chan's relation to the world remains a totality. He cannot sort, categorize, and objectify others. It does not matter, for Buber or Haslam, whether the relation is one-sided (Buber writes of I-Thou encounters with trees, for example). Here, relation is not a conscious choice, which would require certain intellectual capacities, but a presence, which awaits a response. Chan responds to Philip's presence with "awake behavior." Philip responds to Chan with activities of care, and this marks their relationship as one of genuine humanity. For Haslam, if Philip abused Chan, their relationship would degenerate from one of genuine humanity into an I-It relation.[46] Haslam's relational anthropology, then, is "not a capacity, but participation in the meeting between responsive partners."[47]

Haslam critiques Yong's emergentist anthropology because it implies a telos for development: the soul, which can reflect on itself. As Yong puts it, humans are "bodies who know themselves as such" and "thinkers or feelers who are nevertheless constituted by their bodies."[48] She poses the challenge: "The question . . . is not whether individuals with profound intellectual disabilities are aware of the

44. Haslam, *Constructive Theology*, 69.
45. Ibid., 75. For more on the spirituality of persons with profound intellectual disabilities, see Jill Harshaw, *God Beyond Words: Christian Theology and the Spiritual Experiences of People with Profound Intellectual Disabilities* (London: Jessica Kingsley, 2016).
46. Haslam, *Constructive Theology*, 112.
47. Ibid., 53.
48. Yong, *Theology and Down Syndrome*, 183.

world around them or of the position of their bodies within it. . . .The question, rather, is whether these individuals are aware that they are aware."[49] For Chan, who shows no evidence of communication, intention, or awareness of how he affects the world around him, the answer would be no. He does not meet the benchmark of self-reflection.

The non-dual Saivism would come under a similar critique insofar as it, too, emphasizes practices that enable practitioners to know themselves as microcosms of Siva-Sakti's self-consciousness. Thinking along with Haslam's critique, however, we might consider angles earlier thinkers may have neglected. The conscious body is like an interesting, sparkling stone that a theologian can hold up to the light and view from different sides. Doing so encourages recognition that each state of awareness is an important part of being human. Each reflects God's experience. Each is worthy of attention in its own right, regardless of its potential to develop into self-recognition or any other cognitive capacity. Instead of lack, a theologian might see distinct ways of being.

It does not romanticize disability to observe that those of us with profound intellectual disabilities may in fact be *more* able to image God in terms of unmediated awareness than people with higher levels of intellectual function. "Chan's awareness of and responsiveness to those around him would be more like the 'being present' that Buber speaks of as characteristic of I-Thou relations," Haslam contends.[50] He does not erect obstacles to I-Thou relation because he does not conceive of himself as distinct from his surroundings.

These observations indicate that the various dimensions of the *imago Dei* can be experienced by the collective body of humanity in different seasons of life, with greater or less ease, and with more or less permanence. This does not thereby imply that anyone lacks the fullness of the divine image, but only that the nature of an individual's participation in that image—because of its very multiplicity—will necessary differ from that of others and may change over time. Although it is difficult to imagine how such fluidity and

---

49. Haslam, *Constructive Theology*, 63.
50. Ibid., 78.

difference does not detract from the image itself, I will propose in the next two chapters that they, too, are part of the divine image.

Each part of the conscious body images the divine body. An anthropology that takes this principle seriously will include self-recognition as a mirror of divinity but will not take it as the only reflection of the divine in humanity. By expanding the comparison to all thirty-six body parts, we shine a light on all dimensions of embodiment as mirrors of the divine. The circle widens. Full humanity is no longer modeled on the autonomous, rational, (male) agent but encompasses women, children, and people with intellectual disabilities who have been viewed as derivative of this ideal.

PRACTICES OF ATTENDING
TO THE CONSCIOUS BODY

Transcendence of subject-object duality eludes many people in their waking state. People with profound intellectual disabilities experience it intimately. Infancy and deep sleep involve these modes of consciousness. (These observations do not entail "infantilizing" people with disabilities.) Strong emotional experiences of awe, terror, or sublimity might also throw one into the void. But how can people who do not ordinarily experience subject-object boundaries as permeable, or who do not routinely care for someone who experiences the world in such a permeable way, gain embodied understanding of this dimension of the human relation to God?

A new paradigm can expand Christian theological anthropology, but on their own, new metaphors are not enough. A theological anthropology that includes the conscious body will remain counter-intuitive without practice. The wisdom work of contemplation must complete the intuitive shifts toward seeing all people as created in the image of God. The early Augustine recommends, "descend into yourself, enter your secret place, your mind, and there see what I want to say, if you can. For, if you are yourself far from yourself, how can you draw near to God?"[51] Augustine does not recommend any

51. Augustine, *Tractates on the Gospel of John, 11–27*, trans. John W. Rettig (Washington, DC: Catholic University of America Press, 1988), 223 (23.10).

specific techniques, but he is describing a practice of self-recognition, in which the structure of consciousness reflects God's transcendence and unity. By experiencing the structure of subjectivity, one draws near to God.

Hindu and Buddhist traditions excel at devising techniques that allow the practitioner to experience the unity of consciousness and the self's multiple ways of relating to it. These methods are not complicated; often they only require attention to mundane occurrences such as perception. The content of the perception does not matter. Rather, the practitioner observes how perception arises and passes away. The first five body parts name the moments in the process. The will to perceive occurs first, followed by graduated steps in which the object comes into focus for the subject. The process reverses as attention withdraws from the object. One can observe the same chain of awareness in the senses and as a thought arises and passes away. Even breathing—beginning with a glimmer of desire to inhale—replicates the pattern.

Abhinavagupta's Saivism is a tantric tradition, meaning that it treats activities that are ordinarily taboo, or at least not ordinarily connected with the sacred, as conduits for glimpsing ultimate reality. For advanced practitioners, tantric rituals involving meat, alcohol, or sex inculcate the ability to focus on the movement of consciousness. The experience of strong emotions, such as pleasure or desire, ordinarily distract the mind and create a strong sense of duality between people and the things they want. However, the pattern of the movement of consciousness is the same in desire as in perception or thought. The challenge, then, is to maintain awareness of this movement in every situation, whether enjoying food, viewing a powerful work of art, or making love. Each experience offers a window into the ultimate nature of reality, because each encapsulates the pulsation of subject-object union and differentiation.[52] Importantly for our theological anthropology, these practices enable a person to observe and experience the subtle states of consciousness in which some of us dwell on a daily basis.

John Dupuche, a Catholic priest and theologian, explores Christian

---

52. Many of the practices are described in Jaideva Singh, trans., *Vijñanabhairava or Divine Consciousness: A Treasury of 112 Types of Yoga* (Delhi: Motilal Banarsidass, 1979).

theology and practice in light of mantra meditation in non-dual Saivism. Ancient practices of chanting the Jesus prayer or repeating phrases such as "Maranatha" tap into a distinct mode of consciousness. Dupuche describes this practice in Christian and biblical terms, such as going into the desert (Exodus), the birth of the Word (John), the poverty and abandonment of Christ in his passion, and the "stillness of the tomb" on Holy Saturday.[53] Following a tradition of mystical theology in Christianity, he uses paradoxical language to describe how mantras enable the practitioner to transcend sense and intelligence and meet the God who dwells in light inaccessible (1 Tim 6:16): "only a luminous darkness leads through the unknown."[54]

In Dupuche's analysis, the first degrees of consciousness are important for knowledge of God. Mantra practice taps into a basic mode of consciousness that everyone has experienced as a newborn child: "Spontaneously and naturally he begins to stir and opens his eyes; his mind begins to observe and organize the impressions that flood in. . . . The meditator who enters into the silence, drawn there by the newborn Word, returns to a pre-cognitive stage."[55] Hindu traditions often describe the first stages of manifestation in terms of a primordial "unstruck sound." One can discern the influence of this tradition in Dupuche's description of the divine grace that precedes such a prayer practice. Echoing the notion of the primordial sound/Word, he writes, "The gift was given from the beginning, little did the meditator realize. It was indeed the silent sound that resonated at the start and called to the journey of faith."[56]

The debate in my theology class is far from over, but this comparison has made progress. Comparison of imaginative portraits of reality from two traditions has yielded an enriched view of the dignity inherent in every person. The unitive states of consciousness experienced in infancy or in a coma now shine forth as aspects of the human experience that mirror the divine image. As Dupuche puts it, "[The]

---

53. John Dupuche, *Jesus the Mantra of God: An Exploration of Mantra Meditation* (Melbourne: David Lovell, 2005), 15, 53, 72, 76.

54. Ibid., 7.

55. Ibid., 58.

56. Ibid., 8. For more on the importance of word, sound, and speech (*vac*) in non-dual Saivism, see André Padoux, *Vac: The Concept of the Word in Select Hindu Tantras*, trans. Jacques Gontier (Albany: State University of New York Press, 1990).

self is given from the start; [the] self-knowledge comes gradually."[57] I would add, "if it comes at all." It may not, but this would not make any person less than a full bearer of the divine image. The image is present in any degree of consciousness of God, self, or other—some degrees of which are more readily accessible to persons with certain disabilities. The dignity of the self is not dependent on whether or to what extent self-knowledge emerges.

For those of us to whom unified or undifferentiated modes of consciousness do not come easily, except perhaps in deep sleep, contemplative practices break up the habitual way of seeing others (and God) as external to us. Perhaps, with Dupuche, we are "called to sit in stillness and allow the Word to penetrate, transforming [us] into the Word," and "to dwell in the sweetness of the One who is called the 'Void.'"[58] Beyond the mantras he explores, other practices such as centering prayer are being recognized for cultivating this non-dual effect.[59]

The conscious body can help Christians imagine, with greater nuance and humility, the union in Jesus's prayer "that they may be one, as we are one" (John 17:22). Glimpsing it through contemplation, creatures on this side of the creator-creation divide may only hope for it its full unveiling: "now we see in a mirror, dimly, but then we will see face to face" (1 Cor 13:12).[60] We turn now to the veil that dims our apprehension—the limitation of consciousness that Indian thinkers call *maya*. How it gives rise to other features of limited, embodied experience, and how even these limitations image God, is the subject of the next two chapters.

---

57. Dupuche, *Jesus the Mantra*, 59.
58. Ibid., 10, 15.
59. See Cynthia Bourgeault, *The Heart of Centering Prayer: Nondual Christianity in Theory and Practice* (Boulder: Shambhala, 2016).
60. Cf. Augustine, *The Trinity*, 390 (14.5).

2.

The Limited Body (Part 1)

In the biblical fall narrative, God instructs Adam and Eve not to eat—not even to touch!—the fruit of the tree in the middle of the garden. The penalty for transgressing this rule would be death (Gen 3:3). Although they do not die immediately, "death" includes a range of difficulties regarding birth, family, and livelihood (Gen 3:19). As a bookend for this narrative, Augustine imagines heaven as a place where such limits are overcome, "where no evil at all can touch us, no good will be out of reach; where life is to be one long laud extolling God, who will be all in all; where there will be no weariness to call for rest, no need to call for toil, no place for any energy but praise."[1] He writes of imperishable bodies, vigorous minds, and a freedom of the will that "sin will have no power to tempt."[2]

Limits appear to be the effect of sin in this familiar narrative. Limits seem to depart from God's intent for humanity to be healthy, whole, even immortal. In addition to individual physical and mental limits, collective limits are also attributed to sin, as when God creates linguistic differences after the people of Babel attempt to build a tower reaching heaven (Gen 11:9).

Jesus moderates, but does not entirely abrogate, this theme. His opponents challenge him with the case of a man born blind: "Who

---

1. Augustine, *The City of God, Books XVII–XXII*, trans. Gerald G. Walsh and Daniel J. Honan, Fathers of the Church 24 (Washington, DC: Catholic University Press of America, 2008), 22.30.
2. Ibid.

sinned, this man or his parents, that he was born blind?" Jesus appears
to reject the reasoning behind the question: "Neither this man nor
his parents sinned; he was born blind so that God's works might
be revealed in him" (John 9:2–3). Physical limitation, at least in this
case, is not punishment. Nevertheless, Jesus grants the man sight, and,
adding to the confusion, he elsewhere tells the recipients of miracu-
lous healings, "Your faith has made you well" (see Mark 5:34, 10:52).
Does salvation guarantee healing? Will God remove limitations, if
one only has enough faith?

Western thinkers after the Enlightenment aimed to transcend limits as they flirted with the idea of boundless human progress. An
increase of knowledge and innovation could throw off the shackles
of the past, uncover the laws of nature, and create a society free of
conflict and disease—a salvation of our own making, in which limitation would be overcome. However, as modern optimism waned
with the twentieth century, Christian theologians again needed to
come to grips with the limitations inherent in the human condition.
How could supposedly enlightened societies harbor such prejudice
and, aided by technology, wreak such destruction? How could new
freedoms usher in unprecedented economic inequality? How could
the best minds have missed the unforeseen ecological and health haz-
ards harbored within the Trojan horse of scientific innovation?

Questions such as these prompted twentieth-century Christian
ethicist Reinhold Niebuhr to offer up a paradoxical view of human
nature as simultaneously finite and free, temporal and transcendent,
creature and the image of God. For him, this paradox lies behind
modernity's quandaries. It also provides individual and collective
occasions for sin. Niebuhr remains one of the most admired Christian
public thinkers in the United States. His impact on subsequent ethical
and political thought offers a substantial opening in the Christian tradition for reconsidering the role of limitation in theological
anthropology.

NIEBUHR, LIMITS, AND THE *IMAGO DEI*

The paradox of finitude and freedom is evident in Niebuhr's treatment of the *imago Dei*, which he defines as self-transcendence. In his analysis, the human person is not only able to will and think, as in models of the divine image as the rational soul, but is also *aware* of thinking and willing. This existential orientation allows a person to transcend nature by relating to a supernatural end, but it exists in tension with human finitude.

For Niebuhr, this paradox leads to errors on both sides. On the one side lies an overinflated view of human nature. Neoplatonist Christian thinkers, for example, hone in on humanity's inherent connection to God, but they tend to forget the limits of creaturehood. When the early Augustine "sought God in the mystery of self-consciousness," for instance, he came dangerously "close to the deification of self-consciousness."[3] On the other side, we can err by deprecating created existence, as when the apostle Paul associates death with sin and the later Augustine gets mired in ambivalence about sex and the body. These great thinkers contradict a basic biblical teaching "that the created world, the world of finite, dependent and contingent existence, is not evil by reason of its finiteness."[4] Finitude and limitation must not be equated with sin, because they are part of God's good creation.

Though part of creation's goodness, finitude nevertheless becomes the occasion for sin, says Niebuhr, especially sins of pride. Because no one is the whole of reality, we are anxious. Our perspectives are necessarily limited, conditioned by our time and place in history and our community of origin. We cannot be conscious of all things, as if from a God's-eye view. Lacking self-sufficiency, dependent individuals are driven by anxiety to shore up the self. In our insecurity, we do our best to contradict the basic truth of our contingency, but we cannot do this "without transgressing the limits which have been set for [a] life. Therefore all human life is involved in the sin of seeking

3. Reinhold Niebuhr, *The Nature and Destiny of Man: A Christian Interpretation*, vol. 1, *Human Nature* (New York: Charles Scribner's Sons, 1964), 157.

4. Ibid., 167. Niebuhr qualifies his critique comparatively: "This contrast . . . is never a corruption of an original divine unity and eternity, as in neo-Platonism; nor is it evil because of the desire and pain which characterize all insufficient and dependent life, as in Buddhism" (ibid., 169).

security at the expense of other life."[5] When we deny our limits, we become proud. If we have the ability to dominate others, we usually will.

Subsequent generations have appreciated the freshness and relevance of Niebuhr's ethical insight, but they have also observed his own limitations. We will explore in the next chapter how, even as Niebuhr challenges many of the class-based ideologies of his day, he lacks resolve in the face of racial injustice. His persuasive analysis is limited by his own time, place, and privilege. Perhaps most striking, Niebuhr's emphasis on self-transcendence leaves bodies out of the picture, thus leaving a gap too easily filled by ideology. Other voices have, therefore, been necessary to identify how factors such as race, gender, nationality, sexual orientation, and ability contribute to these dynamics.

From a critical disability perspective, the centrality of self-transcendence in Niebuhr's anthropology betrays an ableist orientation. For him, the paradox of human nature is that, even as our limits constrain us, we humans can imagine transcending them. But, as discussed in the last chapter, because only some of us can imagine this, Niebuhr's ideal of self-transcendence as the *imago Dei* falls short of an inclusive theological anthropology. Like other anthropologies that reduce the image of God to a substance or capacity—here, awareness of oneself, others, and God—it excludes people who do not exhibit it—most particularly people for whom profound intellectual disabilities make them unable to differentiate themselves from their environment. His view, like all views, is partial—showing vividly why a variegated model of the human being is so important for Christian thought.

This chapter approaches such a variegated model by putting Niebuhr in conversation with Deborah Creamer's Christian theology of disability and with the non-dual Saiva categories of the limited body. Each adds a layer of analysis that supplements the others to build toward an inclusive *imago Dei*.

---

5. Ibid., 182.

A LIMITS MODEL OF HUMAN BEING

Christian theologians of disability, like Niebuhr, refute the idea that limits are evil or that God imposes them as punishment for sin; yet in churches, popular suspicion lingers that disability might indeed be the result of sin or unbelief. In order to shift away from the logic of blame that has often governed Christian thinking about disability, theologians of disability further unravel the associations between sin and human limits.

Perhaps most significantly for theological anthropology, disability studies refuses to place disability in a dichotomous relation with normality. Not only is everyone finite and, therefore, limited, but all people also experience disability at some point in their lives. Childhood, old age, injury, and recovery from illness inevitably incapacitate people to various degrees. As Elizabeth Stuart reframes the category, "The contrast is not between the able and the disabled but between the temporarily able and the disabled."[6]

Accordingly, Deborah Creamer's limits model for theological anthropology starts from the premise that human limitations are normal. Noting that "disability is actually more normal than any other state of embodiedness," she suggests that a theological anthropology should "start with the human variations of ability as the norm, and to build theory and theology from that starting place."[7] This model can attend to people's movement in and out of various degrees of ability and the various ways people might identify with their limits.

Creamer distinguishes her approach from other models in the disability rights movement. In the early stages, the movement assumed a medical model that defined disability in terms of the individual body and its functionality. Developed concurrently with "professional and academic disciplines that concentrate upon the management, repair, and maintenance of physical and cognitive capacity" this model aims to "normalize" people with disabilities, for

6. Elizabeth Stuart, "Disruptive Bodies: Disability, Embodiment and Sexuality," in *Good News of the Body: Sexual Theology and Feminism*, ed. Lisa Isherwood (New York: New York University Press, 2000), 168.

7. Deborah Beth Creamer, *Disability and Christian Theology: Embodied Limits and Constructive Possibilities* (Oxford: Oxford University Press, 2009), 32.

example through vocational training or prostheses to enable participation in the workplace.[8] Disability and normality remain polarized
in the medical model. Furthermore, by emphasizing the functionality
of particular body parts, the medical model plays into the late capi-
talist implication that a person's worth lies in their productivity and
ability to "contribute" to society. This narrow focus on impairment
risks neglecting the whole person and the contexts in which she lives.

The experience of disability goes beyond physical or mental
impairment and includes social conditions that handicap people by
failing to accommodate diverse bodies. In response to the shortcom-
ings of the medical model, the minority model of disability considers people with disabilities as a social group that shares experiences
of discrimination. This model contributed to the development of
the Americans with Disabilities Act of 1990, which legislates against
certain forms of discrimination, such as in employment and college
admission, and requires means for access of people with disabilities in
public spaces, such as elevators and ramps. Here, "individuals are considered disabled insofar as they experience prejudice and exclusion."[9]
The site of disability here shifts from impairment to social structures
that presuppose able bodies with typical abilities.

Creamer observes that, like the medical model, the minority model
can obscure people with disabilities as whole people. A focus on social
attitudes and barriers can cause the "very real bodily experience of
impairment," and the particular challenges individuals face as they
move through life with a disability, to disappear.[10] Theological
anthropology should not gloss over the "complex relationship" people
have with their disabilities. If "the minority model suggests that
all people with disabilities should accept and even embrace their
own disabilities/impairments,"[11] then there is little room to negotiate
ambivalent or negative attitudes toward impairment.

Both the medical and minority models essentialize disability: one
reduces it to "physical attributes/function" and the other to "social
location/minority status."[12] Both fail to capture people's holistic

8. Ibid., 23.
9. Ibid., 25.
10. Ibid., 27.
11. Ibid.
12. Ibid., 30.

experiences of disability. Just as the category of "normal" is a moving target, Creamer prefers to treat disability as a fluid category, in which individuals participate to various degrees, in differing settings, and at various times in their lives.

In a theological anthropology that starts with limitation, limits are neither obstacles in the quest for an impossible perfection nor immutable identities that position groups of people over and against one another. Creamer writes of limits as both "unsurprising and . . . worthy of theological reflection."[13] This important theological point is also central to Abhinavagupta's cosmology and anthropology, which include limits as part of the reflection of the divine in each person.

THE LIMITED BODY

A limits model of human being might be usefully expanded by conversation with non-dual Saiva notions of limitation at the divine, cosmic, and human levels of reality. Recalling that Christian thought has always borrowed from culture, particularly Jewish, Greek, and modern scientific worldviews, this metaphysic might similarly function to inspire Christian theology to include diverse forms of human embodiment within the *imago Dei*.

Theologians in this Saiva tradition imagine divinity in a process of unfolding into multiplicity and refolding into unity. In the last chapter, creation emerged with a glimmer of awareness that expanded into five, increasingly differentiated degrees of subject and object. In the next phase, six more parts emerge, giving the cosmos additional definition and creating the conditions for the tangible bodies that will emerge in a later phase of divine creativity.

I have designated these parts *the limited body*. In this phase of creation's emergence, all-pervasive, universal divinity makes it possible for other things to exist. Within the world, divine omnipotence is expressed as limited power. Omniscience operates as limited knowledge. Divine fullness opens up to desire. In contrast to ideals of divine omnipresence and infinity, bodies—including divine bodies—are

13. Ibid., vii.

limited in time and space.[14] Outside the glimpses of unity described in the last chapters, humans move within a world of diversity made possible by this series of divine self-limitations.

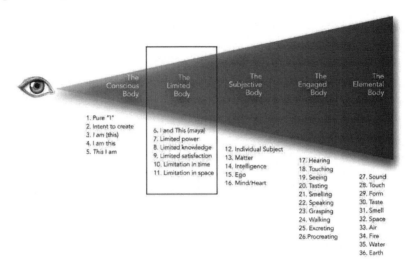

Fig. 3.

This story of creation builds limits into the very fabric of the world. The concept is simple: discrete selves—whether divine or human—require limitation. One cannot relate to another if they cannot find their boundaries. A person cannot remember without a sense of time. Although people might become frustrated with the inabilities be all places at once, to know all things, and to do everything they might like to do, limits are not evil. However much one might struggle against these laws of nature, they are the very conditions of our constitution as individuals.

Abhinavagupta's map of consciousness will guide our consideration of how, specifically, a Christian theology of limitation might include the full range of human and divine embodiment. In his cosmology, limited consciousness (*maya*) unfolds into par-

14. Lists of the sheaths are not always complete or consistent. PTv and PTlv list four limitations, whereas Abhinavagupta's *Tantrasara* and contemporary scholars of this tradition tend to list the six discussed here. For one of Abhinavagupta's discussions of the six, see Abhinavagupta, *Introduction to Tantric Philosophy*, 130–38.

ticular sheaths (*kancukas*) that limit power, knowledge, satisfaction, time, and space. Each is a body part (*tattva*, category) in its own right. Following this map as a provisional guide, we will inquire what each contributes to an inclusive anthropology.

ROOT METAPHOR: LIMITED CONSCIOUSNESS

The root of all limitation, in Abhinavagupta's tradition, is the limitation of consciousness called *maya*. Consciousness is the basic nature of everything. Siva's eyes open, and he perceives all of reality into being. His eyes close, and the universe dissolves again into undifferentiated bliss. The universe is thus pervaded with divine consciousness. The limited body is necessary because, in order for sentient creatures to emerge as individual centers of consciousness, universal consciousness must be delimited. *Maya* is the initial limitation to divine consciousness and the precondition for creation. *Maya* makes it possible for the divine subject to recognize a distinct object: from "I am this" to "I *and* this."

Indian philosophies sometimes paint *maya* negatively as the "illusion" that veils the unity of reality. After all, that is how human beings experience it. *Maya* functions in daily life to bar human beings from experiencing the omnipotence, omniscience, satiety, and freedom that characterize pure consciousness. *Maya* is also the reason individuals reap the consequences of their actions (*karma*). In some Indian traditions, *maya* has never escaped its negative taint. It obscures the unity of reality, and this delusion can result in greed, lust, and hatred toward others. Other Hindu theologians insist, however, that the veils that adhere to consciousness are not evil.[15] From this perspective, *maya* registers more neutrally as "artifice," the principle of creation and one of Siva-Sakti's powers. Along with the five limitations that follow—limited power, imperfect knowledge, desires, and boundedness in time and space—*maya* contracts universal consciousness so

---

15. Contemporary Hindu theologians continue to wrestle with the tension between *maya* as a source of evil and *maya* as non-different from ultimate reality. For a constructive Hindu reclamation of *maya*, see Anantanand Rambachan, *The Advaita Worldview: God, World, and Humanity* (Albany: State University of New York Press, 2006).

that all of the interesting and variegated beings in the world can arise. Without these limitations as parts of the human body, people could neither differentiate themselves from Siva-Sakti nor transcend the state of insentient earth.[16]

Christian attitudes have also been ambivalent toward this limitation. Christians have been tempted to identify the finite body as the source of sin; yet Niebuhr calls it the "genius" of Christianity that "individuality as separate and particular existence is not evil by reason of being distinguished from undifferentiated totality."[17] As with finitude, the individuation of the self is not evil but a blessing. The blessing of limited consciousness is that there are some things rather than no things. Limitation also makes devotion to a personal deity possible.[18] If humans are to love, worship, imitate, and adore God, then God must self-limit as a discrete Other who can be the object of these actions. If there is to be history, there must be actors distinct from God. Perhaps the very structure of human knowing requires a circumscribed message and messenger suited to the epistemic situation (an insight encapsulated in the paradoxical Christian claim that a universal truth has been communicated through a particular divine incarnation).

Furthermore, limits do not denote incomplete humanity but can evoke its virtues. People often develop "perseverance, strength, and creativity" in relation to them, Creamer observes.[19] Limited consciousness capacitates rich experiences of love, curiosity, and learning. Just as an artist is both constrained and inspired by her medium, working within limits can produce innovative ways of being. Mental and emotional limits can lead to original patterns of relationship. Frustration with limits in an ableist society can provoke reform.

---

16. As the short commentary explains, these powers "maintain the individual soul resting in the middle . . . which otherwise would fall into the condition of complete inertia like a rock, or would ascend into the sky of consciousness like the supreme Lord" (PTlv, 211).

17. Niebuhr, *Nature and Destiny*, 167.

18. Some Hindu devotional traditions affirm that God takes on a limited form to communicate in a particular time and space. As Krishna says in Bhagavad Gita 4.7–8, "Whenever sacred duty decays and chaos prevails, then, I create myself, Arjuna. . . . To set the standard of sacred duty, I appear in age after age." Barbara Stoler Miller, trans., *The Bhagavad-Gita: Krishna's Council in Time of War* (New York: Bantam, 1986), 50.

19. Creamer, *Disability and Christian Theology*, 112–13.

At each turn, limited consciousness provides opportunities for novel forms of survival and flourishing.

FIRST LIMITATION: POWER

Overcoming limited power is the stuff of fantasies: to leap tall buildings in a single bound, to read minds, to learn magic at Hogwarts. We dream of defying the laws of nature. Nevertheless, the divine image does not make us omnipotent. Quite the opposite: because Siva "in a condition of deep sleep . . . is incapable of anything," this body part, limited power, restores a limited capacity for action.[20] Because of limitation, divinity is able to do things it otherwise could not do.

For Niebuhr, although limited powers are not themselves evil, they do provide occasions for sin in the form of pride. Some people relate to limitations by denying them—a temptation he names the *pride of power*,

> in which the human ego assumes its self-sufficiency and self-mastery and imagines itself secure against all vicissitudes. It does not recognize the contingent and dependent character of its life and believes itself to be the author of its own existence, the judge of its own values and the master of its own destiny.[21]

This pretense is often seen in people or institutions that consider themselves beyond the reach of law. A measure of power can delude individuals that they are entitled to exchange influence for money or violate the rights of others. For an institutional example, one need look no further than the big banks, considered "too big to fail," whose recklessness led to global financial crisis.

For other people, deep-seated uneasiness about one's limits can lead to the attempt to compensate by grasping at whatever will grant a feeling of security. For instance, individual greed feeds on the sense that more possessions and a bigger bank account can ward off misfortune. This second variety of the pride of power comes into play on

---

20. Paul Eduardo Muller-Ortega, *The Triadic Heart of Siva: Kaula Tantricism of Abhinavagupta in the Non-Dual Shaivism of Kashmir* (Albany: State University of New York Press, 1989), 130.
21. Niebuhr, *Nature and Destiny*, 188.

a collective level when defense budgets soar beyond all sensibility. In the face of anxiety, it is not enough to have firepower to annihilate the world; a wealthy nation gains a measure of security only when its arsenal can annihilate the world many times over. Although dominant sectors of society can be tempted to both varieties of the pride of power, Niebuhr believes that the people on society's margins, who lack ostensible power, are more prone to this second kind of compensation, in which whatever power can be arrogated over another person or group might assuage the indignities of one's own tenuous position. Intimate partner violence and child abuse, for instance, can sometimes be byproducts of powerlessness or discrimination in the public sphere.[22]

If people with relatively more privilege and security might be tempted to grasp at power in different ways than people with less privilege, *intersecting* power structures complicate the situation. Identity politics sometimes gives the impression that the advancement of one group (women, minoritized ethnic groups, immigrants, working-class people) must detract from the gains of another—when, in fact, no one belongs to any single identity category.[23] These complex connections within and across communities, as results of limited power, can be a source of sin, but they can also be claimed as a source of creativity and solidarity.

Contemporary theology is gradually registering the shift from the fantasy of immutable, self-determined isolation to the richness of relation. As process theologians John Cobb and David Ray Griffin put it, "the perfection of human life involves maximizing our relatedness to others."[24] Existence is relation: we are annexed to the lives of many other people, to other species, to the planet. Species are related to one another at the most profound levels. Human activity, weather

22. Of course, the disenfranchised are not always tempted to pride. They might instead hide their abilities, negate the self, and prematurely foreshorten possibilities. See, for example, Valerie Saiving, "The Human Situation: A Feminine View," in *Womanspirit Rising: A Feminist Reader in Religion*, ed. Carol P. Christ and Judith Plaskow (New York: Harper & Row, 1979).

23. For example, despite the fact that a "greater percentage of black people appear to be disabled," the presumed whiteness of the field of disability studies has impeded alliances. Josh Lukin, "Disability and Blackness," in *The Disability Studies Reader*, ed. Lennard J. Davis (London: Taylor & Francis, 2013), 308.

24. John B. Cobb Jr. and David Ray Griffin, *Process Theology: An Introductory Exposition* (Philadelphia: Westminster, 1976), 17, 21.

events, and global ecology are intimately intertwined. This essential relation to others limits our options, to be sure, but it also becomes grounds for the gratitude and mutual responsibility that make life worth living.

SECOND LIMITATION: KNOWLEDGE

When a hut on the Galehead trail in the White Mountains was made accessible to wheelchairs, a controversy ensued, with one reporter asking "why people in wheelchairs could drag themselves up the trail and not drag themselves up the steps to the hut." Alison Kafer observes, "This challenge to the appropriateness of the Galehead ramp exemplifies the ways in which nondisabled access is made invisible while disabled access is made hypervisible."[25] The configuration of the built world often matches what the nondisabled take as a commonsense perspective. In fact, all structures accommodate particular kinds of bodies. This reporter seems unaware that the original trail and the steps to the hut, not to mention the shape and placement of car doors and the size of computer keyboards, all provide access. The failure to perceive this results from limited knowledge.

Knowledge is limited as an inevitable consequence of having particular bodies, having certain experiences and not others, being situated in a particular place and time, and so on. Pure objectivity eludes the inquiries of embodied beings. Even the hard sciences must come to grips with the theory of relativity, which accounts for the effects of motion in space and time, and the observer effect, wherein phenomena change by virtue of being measured.

Dogs do not seem bothered by the relativity of their perspectives. As far as we can tell, fish teeter toward neither skepticism nor nihilism. Humans, however, know that their knowledge is partial and hide their ignorance by denying it.[26] For human beings, this fundamental uncertainty carries a set of temptations parallel to those related to limited power. Niebuhr calls this the *sin of intellectual pride*, "the pride of reason which forgets that it is involved in a temporal

---

25. Alison Kafer, *Feminist, Queer, Crip* (Bloomington: Indiana University Press, 2013), 137–38.
26. Niebuhr, *Nature and Destiny*, 182.

process and imagines itself in compete transcendence over history."[27] As examples of intellectual pride, Niebuhr refers to a series of philosophers, each of whom criticized his predecessors' limitations but still believed that he had reached the pinnacle of universal truth. However, intellectual pride is not only the temptation of philosophers, political pundits, and other know-it-alls. "All human knowledge is tainted with an 'ideological' taint," he writes. "It pretends to be more true than it is. It is finite knowledge, gained from a particular perspective; but it pretends to be final and ultimate knowledge."[28] When challenged, one is tempted to dig in, fortify the conviction of being right, and admit only the evidence that supports one's position. On a group level, Niebuhr saw this happening in pre-civil rights United States, where white Christians, afraid of losing their status, went to great lengths to rationalize racial discrimination.[29]

Is there a blessing in limited knowledge? The short commentary on *The Goddess of the Three* relates it to the illuminating element of fire: this divine power restores to limitless consciousness the capacity for limited knowledge (PTlv, 211). Because of it, divinity and others can know particular things. Limited knowledge can be a source of gratitude for the lessons of one's particular life. The world looks different to me now than before I became a parent or lived in the American South. Each of these experiences decreases the illusion that my perspective is universal. Just so, the jolt of realization that *stairs provide access*—hikers do not have to climb through the hut's window—transforms the ableist mentality that access is a "problem" that applies only to people with disabilities. Recognition of limited knowledge can instill a sense of curiosity open to learning from the experiences of others.

THIRD LIMITATION: SATISFACTION

Limited satisfaction is another word for desire. The Sanskrit word for this body part is *raga*, desire or attachment. Desire can lead to clinging, greed, and obsession: if only we could eat enough, own enough

27. Ibid., 195.
28. Ibid., 194.
29. Ibid., 198.

clothes, or control our loved ones . . . then we would no longer feel the gnaw of want.

In comparative perspective, limited satisfaction is a good analogue for the anxiety Niebuhr diagnoses as the root of pride. For him, the anxious human condition stems from the paradox between human freedom and dependency, which creates the precondition for sinful pretensions to be self-sufficient.[30] In Niebuhr's theological framework, only God is self-sufficient. He writes that "the contrast between the created world and the Creator, between its dependent and insufficient existence and His freedom and self-sufficiency, is absolute."[31] Human beings can never be the source of their own existence.

Niebuhr rightly contests the modern construction of the autonomous subject, but he overstates the case for divine aseity. As we explore more fully in the next chapter, desire also belongs to divinity. What is desire, if not love? Jeannine Hill Fletcher therefore challenges a theological anthropology structured by the ideal of the self-sufficient Father by attending to the "experience of women in mothering roles." "Our relationality is structured by a 'calculus of concern,'" she writes, "human beings are embedded in networks of relationality to which limited resources are distributed at cost to oneself."[32]

She gives the mundane example from a morning at home. She wakes early so that she can work on an article before her family rises. She hears her son stirring and knows that if she can reach him in time, she can soothe him back to sleep. However, if she moves too quickly, she will wake her daughter, who is asleep beside her. Recognizing multiple limits and needs, she instinctively negotiates commitments between self, family, students, and profession. "The subject-position of motherhood demonstrates that the human condition is one in which we cannot 'have it all,'" she muses.[33] On a good day, the writer-scholar-mother-spouse-teacher might successfully arrive at the study without waking the children and complete

30. Ibid., 191.
31. Ibid., 169.
32. Jeannine Hill Fletcher, *Motherhood as Metaphor: Engendering Interreligious Dialogue* (New York: Fordham University Press, 2013), 51.
33. Ibid., 53.

her article, but that desire may be deferred at any moment by other needs and wants within her network of care. Limited satisfaction is the very condition of embeddedness in the world. Love exposes each of us to lack, conflict, and tragedy—even as it weaves a fragile beauty out of complex relations.

FOURTH LIMITATION: TIME

Death is the horizon of human preoccupation with finitude. All other insecurities point to it. Limited power, knowledge, consciousness, and satisfaction converge here. We do not know the time of our death. If we did, we would be powerless to stop it. We long for deceased loved ones, and we fear being forgotten when we have died.

When Christians claim immortality as their destiny, Niebuhr says, the paradoxical coexistence of finitude and freedom collapses. Death is the ultimate limit, so it should be no surprise that religion would address it with promises of "eternal life" (John 3:16). However, the idea that human beings would be immortal if sin had never entered the world "obscures [the] organic relation to nature and could be made meaningful only if it were assumed that sin had introduced death into the whole of nature," Niebuhr writes. "But such an assumption becomes almost identical with the Hellenistic belief that nature and finiteness are themselves evil."[34] The entitlement to immortality, which developed in exilic Judaism and continued in early Christianity, it is at odds with other biblical themes of human contingency and creaturehood. Could this development be part of humanity's willful tendency to overreach and deny limits?

Disability studies suggest other temporal stances, which more adequately reflect that time is limited and that humans are limited in time. Chronic illness confounds narratives of assured healing. Aging guarantees that if one is able-bodied, the condition is temporary. When one becomes ill in the United States, the "time of undiagnosis" entails "the shuttling between specialists, the repeated refusal of care and services, the constant denial of one's experiences, the slow exacerbation of one's symptoms, the years without recognition or diag-

34. Niebuhr, *Nature and Destiny*, 175.

nosis, the waiting"; the "time of prognosis" then calls the future into question.[35] People with post-traumatic stress disorder or multiple chemical sensitivity "live in a kind of anticipatory time, scanning their days for events or exposures that might trigger a response."[36] In all of these modalities, which Kafer calls "crip time," the lived experiences of people with disabilities throw "normative and normalizing expectations of pace and scheduling" off track.[37]

Temporal limits can reshape the imagination regarding full humanity within a bounded life span. By being realistic about temporal limitations, crip time can engender appreciation for the limited time of life and a loving reinvestment in the present.[38] If one is willing to abdicate "American ideals of productivity at all costs," for example, "imaginative life schedules" centered on the body's needs can emerge.[39] The limits to longevity might become, as Kafer implores, "a call for love and justice rather than a sign of tragedy or shame."[40] Accepting contingency opens other avenues for making meaning.

All flesh is grass (Isa 40:6). How odd that normative expectations would imply anything else! Sharon Betcher challenges her readers: "So draw a line in the sand: let go of the heroics of medicine. Let yourself be mortal. There's something more to the fullness of life than measured by biology."[41] The 'adam of Genesis is, after all, an "earth creature." From dust it came, and to dust it will return. Advances in medicine can alleviate suffering, but they cannot grant immortality. Nevertheless, we can receive the needs and delights of the moment as the gifts of life's fullness.

35. Kafer, Feminist, Queer, Crip, 37.
36. Ibid., 38.
37. Ibid., 27.
38. Kafer highlights Jack Halberstam's study of AIDS narratives in this regard. Ibid., 36–37.
39. Ibid., 39, 38.
40. Ibid., 41.
41. Sharon V. Betcher, "Revisiting Midnight's Children: Critical Disability and Postcolonial Studies Interventions in Christology," Postscripts: The Journal of Scared Texts and Contemporary Words 7, no. 3 (2011): 329.

FIFTH LIMITATION: SPACE

Who among us can be somewhere other than here, now? The Sanskrit word for this limitation is *niyati*, a word with connotations of necessity, fate, and destiny. The place one is born influences—by fate, as it were—what a person or community can become. "The function of *niyati tattva*," one teacher explains, is to give people the impression of "residing in such and such a particular place and not in all places."[42] Spatial limitation is thus related to the contingency we call *culture*. When people are born and where they dwell determine much about them, including their language and the starting point for their assumptions and identity.

We have seen that Niebuhr regards "the pretensions of universality . . . as a sin" because every perspective is "qualified by its 'here and now' relation to a particular body."[43] One's abilities and understanding remain conditioned by one's location in the world. Postcolonial theology illuminates how cultural differences create opportunities for sin. Western European imperialism has been fueled not only by new modes of transport and the hope of economic gain but also by narratives of Western cultural and religious superiority. As the narrative goes, people in other parts of the world are incapable of governing themselves or maximizing their own resources, and they need the superior and benevolent wisdom of the colonizers. It is morally incumbent on the West to bring sanitation, civilization, and salvation to the rest of humanity.[44] The (not so) benevolent paternalism that undergirded both colonialism and the slave system in the United States still weaves itself through contemporary political and religious rhetoric.

One's habits are not superior simply because they are one's own. Niebuhr describes as *moral pride* the permutation of the anxious ego that holds up one's own relative standards as the absolute and only

---

42. Swami Lakshmanjoo, *Kashmir Shaivism: The Secret Supreme* (Albany: State University of New York Press, 1988), 7.

43. Niebuhr, *Nature and Destiny*, 170.

44. For the implication of disability rhetoric in these narratives, see Betcher, "Revisiting *Midnight's Children*," 7.

truth: "Moral pride thus makes virtue the very vehicle of sin."[45] Religious communities in particular are tempted to exempt their own practices, beliefs, and ethics from contingent processes of development and cultural formation. Thus exempted and universalized, they project inferiority or degeneracy upon others. By contrast with this religio-cultural chauvinism, Rabbi Jonathan Sacks encourages an alternative reading of the tower of Babel: God does not impose linguistic, cultural, and religious differences as a punishment for hubris, but rather ensures diversity because it pleases God.[46]

Limitation in space also includes ecological contingency. Reflecting on physical space, Betcher observes that humans now live with the "new 'neighbors' we've loosed into the world—PCBs, nuclear particulate, excess carbon."[47] These material realities are neither temporary nor anomalous, and they challenge the way that the colonial mind maps the world: "Today the South is . . . a harbinger for the North—not its primitive forbearer, but its future."[48] Infirmity, disability, and ecological disaster, long projected onto other continents by able and benevolent Christians in the global North, cannot be repressed or held at bay. The limitations are "ours" as well, and this will require of Christian theologians "a significant psychic adjustment for living into ecological interdependence."[49]

PRACTICES OF EMBRACING THE LIMITED BODY

It is extraordinarily countercultural for white, middle-class Christians in the United States to embrace limits. We learn many academic subjects, from history to the sciences, as a series of obstacles that have been overcome. Theology falls into the same grooves. A nostalgia for a past self, free from impairment, hearkens back to Eden before the fall, and it projects forward to a paradise to come. Some pastors urge parishioners to renounce the limits, contingencies, and vulnerabilities

45. Niebuhr, *Nature and Destiny*, 199.

46. Jonathan Sacks, *The Dignity of Difference: How to Avoid the Clash of Civilizations* (New York: Continuum, 2002), 52.

47. Betcher, "Revisiting *Midnight's Children*," 21–22.

48. Ibid., 19. Betcher develops this postcolonial analysis in *Spirit and the Obligation of Social Flesh: A Secular Theology for the Global City* (New York: Fordham University Press, 2014).

49. Betcher, "Revisiting *Midnight's Children*," 23.

of their lives—to envision what they want, and to "name it and claim it." Can we embrace the limited body as a spiritual practice?

Fantasies of purity disdain anything less than a cure, but the heroes of faith tell another story. Abraham and Sarah were infertile. Moses had a speech impediment. Paul struggled with a "thorn in the flesh." The saints model faith within these conditions. If a person is omnipotent, she has no need for courage. Unless a person gives something, he cannot be called generous. Aristotle's philosophy formalizes this insight. He observes that limitations present opportunities for moral and spiritual formation. Wishing away embodied limits is equivalent to wishing away an intelligible moral universe, for these make justice, courage, generosity, and moderation comprehensible. Much of the adventure and goodness of life is made possible *because* of its ambiguity.[50]

The *kenosis* or self-emptying of Christ provides one model for embracing limits. In the famous Philippians hymn, Christ,

> who, though he was in the form of God,
>   did not regard equality with God
>   as something to be exploited,
> but emptied himself,
>   taking the form of a slave,
>   being born in human likeness.
> And being found in human form,
>   he humbled himself
>   and became obedient to the point of death—
>   even death on a cross.
> Therefore God also highly exalted him
>   and gave him the name
>   that is above every name. (Phil 2:6–9)

Here, Christ begins in a position of fullness, equal with God, but abdicates it in solidarity with humankind. God then exalts him again

---

50. See Martha C. Nussbaum, *The Fragility of Goodness: Luck and Ethics in Greek Tragedy and Philosophy* (Cambridge: Cambridge University Press, 1986), 341. I appreciate my colleague John Senior for reminding me of this ethical tradition, as well as my colleague Elizabeth Gandolfo for calling attention to the flip side of this dynamic: "It is precisely because human goodness and happiness are so closely tied to vulnerability, indeed are only available *in vulnerability*, that the human *telos* is so vulnerable to destruction." Elizabeth O'Donnell Gandolfo, *The Power and Vulnerability of Love: A Theological Anthropology* (Minneapolis: Fortress Press, 2015), 99.

as a reward for his sacrifice. In one interpretation of this logic, humans should imitate divine *kenosis* by humbling themselves, self-sacrificially taking on the limits of the poor and marginalized.[51]

Contemporary exegetes cast a wary eye on the privilege this kenotic approach presumes. Christ's experience of being "in the form of a slave" is unlike the involuntary condition of actual slavery, and his abjection is temporary. With this crucial distinction, Sheila Briggs argues, the Philippians hymn reinscribes the values of a slave society. Christ is honored because of his perfect obedience. The people who stand to benefit from this teaching are the slaveholders, not the slaves.[52] Eiesland observes a similar effect in theologies that advocate self-limitation. Self-limitation might be an appropriate practice for people "who live in abundance and whose consumerist practices defy the reality of global scarcity," but this ethic rings absurd for people whose economic or physical conditions severely limit them.[53]

It is all too easy for an ethic of self-sacrifice to romanticize limitation and acquiesce to the status quo. Instead, the ethical response to oppressive and unnecessary limits is to struggle against them and work toward a society that empowers and liberates people. For the dominant, the privileged, and the temporarily able-bodied and able-minded, this may indeed be a call to self-limit: to keep the presumed universality of one's experience in check, to adjust one's reality to accommodate others, and to use one's powers to remove unnecessary and disabling limits for others.

Most people fall somewhere between the poles of privilege and oppression, with limited ability to remove limitations. We face the conundrum of discernment: which limits must one embrace, which should a society accommodate, and which may we try to remove? How can one take responsibility and avoid the extremes of "apathy and omnipotent control"?[54]

A limits model of human being reframes the polarities: "Rather

---

51. Cf. David Tracy, *Blessed Rage for Order: The New Pluralism in Theology* (New York: Seabury, 1975), 106, 221.

52. Sheila Briggs, "Can an Enslaved God Liberate? Hermeneutical Reflections on Philippians 2:6–11," *Semeia* 47 (1989): 146–47.

53. Nancy L. Eiesland, *The Disabled God: Toward A Liberatory Theology of Disability* (Nashville: Abingdon, 1994), 84.

54. Creamer, *Disability and Christian Theology*, 113.

than thinking of limits solely in a negative sense (what we, or what God, cannot do), this perspective offers alternatives for thinking about boundaries and possibilities."[55] Our comparative framework has highlighted boundaries of ability, knowledge, dependency, and contingency that put parameters on the possibilities. In many cases, limitation simply is. Not every choice is available to us, and unforeseen detours, accidents, and surprises beset our attempts to implement new possibilities. These result not only from prideful human attempts to overcome creaturely insecurity but also from living in a contingent world. Within such boundaries and possibilities, Sharon Welch calls for a "nondualistic vocabulary of strength and weakness, of insight and deception—one that emphasizes accountability, not guilt."[56] We are not to be blamed for our limited time, energy, abilities, and resources, but we are accountable to one another within them.

This reframing should restrain the culture of compulsory cure forwarded by the medical model of disability. Scientific and theological inquiry both aim for human flourishing, but they work at cross purposes when they place blame on people who cannot afford or do not choose to pursue the latest technological advance. This moralizing comes from medical and religious communities alike: "Why don't you just get corrective surgery?" "Of course you are suffering. You won't take your medication." Alongside the ableist desire present in these statements is a failure to recognize that limits apply to medical interventions as well. Every solution—whether medical or social—occurs in the context of limited power, knowledge, and lifespan. Interventions come with unforeseen side effects. Human agents fail to deliver fully on their promises. Much of the time, we must live with less than a cure.

Human acceptance of limits (in ability, knowledge, time, place, and satisfaction), does not thereby negate the quest to cure the diseases and impairments that cause so much suffering. Far from it. Much good has been achieved through vaccines, surgical innovations, pharmacology, prostheses, and therapeutic techniques. Kafer

55. Ibid.

56. Sharon D. Welch, *Sweet Dreams in America: Making Ethics and Spirituality Work* (New York: Routledge, 1999), 43.

acknowledges the "tricky ground" upon which she argues against visions of the future in which disability is eradicated:

> As must joy as I find in communities of disabled people, and as much as I value my experiences as a disabled person, I am not interested in becoming more disabled than I already am. I realize that position itself is marked by an ableist failure of imagination, but I can't deny holding it. Nor am I opposed to prenatal care and public health initiatives aimed at preventing illness and impairment, and futures in which the majority of people continue to lack access to such basic needs are not futures I want. But there is a difference between denying necessary health care, condoning dangerous working conditions, or ignoring public health concerns (thereby causing illness and impairment) and recognizing illness and disability as part of what makes us human.[57]

Limits call not for a single spiritual practice but many—not only acceptance but also protest, solidarity, lament, and healing. As the place of life's passion and adventure, limits do call for courage and acceptance. In many cases, however, limitations result from exploitation or neglect of these basic contingencies. The limits human beings unnecessarily place upon one another call for protest and solidarity. In still other cases, neither acceptance nor protest is adequate. The tragic dimension of our interconnected world entails that, despite awareness of how our daily practices perpetuate global, economic, and environmental harm, we may be unable to extricate ourselves fully from them. For complicity in oppression, lament is also an appropriate practice.

Without returning to compulsory cure, a limits anthropology may also speak of healing as a spiritual practice. Theologians of disability make an important distinction between healing and cure. "Healing happens when the well-being God offers is experienced," Kathy Black writes. "This may entail elimination or alleviation of the illness, but in the case of permanent disability, healing often happens in the midst of managing the disability rather than any kind of 'cure.'"[58] Communities are integral to well-being. One does not heal alone, for "wholeness" comes from "the genuinely inclusive communion that

57. Kafer, *Feminist, Queer, Crip*, 4.
58. Kathy Black, *A Healing Homiletic: Preaching and Disability* (Nashville: Abingdon, 1996), 53.

results from sharing our humanity with one another in light of the grace of God."[59] Limitation belongs to the living matrix in which human beings are called to love one another.

This chapter has encouraged Christians to consider limits as essential to being human. We are neither omnipotent nor omniscient. We need others to survive and flourish. We are born and live out our lives in particular times and places. Our many different kinds and degrees of limitations are part of our created diversity. God affirms this creation as "good," even as its inherent vulnerability also provides opportunities for harmful denial and overcompensation for limits.

It would appear that, even with God's infinite extension in time and presence in all places, God contends with the same world we do: the wild, random world of cancer cells and supernovas, of evolution and dying stars, of prayers and hopes and tears. Can Christians understand limits as part of the divine body as well? Are they part of the image of God in humanity? This is the question to which the next chapter turns.

59. Reynolds, *Vulnerable Communion*, 18.

3.

The Limited Body (Part 2)

Together with the work of Reinhold Niebuhr and scholars of disability, the categories of the limited body remind us that limits are not inherently evil but can be embraced as part of God's intent for creatures. But who is God with respect to human limits? If limitation is part of God's good creation and not a result of sin, does it also belong to the image of God in humanity? Is God limited? Disabled? Nancy Eiesland's well-known epiphany claims as much. She saw

> God in a sip-puff wheelchair, that is, the chair used mostly by quadriplegics enabling them to maneuver by blowing and sucking on a strawlike device. Not an omnipotent, self-sufficient God, but neither a pitiable, suffering servant. . . . I recognized the incarnate Christ in the image of those judged "not feasible," "unemployable," with "questionable quality of life." Here was God for me.[1]

Admittedly, attributing limitation to God seems counterintuitive, even impious. Everyone knows God is perfect, omnipotent, omniscient, and above the fray. If humans are limited, it must be because we are *not* God. Limitation is a marker of our finitude, Niebuhr insists. God is not finite. Therefore, limitation—however good—is not part of how we image God. Eiesland's vision of God as disabled seems to contravene what people—including many people with

---

1. Nancy L. Eiesland, *The Disabled God: Toward a Liberation Theology of Disability* (Nashville: Abingdon, 1994), 89.

disabilities—want and need from their deity. This chapter takes a second look, again taking inspiration from the non-dual Saiva tradition.

The thirty-six part anthropology of this tradition startles Christians with its frank placement of six limitations—limited consciousness, power, knowledge, and satisfaction, and limitations in time and space—squarely within its image of God, world, and humanity. This surprise factor is one of comparative theology's benefits as a method. The unexpected inclusion of limits within divinity invites us to investigate, to know more, to try on the idea that limits are not an afterthought or a deficit in divine perfection but inherent in the divine relation to creation. Perhaps these insights on limitation can be woven into a Christian view of the human person, in which limits do not blur the image of God in humanity but reveal its depths.

This chapter explores openings in contemporary Christian theology that make it possible to imagine each of the six limitations as part of God's experience. As we make our way through the parts of the limited body, a constellation of voices from classical, feminist, disability, and relational theologies will point the way to a Christian model of God that includes limits, as well as a corresponding model of the *imago Dei* in which human limits reflect something of God's experience of the world.

FROM CLASSICAL THEISM TO OTHER MODELS

It is rather commonplace for contemporary theologians to take aim at what has come to be called *classical theism*. Christian theology adopted a set of attributes for God through engagement with the Greek philosophies that were pervasive in the ancient and medieval world. The "omnis"—omnipotence, omniscience, omnipresence, and omnibenevolence—deny any limit to God's power, knowledge, or goodness. The list is rounded out by other descriptors such as immutability, apatheia or unfeelingness, and aseity, the condition of being self-sufficient or self-generated.

According to the logic of classical theism, to feel is to change, to desire is to lack, and to change or lack is to suffer. Classical theists prefer an unchanging, unfeeling God, who cannot suffer, but they must also reconcile these divine attributes with salvation history. God's adventures of covenant, exile, redemption, incarnation, crucifixion, and new community must be made to comport with the notions that God controls everything, does not change, and does not feel. For instance, Thomas Aquinas chooses to deny "real relation" in God, because relationship would entail vulnerability and change.[2] Another strategy is to attribute God's joy, regret, compassion, and surprise in Scripture to anthropomorphism, humanlike expressions placed in the text to help finite readers understand the Infinite. Anselm thus shields God from the entanglements of love by distinguishing God's eternal nature from the human experience of God in history, writing, "Thou art compassionate in terms of our experience, and not compassionate in terms of thy being."[3]

Critiques of classical theism have come from many angles, starting with the observation that, despite the existence of isolated scriptural passages that can be interpreted as teaching that God neither feels nor changes, the biblical narrative does not support these interpretations very well. Salvation history is the saga of God longing for God's wayward people. God is vulnerable to their spurning. Incarnate, Christ becomes a particular person, limited in time, place, and perspective. His ministry culminates with the ultimate vulnerability: torture and execution. Keen to unravel the attribute of divine apatheia, Jürgen Moltmann's path-breaking book, *The Crucified God*, narrates the inner-Trinitarian drama of suffering love. It is not only the human nature of Jesus that suffers. Rather, the second person of the Trinity suffers abandonment to death, and the first person suffers the loss of the beloved Son.[4]

Although the divine attributes of classical theism represent the perfections limited and vulnerable human beings might desire, the God of classical theism is, in fact, limited by the inability to engage in "real relation" with the world. Attempts to protect God from the vulnerability of relation and change, in fact, place limits on God's ability to

2. Aquinas, *Summa Theologiae*, 1.28.

3. Anselm, *Proslogion: With the Replies of Gaunilo and Anselm*, trans. Thomas Williams (Indianapolis: Hackett, 2011), ch. 8.

4. Jürgen Moltmann, *The Crucified God: The Cross of Christ as the Foundation and Criticism of Christian Theology* (Minneapolis: Fortress Press, 1993), 243.

love. A reading of Scripture through the lens of relationship yields a different view. One discerns a compassionate God, who freely enters into relationship with the world, creating new life, responding to injustice with righteous anger, and lamenting tragedy and degradation. The fact that God can suffer these things is not a deficiency but rather a perfection. God's compassionate presence offers comfort, solidarity, and empowerment, which mysteriously transform suffering.[5] If God's loving relation to the world is real, then each of the classical divine attributes must be reinterpreted.

GOD'S BODY

The model of the limited body will again serve as the framework for this investigation. I use the word *model* intentionally, since the apophatic dimension of theology reminds us that language does not describe God, who transcends all categories. Instead, theologians posit metaphors or models for God. In a good metaphor, one thing is shown to be like another in certain ways, and yet the two things remain dissimilar in other ways. When someone describes a football player as a beast, they affirm his physical size, strength, and ferocity. No one actually believes that a grizzly will be suiting up for the game. A metaphor contains dimensions of both "is" and "is not." God is like an ideal human parent in some ways (God generates or adopts other beings, loves them, and cares for them), but not in others (God does not procreate sexually and is not partial to one family over another). In order to remind us of this dialectical nature, theology employs many such images. As Sallie McFague argues, some metaphors have staying power and become useful models over time—so much so that Christians are tempted to forget their twofold character. However, when the "is not" predominates and a model outlives its usefulness, the theologian's task is to propose new metaphors and models for the Christian imagination.[6]

In view of the "is not" character of classical models of God's power and perfection, McFague offers the model of the world as God's body.

---

5. Cf. Johnson, *She Who Is*, 265–70.
6. McFague, *Models of God*, 35.

Drawing upon the metaphor of the relation of self and body, this model understands God to be intimately related to and affected by what happens in the world, while not being reduced to it.[7] God is both transcendent of the world and immanent within it. In this panentheistic model, the world (*pan*) resides in (*en*) God (*theos*)—an important distinction from pantheism, which would equate the natural world with the divine.[8] God retains God's transcendence in a manner similar to the way the self includes but is not reduced to the physical body.

McFague believes that this model can dispose human beings toward the world differently than the old, monarchical model of God as the sovereign but distant ruler over the world. The monarchical model devalues the body, along with the people (women, children, people with disabilities, slaves) associated with the body's functions of birth, labor, feeding, and caretaking. The Earth can be abused and discarded in anticipation of some "new" heaven and Earth. By contrast, the model of the world as God's body claims that embodiment itself is sacred. Because God is not separate from the world, God suffers all of the oil spills, polluted drinking water, choked air, toxic waste, and rising global temperatures that afflict creatures and ecosystems. God feels our negligence and calls us to reverence and care.

Deborah Creamer picks up McFague's model of the world as God's body to point out that, if God includes all of creation within God's existence, then God includes limits. God is no less complete for including death, decay, and finite resources.[9] This claim flies in the face of an ideal of divine perfection that would construe limits as

---

7. McFague, *Body of God*.

8. McFague argues that panentheism better describes God's relation to the world in Scripture than either the uninvolved deity of classical theism or pantheism's natural processes. A variety of thinkers have reclaimed panentheistic themes, including G. W. F. Hegel, Pierre Teilhard de Chardin, Paul Tillich, process theologians, and a number of relational and ecological theologians. Ibid., 150, 254n24.

9. Creamer, *Disability and Christian Theology*, 112. Notably, other interpretations of the self-body metaphor avoid these implications. For an example from the Indian context, Ramanuja uses the self-body analogy to indicate the inseparable relationship of God with the world, the dependence of the world on God, the reality of the world, and the accessibility of God to the world, but he also emphasizes God's essential difference from the world and an immutable and impassible core to the divine being that is not affected by suffering, *karma*, and change. Eric J. Lott, *God and the Universe in the Vedantic Theology of Ramanuja: A Study in His Use of the Self-Body Analogy* (Madras: Ramanuja Research Society, 1976), ch. 10.

defects. People naturally hesitate to ascribe defects to the God they worship. The association of limitation with defect implies "that the more limits we have, the less we are like God," an implication that has been particularly damaging to people with disabilities.[10] A view of divine perfection that includes limits challenges this ideal.

Other theologians, seeking a theology that can remain vibrant alongside the truths of scientific discovery, have also gravitated toward the explanatory power of the world as God's body. Charles Hartshorne describes God's relation to "God's cosmic body" this way: like "the supercellular individual of the cellular society called a human body, so God is the super-creaturely individual of the inclusive creaturely society."[11] God's experience of the world is akin to the self's "sympathetic participation in cellular feeling" of sensation, pleasure, and pain in the body. God's influence on the world is like the mind's influence over the creation and development of the body's cells.[12] This, too, is a panentheistic model in which God's immanence can be affirmed alongside God's transcendence.

Abhinavagupta's teaching that the divine body of consciousness is entirely recapitulated in the cosmic body and the human body adds to these Christian discourses. He affirms that limits are part of divinity's reflection in humanity. He also acknowledges how counterintuitive the idea of divine limitation can be, especially in light of other systems of Indian philosophy in which the six sheaths (kancukas) of the limited body are denied of the ultimate reality.[13] He therefore explains that the parts of the limited body "are also known as dharanas, because they make . . . the empirical individual think [dhr] of the universal powers of [Siva] differently" (PTv, 98, cf. 100). From the divine perspective, the sheaths are Siva's own powers (saktis) of limitation. Without them, Siva would simply be pure consciousness, without an

---

10. Creamer, *Disability and Christian Theology*, 112.

11. Charles Hartshorne, *Omnipotence and Other Theological Mistakes* (Albany: State University of New York Press, 1984), 59.

12. Ibid., 61.

13. Indian thought prior to the non-dual Saivism of Kashmir is familiar with the kancukas as part of the human person. Buddhist traditions use them to account for why individuals view themselves as separate beings despite being profoundly connected. However, while many Buddhists deny the existence of a divine being underlying apparent difference, this branch of Saivism views the limitations themselves as a mirror of the divine reality that pervades everything.

object. Limitation enables divinity to experience things in a way a self-contained being never could.

Limited consciousness, already appeared in incipient form in chapter 1. The Trinitarian analogy suggested that the three divine persons can know each other because divine consciousness remains unified while nevertheless contracting into subject and object: "I am this." The distinction between creator and creature, which non-dual Saivas call the divine attribute of *maya*, further distinguishes self and other. Here, the individuation is complete: "I *and* this." It is important to remember that even as both traditions affirm a shared existence between the divine creator and the creatures, and even as liberation consists in realizing or participating in that shared existence, both traditions also affirm the reality of difference between God and creation. Created diversity is real. "I and this" is a legitimate way to apprehend the external world. For Christian theology, just as Trinitarian difference is the basis of the recognition of the *imago Dei* in human relationality and sociality,[14] recognition of the distinction between God and the world further affirms the importance of respecting the limitations that distinguish self from other.

We are left with the task of imagining, with our constellation of Christian theologians, how limitations in power, knowledge, time, space, and satiation also belong to God's body.

LIMITED POWER

Notions of limited divine power in non-dual Saiva and contemporary Christian theologies can work together to affirm that limited power does not contradict the image of God in humanity but is part of it. In the Saiva logic, limited power flows from limited consciousness. To be an individual center of consciousness—whether divine or human—is to experience the impediments and opportunities of limited power: others are not me, and the world does not always conform to my wishes.

Conflict and loss (what theologians sometimes call sin or evil) result from this situation. Decisions made by limited centers of

14. See my discussion of the engaged body in chapter 5.

consciousness do not always accord with the divine perspective. Furthermore, what is good for some creatures conflicts with what is good for others (think of the lion and the gazelle). God's role in this process is not to manipulate the puppet strings or force free beings to choose one thing over another. This does not mean that God is powerless, but it does modify what divine omnipotence might mean. Process thought articulates this dynamic well with its dipolar view of God. One pole is primordial or abstract; it contains all possibilities. The other is consequent or concrete; it includes all actual events. Divine power does not dominate or control creation in the concrete pole but lures and persuades. It holds out possibilities, along with a vision of the good, for creatures to choose. Concrete conditions partially determine what is possible in the future. Nothing is inevitable, but genuine creativity and novelty remain possible at all times.[15] When creatures choose from among numerous options, God remains in the moment, again beckoning toward beauty, novelty, and richness of experience for all creatures.

Many Christians are uncomfortable with the suggestion that God's freedom and power might be limited by God's relation to the world. In contrast to the *intrinsic* relatedness to the world described here, some theologians insist that there is no constraint on God to love the creation. Thus, although God *freely chooses* to love, God could have chosen otherwise. Freedom and power precede the choice to relate.

Such a commitment to divine freedom appears even in some theologians who want to avoid the domineering, unrelational God of classical theism. Feminist theologian Elizabeth Johnson, for example, insists that, in contrast to the relational burdens society places on women, redemptive, reciprocal, and mature relationships must be freely chosen: "a relational God who loves in freedom" is reflected not in the "stereotype of natural caregivers, who necessarily deny and sacrifice themselves for others," but in "the importance for every woman of centering herself, affirming herself, and choosing her own life's directions."[16] Thus, God and human beings must freely choose to be in relationship with others.

---

15. "This doctrine of the partial self-determination of every actuality reconciles efficient and final causation, real influence with real freedom." Cobb and Griffin, *Process Theology*, 25.

16. Johnson, *She Who Is*, 226.

This notion of divine freedom of choice differs significantly from the notion of divine freedom (*svatantrya*) in non-dual Saivism. Siva-Sakti's free act of creation manifests as the natural, spontaneous arising of consciousness: "Consciousness and freedom are a fundamental pair. . . . The mastery of Siva expresses itself in doing what is impossible and extremely difficult[,] taking on the form of limited subjects. . . . The will (*iccha*) is not involved."[17] In this view, divinity's primary freedom is the freedom to break out of the dualities of finite and infinite, material and immaterial, that might otherwise seem to separate God and the world. The world is part of God's being, so that God experiences each creature's ecstasy and pain.

Relation to the world renders divinity in certain respects vulnerable. Elizabeth Gandolfo reconciles a feminist view of God with the inevitable vulnerability of relation by reading divine love through the tender, fierce, and bittersweet experience of motherhood. Like a mother, God nurtures fragile life in the full knowledge that this life can be wounded or extinguished by any number of circumstances. She finds Johnson's logic contradictory: divine love is essentially vulnerable to the world's suffering, and yet relation is a product of divine choice, "*as if* God could choose otherwise."[18] Gandolfo affirms the importance of free choice to resist imposed self-sacrifice and enter into solidarity with the oppressed. However, even for the most empowered, life's fragility entails inevitable loss and harm. She proposes, then, that "the invulnerability of divine love's free self-expression is most fully manifested in creation when it does precisely what it is in love's essence to do—enter into vulnerable relation with the beloved, even when to do so seems to contradict the invulnerability of the divine essence."[19]

Gandolfo's view of divine vulnerability shares certain features of the process account of divine power in its primordial and consequent poles. She proposes a Trinitarian solution to the question of divine power, in which divinity is invulnerable "in its primordial dimension."[20] This first dimension of God's being preserves the dig-

---

17. Dupuche, *Abhinavagupta*, 36–37.
18. Gandolfo, *Power and Vulnerability*, 223.
19. Ibid., 224.
20. Ibid., 212. This distinction bears resemblance to a strategy of earlier theologians on this

nity of the *imago Dei* in the face of dehumanizing suffering.[21] The primordial divine invulnerability is only "a limited power," however, because it "precludes values and powers that are only available in the vulnerable realm of humanity"[22] In the second mode of divine love, God enters into the powerless and dependent condition of a human infant. This paradoxical action not only reveals divine solidarity with vulnerable life but also manifests the creator's motherly love for every suffering creature. The vulnerability of human life, then, is part of the *imago Dei*. The power that flows from this relational God is the third mode, the "Spirit of creative transformation," who frees people from fear, grants them courage to make peace with the vicissitudes of life, and empowers them to build compassionate communities.[23]

This Trinitarian rendition suggests that, while Abhinavagupta's philosophy emphasizes the image of the divine in the individual, we might expand the relational implications of this comparison for individuals in communities. For relational Christian theologies, just as each person is constituted in community, God's agency is tangled up with all of the other agents in existence, from cells to humans to tectonic plates. Therefore, divine power is a relational power-with. In a relational world, human beings can abuse this power and exploit and oppress one another and the Earth. However, God invites people to cooperate not only to ensure individual liberation but to empower the mutual flourishing of communities.

Together, these views allow us to revisit Eiesland's image of the disabled God, which she grounds in God's self-limitation in the incarnation: Christ is divine yet human, both God and a helpless infant, almighty yet a violable body subject to abuse. She avoids either romanticizing disability or idealizing Christ as "suffering ser-

---

issue. William of Ockham distinguishes between the absolute power of God, which existed before God commits to a course of action, and the ordained power of God, which is the order God has established in the world and now limits God's options. Deism's divine watchmaker, who, after setting the laws of the universe in motion, refuses to intervene in it, is one version of this idea. Another version is expressed by C. S. Lewis, who affirms that once God has opted to do certain things or to behave in a certain manner (such as to be just), other possibilities (perverting justice) are excluded. See Alister E. McGrath, *Christian Theology: An Introduction*, 5th ed. (Oxford: Wiley-Blackwell, 2011), 209–15.

21. Gandolfo, *Power and Vulnerability*, 27, cf. 189. Of course, our experience of divine love is "not invulnerable, for it is still subject to manipulation, distortion, and despair" (ibid., 196).

22. Ibid., 213.

23. Ibid., 259–60.

vant, model of virtuous suffering, or conquering lord."[24] Rather, the risen Christ reconfigures notions of perfection and wholeness "as unself-pitying, painstaking survival."[25] When the resurrected Christ reveals his wounds to his disciples, he reveals his full humanity. Human embodiment in all its contingency, ambiguity, and impairment is the site of salvific connection to God.[26] Although God's surviving love may not be the power we fantasize, it is powerful nonetheless.

The classical attributes of divine self-sufficiency and omnipotence might retain a place in the doxological language of praise, as when the children sing, "Little ones to you belong. They are weak, but you are strong." However, these attributes are perhaps best located within the tradition of negative theology. To say that God's power is not like our power, that God is not dependent in the same way that we are dependent, guards against using human analogues for God as if they were a direct description of the divine reality. However, these "negative" attributes, too, are the ideals of limited humans, projected beyond daily realities of dependency onto the divine screen; this particular language of negation errs when it construes perfection as a hermetic seal against relation to others.

LIMITED KNOWLEDGE, TIME, AND SPACE

Once God's relation, both to Godself and to the beloved creation, becomes the starting point, the other parts of the limited body begin to fall into place. As with limited power, limited creaturely knowledge is often taken as a mark of difference from the Creator. God's omniscience checks human hubris: we do not have the God's-eye view. This principle of divine omniscience is often stretched to its breaking point, however. If God knows everything that will happen, even before it happens, why does God not act (omnipotently) to prevent it? Does divine foresight concede divine will?

24. Eiesland, *Disabled God*, 94, cf. 102.
25. Ibid., 101. Other theologians of disability who reconfigure the divine attributes include Creamer, *Disability and Christian Theology*, ch. 4; Jennie Weiss Block, *Copious Hosting: A Theology of Access for People with Disabilities* (New York: Continuum, 2002); and Black, *Healing Homiletic*.
26. Eiesland, *Disabled God*, 100.

Hartshorne calls this entire line of questioning a mistake. It assumes God's immutability: if God does not change, then the unfolding of history cannot add anything to God's knowledge. The future is definite and known by God. From a process theological perspective, however, "The creative process produces new realities to know."[27] God grows in knowledge, and God's experience is enriched through the genuinely novel decisions of creatures. In this sense, limitations in human knowledge mirror that of the divine. We, like God, can know only what there is to know. The future has not yet happened. When it does, it will exist as a thing to be known. We, like God, also have a sense of probability of what will happen in the future. For instance, once yellow flowers appear on my garden plants, I know that cucumbers, squash, and tomatoes will appear in a few weeks. At least, that has been the sequence for several years in my garden. But an unexpected hailstorm or invasion of hungry rodents might thwart my expectations. Similarly, I am fairly certain that my daughter will be grumpy until she has eaten breakfast because I have experienced this pattern for six years. However, occasionally she will surprise me with a cheery stream of stories when she climbs out of bed. Even more, God's familiarity with the patterns and tendencies of the entire cosmos provides grounds for a robust sense of divine foreknowledge that does not rule out novelty or free will.

The analogy of limited knowledge has an "is not" dimension as well. God's knowledge is not limited in the same way that human knowledge is. McFague posits that because God has the whole world for God's body, the experiences of all creatures are equally present to divine consciousness in a way they could never be to individuals. Through this intimate knowledge, God holds the good of all of creation in mind at once.[28] This also means that although God's special concern for the marginalized can feel threatening to people entrenched in power and wealth, divine love is not susceptible to ideological taint. God's option is for the flourishing of all creation.

Limited knowledge is related to the contingencies of living in a particular time and place. For non-dual Saivas, human temporal exis-

27. Hartshorne, *Omnipotence*, 27.
28. McFague, *Body of God*, 174–75.

tence is a reflection of the divine ability to experience time (*kala*). Divinity must become limited if anything at all is to happen. Christians affirm these limitations in God in a special way in the incarnation: divinity took flesh for a period of approximately thirty years in first-century Palestine. Jesus experienced infancy, childhood, youth, and adulthood. He changed. He died. He knew what it was possible to know from the perspective of a working-class Jew in a small corner of the Roman Empire. God was uniquely present to, and experienced the limits of, that slice of history and geography.

In Augustine's notion of the eternal present, divine incarnation within time is a onetime exception. According to his speculation, all moments appear to God at once.[29] Past, present, and future are laid out like a timeline in a textbook on the history of everything—or like a serial program one can stream online. Although God has seen this show an infinite number of times, God can drop in for this or that episode, fast forward, rewind, and skip the commercials. There are no surprises for God—even in the incarnation—because every seemingly random or tragic event, every purportedly free choice, has been known from eternity.

The eternal present is an odd construction when placed next to the scriptural narrative, where God clearly participates in time. It is hard to imagine why God would want to watch the same story for all eternity, unless it were actually unfolding with opportunities for relation and redemption. Relational theologians reconceive the divine perfections in a way that makes better sense of salvation history, of the twists and turns of evolution and history, and of the genuine delight that comes from novelty. Time is where the drama of betrayal, tragedy, and redemption takes place. People pray and God responds. God promises and people hope. Adventure, novelty, and zest replace the static condition of the eternal present as divine attributes.[30]

Rather than a onetime exception, the incarnation "is radically the

29. Augustine, *Confessions*, trans. Henry Chadwick (Oxford: Oxford University Press, 1991), 11.16.

30. Cf. Alfred North Whitehead, *Process and Reality: An Essay in Cosmology*, ed. David Ray Griffin and Donald W. Sherburne, corrected ed., Gifford Lectures (New York: The Free Press, 1978), 351.

way God works in the world," Marjorie Suchocki claims.[31] She explains, "If God offers a possibility drawn from the resources of the divine life, then one could imagine that by receiving the influence of God, the reality that then embodies that influence is to one degree or other an incarnation of God in the world. Incarnation, then, would be radical, not limited to a single person, but possible throughout existence."[32] In other words, in the creation of each being, which participates in the life of God insofar as it exists at all, God is constantly becoming. God, in turn, beckons each being into a future that is made up not only of the past but of genuinely new possibilities.[33] The particular and the local are not deficiencies compared to some abstracted and disembodied ideal but the very nature of divine omnipresence.

Cultural differences are a salient feature of contingent human existence. Although some would see them as impediments to human flourishing in the world, even precursors to an inevitable clash of civilizations, Suchocki views these different ways of being human as part of the dynamism of incarnation. Divine limitation in time and space means that "God is involved in the development of culture."[34] She continues, "Will it be a universal reflection of God? Of course not. It is a timely reflection. Will it be a full reflection of God? Of course not. It is an adaptation of the purposes of God as suitable to this time, this place. But it is nonetheless an incarnation of God in the world."[35] In human cultures, the processes by which language, stories, and rituals are produced, as well as the manner of our relationships to one another and the Earth, are influenced by God. Every language, culture, and religion bears the trace of its response to the divine presence and call. The truths of the world's religions are thus rooted in the diversity of God's radical incarnation in every time and space.[36] To identify where and how this incarnation shines forth, human beings must continue to discern and respond to the divine call.

31. Marjorie Hewitt Suchocki, *Divinity and Diversity: A Christian Affirmation of Religious Pluralism* (Nashville: Abingdon, 2003), 40.
32. Ibid., 47.
33. Ibid., 46.
34. Ibid., 47.
35. Ibid.
36. Ibid., 40.

Life is an adventure, especially for God. Communities live into the *imago Dei* when they open their knowledge to the experience of the world and diverse neighbors, and when they allow these experiences to develop the virtues of humility, responsibility, creativity, and dialogue in them.

THEOLOGICAL IMPLICATIONS: SIN AND TRAGEDY

Thus far in our study of the limited body, I have argued first that limits are not inherently evil but integral to being human. Beyond this, I have proposed that they are actually part of the way that the creation mirrors the creator. Limits are part of the *imago Dei*. This argument expands Niebuhr's affirmation that human experience "may reveal elements of the image of God even in the lowliest aspects of . . . natural life" and posits a profound relation of God's limits to ours.[37] Although the limits are asymmetrical, divine limitlessness and creaturely dependence are no longer absolute categories.

Limits in the *imago Dei* render God quite differently than classical theism. Contemporary theology's imagination of a profoundly relational God, who feels and incorporates all of the world's collective experiences, resonates well with the limited body. Even as God experiences adventure, novelty, and loss, and thus undergoes change, God also transcends the world. Unlike the limits of human knowledge, "God knows everything there is to know," including the possibilities that may occur in the future.[38] God has been present in time since its beginning and will remain present far beyond us mortals. Feminist and relational theologies add a direction and purpose to the unfolding of creation. Unlike waxing and waning human abilities, God's loving power of persuasion is steadfast. It continues to lure creation toward the good, regardless of the choices creatures make.

These critical shifts in God-talk ripple outward into other topics of theological reflection, most notably those of sin and evil. The primary benefit of including limitation as a category within the *imago Dei* is to decouple limitation from sin, shame, and guilt, as Jesus did

37. Niebuhr, *Nature and Destiny*, 150.
38. C. Robert Mesle, *Process Theology: A Basic Introduction* (St. Louis: Chalice, 1993), 37.

with the man born blind. This model calls "attention to the fact that we all experience limits, that these limits differ, and that these limits are experienced and lived in multitudinous ways."[39] With limitations as divine body parts, the *imago Dei* includes a wider cross-section of human difference: to various degrees, both humanity and divinity participate in a range of intersecting limits.

Sin nevertheless remains an important category in this theology because limits expose human beings to many opportunities to neglect and exploit them. As Creamer suggests, "Sin might now be redefined as an inappropriate attitude toward limits as we both exaggerate and also reject our own limits and the limits of others."[40] For example, Niebuhr's description of pride, which denies one's own finitude and asserts power over others to soothe one's own insecurity, is a relevant example of both rejecting one's own limits and exaggerating the limits of others. Humans can also exaggerate their own limits to the point of failing to develop their gifts, as Niebuhr's feminist critics have observed.[41]

Although sin is often associated with willful transgression, Hindu and Christian traditions both recognize more at play. Contingent beings are inevitably embroiled in finite awareness and ability. Hindus describe the distortions entailed in limitation when they diagnose the human condition as ignorance, especially insofar as humans remain insensate to the truth about themselves and others. Individuals can be unaware of the personal or group biases that harm others. When they are made aware of these biases, individuals can make better choices; yet, overcoming structures of privilege and oppression is more than a matter of individual choice. Because we live and move within social structures that can only be partially transcended, the Christian language of original sin might retain a place in this limits model.

The doctrine of original sin has an unfortunate legacy because so many Christian theologians have associated it with the body and sexuality. Instead, original sin can be construed as *the conditions within which* humans inevitably overreach their limits or fail to grasp the

39. Haslam, *Constructive Theology*, 12.
40. Creamer, *Disability and Christian Theology*, 33.
41. Most notably, Saiving, "Human Situation."

graced nature of finite existence. We are born into these conditions of limitation—they are "inherited," in a manner of speaking. Understanding original sin "analogically . . . as the law of imperfection and suffering in a contingent world [that] has existed from the first moment of creation," Nathan Halloran compares it with *maya*.[42] As the substrate for creation, *maya* ensures that every individual is born with limited consciousness, a sense of separateness, and habits that reinforce these impressions.[43] These things have the effect of making it difficult to ascertain the unstained luminosity that is the deepest truth of the self. The limitations predispose individuals to hoard security at the expense of others. Even as these conditions constrain us through no fault of our own, they are the matrix within which redemption and reconciliation must be found.

The Christian and Hindu traditions, thus viewed together, highlight the tragic dimensions of existence within which human beings exercise agency. Agency is bound up in questions, raised in the last chapter, about when one should accept limits and when one should struggle against them. Gandolfo offers clues when she writes, "Our basic human condition is one that exposes us to great suffering, but it is not the condition itself that we ought to reject; rather, it is the exploitation, abuse, mismanagement, and neglect of our condition that ought to be resisted."[44] A theology that embraces limits retains a place for struggle and protest, even in the face of terrible and incurable suffering. It is not a passive theology, and God is not passive when we suffer tragedy. To fathom how this might be the case, we

---

42. Nathan Halloran, "*Maya, Anava Mala* and Original Sin: A Comparative Study," *Journal of Hindu-Christian Studies* 26, no. 1 (2013): 75.

43. These three features are known as the *mala*s or "impurities" that are inherent in *maya*. The first, *mayiya-mala*, is related to the subject-object distinction that veils the unity of reality. The second, *anava-mala*, gives a person a sense of being an individual. The third, *karma-mala* denotes the influence that consequences of past deeds (*karma*) have on present existence. The translation "impurity" for *mala* can be misleading alongside the concept of original sin, which traditionally carries notes of moral stain. Rather, *mala*s are smudges on the clear mirror of consciousness. Here, non-dual Saivism differentiates itself from its sister religion, Saiva Siddhanta, which associates the *mala*s with evil and the created state with slavery. For Saiva Siddhanta, there is a basic dualism between God (*pati*) and the bond or fetter (*pasa*). The human being (*pasu*), bound by the impurities of *maya* (the *mala*s), needs divine grace to be liberated from them. By contrast, the non-dual perspective views the veils of creation as God's own powers. See Halloran, "*Maya, Anava Mala*," 68.

44. Gandolfo, *Power and Vulnerability*, 8, cf. 125.

must consider one remaining limit within the image of God: the limitation of divine satisfaction—in a word, desire.

DIVINE DESIRE (LIMITED SATISFACTION)

If divine power has the character of persuasion rather than coercion, then there is some degree to which God *cannot* prevent sinful choices and tragic events. At the same time, God does not cause those things to happen. God could not create a world of free and interrelated beings without the possibility of hurricanes, genocide, or the body's immune system attacking healthy cells. If the world is God's body, then each of these tragedies also occurs within God. Although God neither causes nor prevents suffering, God is always present within it. There is good news in the fact that every limitation is an object of divine consciousness, or as Reynolds puts it, that in Christ God demonstrates "unconditional *regard* for all persons."[45]

Nevertheless, there is an aspect of the human spirit that rails against the suffering, for instance, of a child whose genetic condition ensures a short life shot through with excruciating pain. It is indeed tragic that the free and evolving agency of creation makes such things possible. The anguish of this child and the parents is also felt by God, not only as pain but as compassion. This ability to *feel*, contrary to the classical attributes of apatheia and aseity, entails a sense of lack. This limited satisfaction (*raga*), which belongs to the limited body, is more positively named *desire*.

The early medieval Christian thinker known as Pseudo-Dionysius holds up the name *Yearning* as one of the highest titles for God. Divine yearning, he says, "is a capacity to effect a unity, an alliance, and a particular commingling in the Beautiful and the Good."[46] God's desire exists before the world: God is "beguiled" into creating the world and "comes to abide within all things."[47] This variety of divine love is called *eros*, a powerful, self-diffusing love that moves outward, toward an other. It is the inherent mechanism that moves beings

45. Thomas E. Reynolds, *Vulnerable Communion: A Theology of Disability and Hospitality* (Grand Rapids: Brazos, 2008), 211; my emphasis.
46. Pseudo-Dionysius, "The Divine Names," in *The Complete Works*, 81.
47. Ibid., 82.

toward the goodness and beauty in one another and, ultimately, in God.

If God's nature is love, then limited satisfaction must be part of God's experience. God's relation to creation entails limits to divine power and satisfaction from the moment God calls forth light from the deep and separates the waters in the messy, ongoing work of creation.[48] Love's satisfaction is limited, first, simply because it is love. The old myth imagines Eros as the child of Poverty and Resource because limitation urges divine love toward new and creative efforts to attract the world to itself. The divine *eros* flows into every corner of creation, but this desire often goes unreturned. As the Bible narrates the divine love affair with the world, love puts God at the mercy of created beings. God goes to great lengths to win back the hearts of the people who choose to turn away, forsake the divine commandments, and worship other gods. Anselm's protest notwithstanding, Scripture's testimony that "God is Love" (1 John 4:8) does not negate all ordinary sense of what loving is like.

Desire thus propels both the creation and the redemption of the world. God's desire never becomes fixed on anything other than the good of creation. The human protest against suffering participates in this divine yearning, and human responses to suffering answer the divine desire for the good. The very ability to ask whether something could be different is part of the *imago Dei*. Research into ways to alleviate physical and emotional suffering participates in this divine longing. Patents and profits represent other, competing desires, and when the restless heart seizes upon these inferior goods, it diverts from the depths of divine compassion from which it springs. Nevertheless, divine love remains with suffering creation, opening possibilities for new life.

Love is not autonomous but accomplishes its aims in relation. The possibilities God envisions become actual only through partnership with the beloved creation. Real power—divine power—is empowerment, not power-over. We know divine love by loving. The tender-fierce commitment of parents for their children. The

48. For a compelling reading of the creation story against the classical teaching of *creatio ex nihilo*, see Catherine Keller, *The Face of the Deep: A Theology of Becoming* (London: Routledge, 2003).

spark of attraction between lovers. The steadfast faithfulness between partners. The passion of solidarity in the face of injustice. All such relationality, "in its potential and its possibilities, *is the presence of the divine among us.*"[49] And so God depends on these lovers, parents, sisters, brothers, allies, and colleagues to extend the divine intent to nurture and prosper creation to one another in mutual care and responsibility.

PRACTICES OF IMAGINATION

A famous figure of Siva depicts him dancing. His hair flies wildly around his head. With one of his four hands, he beats the rhythm of creation on his drum. With another, he makes a gesture that says, "Do not fear," and with another he welcomes the viewer to worship at his feet. The fourth hand holds the fire of cosmic destruction. The entire image is ringed by this fire—a fearsomely beautiful icon of the circle of life. The more serene image of Siva sitting in meditation depicts the same process: eyes open, creation unfolds; eyes closed, creation dissolves into single-pointed concentration. In either case, endings—even the end of the world—are framed with equanimity as part of the awesome but nevertheless ordinary way of things.

Images can exceed their original intent. A Christian student of mine once made a creative connection between these two Hindu metaphors. "Isn't it true," she mused, "that destruction comes from closing our eyes to one another?" For her, this metaphor contains the ethical imperative to overcome limited consciousness, to the extent possible, by training our gaze upon one another. Human beings can overcome some dimensions of our contingency (such as cultural biases) and indeed must overcome them if our self-serving attitude harms others. Limited perspective does not excuse bigotry but calls for widening the scope in order to live in just, compassionate relationships with others. Concomitant with the practices of embracing limits in the last chapter, then, I would like to propose that *imagination* can be a virtuous practice for expanding the capacity to recognize the image of God in all people.

49. Hill Fletcher, *Motherhood as Metaphor*, 59; my emphasis.

This proposal brings us full circle to Niebuhr and his own limited perspective. Recall that Niebuhr's genius was to identify modern anxieties, rooted in limited power and knowledge, as the source of prideful assertions over others. He looked to religion to "[produce] the kind of social imagination" that could "help us to live together decently with members of other races and groups."[50] James Cone cites this passage from Niebuhr's editorial in the *Detroit Times* as evidence of the paradox, even hypocrisy, of the great ethicist's life. In the church he pastored in Detroit, Niebuhr failed to move the needle on racial integration. Later, in New York City, he did not reach out to activists in the Harlem neighborhood only blocks from his office. He did not engage black intellectuals in his work. He urged "gradualism, patience, and prudence" in reforms of Jim Crow. Most damningly, he failed to speak out about the terror of lynching.[51]

Elsewhere, Niebuhr invokes imagination as an important theological practice, writing that "One needs a powerful imagination to see both tragedy and beauty, futility and redemption in the . . . terrible beauty of the cross."[52] In this regard, Cone is astounded at Niebuhr's failure to recognize "the visual and symbolic overtones between the cross and the lynching tree, both places of execution in the ancient and modern worlds."[53] The crucifixion was being reenacted all around him, and he did not seem to notice. Like other white theologians and preachers, he "lacked imagination of the most crucial and moral kind"[54]—the imagination that would not only give him "'eyes to see' black suffering," but also "the 'heart to feel' it as his own."[55] Today's contexts demand no less: if white Christians could perceive Christ in every instance of police brutality against black men, women, and children, could these atrocious routines be tolerated any longer?

An inclusive and just theological anthropology must spur the imagination to recognize all people as fully human. M. Shawn

---

50. James H. Cone, *The Cross and the Lynching Tree* (Maryknoll, NY: Orbis, 2013), 44.
51. Ibid., 39, cf. 38–42.
52. Ibid., 37.
53. Ibid., 94.
54. Ibid.
55. Ibid., 41.

Copeland's definition of racism demonstrates the crucial connection of imagination to this doctrine. In a racist ideology,

> One racial group is contrived as "the measure of the human being" and is deemed normative. Meanings and values have been embedded in those differences so as to favor the group that has been contrived as "the measure of the human being." Virtue, morality, and goodness are assigned to that racial group, while vice, immorality, and evil are assigned to the others. Entitlement, power, and privilege are accorded that racial group, while dispossession, powerlessness, and disadvantage define others.[56]

More specifically, white culture in the United States elevates one slice of God's image in humanity as the standard for all of the diverse embodiments of that image. It narrows humanity into two categories: white and nonwhite, obscuring both the shared image and its refraction through other facets of human difference. Not least, it normalizes violent and dehumanizing forms of public life.[57]

To tell the truth about humanity, Christians from all manner of limited perspectives must exercise the imagination. But how? The arts can animate this practice. To help his readers recognize God's presence in "every lynching in the United States," Cone draws on works of "the Black literary imagination," which span literature, journalism, sermons, spirituals, and other genres, and which employ "the imagination to relate the message of the cross to one's own social reality."[58] In a similar vein, Gandolfo recommends that Christians cultivate dangerous memories of suffering through practices of lament. She points to contemplative practices that can replace habitual discourses about identity, as well as practical means of solidarity with vulnerable others. Such "existential and practical resources for resilience to harm and resistance to violence," which incorporate the imagination to see self and other as beloved of God, inspire responsive love toward vulnerable humanity.[59]

---

56. M. Shawn Copeland, "The Critical Aesthetics of Race," in *She Who Imagines: Feminist Theological Aesthetics*, ed. Laurie Cassidy and Maureen H. O'Connell (Collegeville, MN: Liturgical, 2012), 81.

57. Kelly Brown Douglas (*Sexuality and the Black Church: A Womanist Perspective* [Maryknoll, NY: Orbis, 1999], ch. 3) gives the example of homophobia to show how racialized minorities can absorb hegemonic norms as their own.

58. Cone, *Cross and the Lynching Tree*, 158.

59. Gandolfo, *Power and Vulnerability*, 6, cf. 266.

The imagination is like a muscle that must be exercised. It can be disciplined, trained, and transformed. If the imagination is to do more than project and reinforce one's own bias, I suggest that practices of the imagination must contain a critical component that attends to one's own limitations. Imagination, after all, begins from a place of limitation, asking, How might things be different? Where are these dehumanizing images coming from? How does Scripture transform these habitual ways of seeing the world? What possibilities have my community not yet envisioned? Whose stories could help me understand things differently?

Furthermore, the products of the imagination should be interrogated, says Copeland: "any appeal to the empirical or visual in the effort to understand human being is never innocent, never ahistorical, and never divorced from power."[60] Laurie Cassidy illustrates how privilege operates in the production of images. Writing with reference to a photograph of a starving child, she cautions,

> Our passive and uncritical gaze upon suffering human beings in photographs may reinscribe the role of viewer as spectator and "normalize" the suffering of the persons upon whom we gaze. This divide between spectator and "sufferer," between agent and object, subverts the fundamental claim and responsibility of the dignity and radical sociality of being made in God's image and likeness.[61]

The privileged assume that to see is to know, and this knowing gaze can be manipulated to reinforce the status quo.[62]

Images and imagination do hold the potential to transform the viewer. To navigate complicity and transformation, Cassidy offers a set of questions for Christians to ask of images so that they will encounter others as the image of God. Faced with an image of suffering, one might ask, for instance, "Does this image interrupt or reinscribe the stereotypes of people who look like this or share this social position?" This question acknowledges one's own vulnerability

---

60. Copeland, "Critical Aesthetics of Race," 82.

61. Laurie Cassidy, "Picturing Suffering: The Moral Dilemmas in Gazing at Photographs of Human Anguish," in *She Who Imagines: Feminist Theological Aesthetics*, ed. Laurie Cassidy and Maureen H. O'Connell (Collegeville, MN: Liturgical, 2012), 105–6.

62. Kafer's analysis of images of disability in the "Pass It On" billboard series illustrates this point as well. Kafer, *Feminist, Queer, Crip*, ch. 4.

to conditioning by social situation and shifts viewing from a passive to an active task. Second, "If I or a loved one were in this photograph, how might I want this image to be different?" Here, one imagines oneself in the same situation, recognizing shared vulnerability not only to suffering but to its exploitation and representation. This painful exercise can open the viewer to lament and create a sense of responsibility to others. Third, "Is this suffering avoidable and how so?"—a question that refuses to normalize the suffering of an individual or group of people.[63]

Each of these questions is a work of imagination that acknowledges the limits of the imaginer. Accompanied by the hard, daily work of building diverse communities in which people imagine together, such questions fruitfully employ the very limitations and vulnerabilities that might otherwise be abused. The practices of imagination pivot our attention now to the next set of body parts, where the mental faculties come under consideration as parts of the image of God.

63. Cassidy, "Picturing Suffering," 121–22.

4.

The Subjective Body

The limitations discussed in the previous two chapters—limits in scope, power, knowledge, satiation, time, and place—apply to all of the subsequent body parts. This anthropological claim is immediately put to the test in the next set: the subjective body. In the West, we have accorded extraordinary powers to the mind. We hold it to be the clear, objective arbiter of truth. Set apart from its supposed opposites—the body, emotion, and animality—its purported lack of limits has continued to be a staple of modern dualistic thinking, from Descartes to the present.

The tenacity of these dualistic roots can be discerned in popular explanations of what goes "wrong" in instances of mental illness. Andrew Scull demonstrates the perennial return of *physical* accounts of mental illness that pinpoint the cause within the humors, the brain, or the body's chemistry. Notably, while these explanations help to reduce the stigma of mental illness, they also insulate part of the person from limitation. In the version of metaphysical dualism that emerged with European rationalism,

> The rational mind, identical to the immortal soul (and both *'l'âme'* in French), stood in contrast to the material, mortal body. By definition, the former was incapable of error (or could be drawn into error only by the failures of its means for perceiving the world and organizing humans' response to it, the brain and the nervous system). Madness, thus, was rooted in the body, the natural province of the physician. To argue

to the contrary was to imply that the mind was subject to disease, debility, or even (in the case of outright idiotism) death; in other words, to contradict the very foundation of revealed religion and morality, the belief in an immortal soul.[1]

Medical accounts of mental illness capacitate the distinction between the body and a person's true self, encapsulated in the nonphysical mind or soul.

The latest return of physical accounts of mental illness has taken the form of biological reductionism. In the twentieth century, the developing field of genetics offered new etiologies. To prevent undesirable traits in the population, many people deemed mentally ill or defective were sentenced to involuntary sterilization in the United States.[2] Biochemical etiologies rule the day in the twenty-first century, and a steady supply of drugs incentivized by the pharmaceutical industry capitalizes on the hypothesis that a chemical imbalance in the brain is the underlying cause of many conditions.[3]

Of course, the pendulum periodically swings toward other models. Psychoanalysis employs talk therapy as a means to explore psychological distress. Foucauldian and feminist theories fault society, rather than the individual, as the source of pathology. But, like gravity, the special association of limitation with physicality pulls in a dualistic direction.

The uptick in use of the expanded Diagnostic and Statistical Manual of Mental Disorders illustrates this trend. The DSM-5, as it is known, correlates symptoms of psychological distress to hundreds of medical diagnoses such as schizophrenia, bipolar disorder, and

1. Andrew Scull, *Madness: A Very Short Introduction* (Oxford: Oxford University Press, 2011), 35, 37. Cartesian dualism is not the only version of this way of thinking, of course: variations on an Aristotelian-Thomistic model persist, in which the faculties are more intimately related to one another as form to matter, and emergent dualisms allow the mind or soul to originate in the brain but endure as a genuinely new entity, even beyond physical death. What the dualistic proposals share, however, is one part of the human subject that escapes limitation by the others.

2. Justice Oliver Wendell Holmes's opinion in a eugenics case that "three generations of idiots are enough" and Hitler's gassing of mental patients are notable examples. Scull, *Madness*, 6.

3. Some critics point out that the medicalization of mental illness may even be doing more harm than good. Although pharmacology might ameliorate certain symptoms, the underlying theory has eluded proof; and often the side effects of the drugs contribute to far-reaching health problems in the populations that take them. See, for example, Marcia Angell, "The Epidemic of Mental Illness: Why?" *The New York Times Review of Books*, June 23, 2011, http://tinyurl.com/y9g4nbez.

depression. Increasingly, insurance companies require a medical diagnosis corresponding to its categories before they provide coverage. Critics charge that although the DSM-5's classifications are presented as scientific, they are in fact hotly debated (homosexuality was only completely removed from the manual in 1987, while new categories are added with every revision), and much more research in genetics, neuroscience, and psychology is necessary before its use as a diagnostic tool can be considered reliable.[4] Nevertheless, practitioners and patients by the millions put their faith in it.

The medicalization of mental illness concerns theological anthropology because it contributes to a prevalent view of the human person. The current biological reductionism differs from its dualistic predecessors in that it is agnostic about the existence of a nonmaterial soul, but it also fits well with a popular variation on body-soul dualism. To say, "It's not him; it's the illness" is one means to reduce stigma via biochemistry. By isolating the ailment to the body, like heart disease or asthma, the person is left essentially untainted—but there are also costs to this hypothesis. Biological reductionism of mental illness reinforces a view that, whatever the image of God might be, it lacks limitation or impairment.

The previous chapters have labored to argue that limits belong to divinity and the divine image. At a time when some studies estimate that "more than half of Americans will develop a mental illness at some point in their lives," this insight must also be allowed to penetrate beyond the vulnerable physical body.[5] Regardless of the reasons behind the increase, the result is that more people than ever are experiencing the theological stigma of mental and behavioral health disorders. This chapter urges Christian theology to admit that the individual soul—that peculiar construct—itself is limited, that the subjective faculties can be impaired, and that such limitation and

4. See, for example, Steven E. Hyman, "The Diagnosis of Mental Disorders: The Problem of Reification," *Annual Review of Clinical Psychology* 6, no. 1 (2010): 155–79; and, for a concise summary of the critiques, Division of Clinical Psychology, "Division of Clinical Psychology Position Statement on the Classification of Behaviour and Experience in Relation to Functional Psychiatric Diagnoses: Time for a Paradigm Shift," May 2013, PDF, http://tinyurl.com/ycc9kypg.

5. Benedict Carey, "Most Will Be Mentally Ill at Some Point, Study Says," *The New York Times*, June 7, 2005, http://tinyurl.com/y8v72gzd.

impairment do not diminish the extent to which a person participates in the divine image. The Indian typology helpfully frames these faculties in concert with the limits model of the human being we are developing.

With the subjective body, we move from categories distinctive to non-dual Saivism and into a view of the person that is shared more widely among Indian philosophical schools. The ancient Samkhya philosophy in India, which undergirds the practices of Yoga and such central Hindu scriptures as the Bhagavad Gita, begins its cosmology here, with the individual subject (*purusa*), matter (*prakrti*), intelligence (*buddhi*), ego (*ahamkara*), and mind/heart (*manas*). These five parts of the subjective body emanate from one another in the order shown in the chart: the individual subject appears with the material realm, which emits the intelligence, which produces the ego or sense of "I," which emanates the mind or heart.[6]

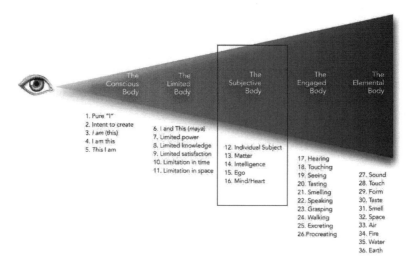

Fig. 4.

6. The difficulty of recognizing differences between these capacities lies partially in language: one teacher of Trika Saiva philosophy uses the single English word "mind" to translate both *buddhi* and *manas*. See Deba Brata SenSharma, *The Philosophy of Sadhana: With Special Reference to the Trika Philosophy of Kashmir* (Albany: State University of New York Press, 1990), 176, 179.

The subjective body surfaces several helpful features for a contemporary theological anthropology. Its parts are first of all *multiple*, encompassing five dimensions of subjectivity that include but neither center on nor privilege rationality. Second, these variegated parts are *unexceptional*; their presence in the animal world calls into question the Christian tendency to limit the image of God to humanity. Third, contrary to the fantasy that the "thinking part" of the divine image is somehow untouched by finitude or materiality, each of these parts is *limited*. This teaching undermines the basis for our society's tendency to treat people who struggle with mental illness, or whose rationality is impaired in some way, as less than fully human. Through conversation with the Indian categories, an expanded Christian theological anthropology can ameliorate the dualisms, exclusions, and stigma created by the tradition's elevation of the rational soul as the unique locus of the *imago Dei*.

MULTIPLE

The first point evident from this model is that subjectivity is multiple: it does not reduce the divine reflection to a single, mental capacity but draws attention to a range of faculties. These five body parts grant an individual a sense of selfhood and the abilities to intuit, think, and feel.

The first two body parts, individual subjectivity (*purusa*) and material nature (*prakrti*), manifest simultaneously. This pairing is how divine consciousness and its object (Siva and Sakti) present themselves in the realm of limitation. As the principle of individual subjecthood, *purusa* has a special relationship to the first principle, the divine subject, Siva.[7] Having become aware of objects in the conscious body

---

7. As a philosophical term, *purusa* carries an ancient pedigree that precedes this interpretation. In Samkhya, *purusa* is the highest *tattva* and in a class all its own: "Higher than the person (*purusa*) there's nothing at all. That is the goal, that's the highest state" (*Katha Upanisad* 3.11). Patrick Olivelle, trans., *Upanisads* (Oxford: Oxford University Press, 1996), 239. In Samkhya and Yoga philosophies, *purusa* lacks any connection to *prakrti*, neither acting on matter nor causing it to come into existence, but merely witnessing or observing it. In several late additions to the Vedic scriptures, *purusa* is imagined in corporeal form. A famous hymn, the Purusa Sukta, imagines it with "a thousand heads, a thousand eyes, a thousand feet," pervading "the earth on all sides" (*Rig Veda* 10.90.1). Wendy Doniger O'Flaherty, trans., *The Rig Veda: An Anthology*

and undergoing constriction in the limited body, universal consciousness is now localized in particular centers of consciousness.
There is not one but innumerable *purusa*s, each an individual subject
with the ability to become aware.[8]

Previous comparative work has begun to explore resonances
between *purusa* and the human person. Nicholas Bamford hones in
on the *purusa tattva* to suggest that human personhood can be seen as
the image of a personal deity. Here, God is not only to be contem-
plated beyond words and images but can be addressed as a "you" with
characteristics worthy of devotion. Bamford extends this principle
into his Christology: in Christ, the divine person (hypostasis, *purusa*)
unites with the human person (hypostasis, *purusa*).[9] This Christology
in turn serves as the template for salvation as realizing union with
God: *recognition* in non-dual Saiva parlance, or the process of *deification* in Orthodox Christian terminology.[10]

Bamford's analysis can be augmented by drawing out the importance of the other parts of the subjective body. His soteriology, which
recognizes in the *purusa* an inherent relation to divinity that has been
obscured or lost, can be extended throughout the entire divine image.
Each of its faculties could be employed in practices of recognition.
What, then, can we learn from *prakrti*, intelligence, ego-sense, and
mind/heart?

(New York: Penguin, 1981), 30. In a myth of origins, Vedic sacrifices, animals, heavenly bodies, gods, and four major caste groupings (*varna*s) are subdivided through the sacrifice of *purusa*.
It is important to note this *purusa* lacks any attributes of lordship or personal deity (Isvara),
which is a separate idea in Samkhya and Yoga schools. Only much later do certain communities
equate the *purusa* that creates and pervades the universe with the supreme deity who receives
devotion (cf. *Bhagavad Gita* 8:22).

8. In the microcosm of the individual, this shared pattern makes possible knowledge of the
whole: "Without it, who would perceive the objects of knowledge beginning with 'earth'?"
(PTlv, 211). Also see Bamford, *Converging Theologies*, 131.

9. Bamford, *Converging Theologies*, 93–94. In this line of reasoning, Bamford correlates the
first *tattva* (*Parama Siva*) with the Supreme Person (*parama purusam*), the personal deity in theistic Hindu traditions. He then looks to the Christian doctrine of the incarnation: if Christ is cast
as the Supreme Person, then the term *purusa* can be seen as analogous to *hypostasis* in Christology.

10. Ibid., 117–20. *Recognition* more accurately describes the non-dual Saiva situation, where
the identity is only veiled, not lost. From his perspective as an Orthodox theologian, by contrast, Bamford writes of the image of God—which is not identity with God—being "lost" or
"corrupted," then "restored" through grace (ibid., 46). The work of deification is an ontological
change that goes beyond this movement, whereby not only is the image restored but people
also receive likeness to God (ibid., 47).

In the dualistic Samkhya philosophy, *purusa* is utterly separate from the material realm, or *prakrti*. By contrast, the non-dual Saivism of Kashmir places them together along a continuum of manifestation and envelops them in the eleven principles discussed in the previous chapters (Siva through the limitations).[11] The remaining twenty-four categories in the schema fall within the realm of material nature (*prakrti*). The fact that the first three modifications of *prakrti* are the intelligence, ego-sense, and mind/heart, which together are known as the principles of inner awareness (*antahkarana*), can help to reframe the common mental habit of mind-versus-matter. Residing within the realm of material reality, the "mind" never achieves the purity from material constraints that has been idealized in the West.[12]

The first principle of inner awareness, *buddhi*, can be translated as intelligence, wisdom, will, or even intuitive knowledge.[13] The Buddha is so called because, awakened, he perceives everything. Mirror-like, *buddhi* "is capable of receiving reflection from all sides so that it receives the reflection of the light of the self from within as well as that of the external objects from without."[14] Because it receives the images generated by all of the senses, including the mind (*manas*), it houses memory, intuition, language, imagination, and dreams. Because it also reflects the light of consciousness within, it serves as the center of religious awakening. As such, it embodies at the level of the human being the divine power of all-pervasive consciousness (PTv, 66). Although this intelligence is a mighty power, it is not uniquely the divine image. Like the other body parts, its mir-

11. With this move, the non-dual Saiva tradition demotes *purusa* from its perch as the supreme witness and makes it one of many objects for Siva's consciousness. As the short commentary puts it, "The individual consciousness, even though it is a limited perceiver, is here reckoned as belonging to the group of knowable objects" (PTlv, 211).

12. Furthermore, material nature cannot be reduced to things that can be seen or touched. It would also be misleading to imagine *prakrti* as an undifferentiated mass of "stuff" existing somewhere in the universe. Instead, like all of the *tattva*s, it is the principle within which the stuff appropriate to each body part (whether intellectual, mental, sensory, or elemental) can emerge.

13. Singh provides the following range of definitions: "the intellect; the ascertaining intelligence; sometimes the higher mind; the super personal mind; intuitive aspect of consciousness by which the essential Self awakens to truth." Jaideva Singh, *The Yoga of Delight, Wonder, and Astonishment: A Translation of the Vijñana-Bhairava* (Albany: State University of New York Press, 1991), 156.

14. Kanti Chandra Pandey, *Abhinavagupta: An Historical and Philosophical Study*, 2nd ed. (Varanasi: Chowkhamba Sanskrit Series, 1963), 378.

ror is at least partially clouded by the obscuring role (*mala*) of limited materiality as well as by the individuality that comes with personhood. Being embedded within particular centers of consciousness, the intelligence reflects the light of consciousness from a particular angle, not from a universal vantage point.

The second principle of inner awareness, the ego-sense or *ahamkara*, is made up of two words, "I" (*aham*) and "making" (*kara*). This body part is responsible for forming the awareness of oneself as a distinct "I." Without this differentiation of selfhood, it would be impossible to function as an agent in the world. And yet it also gives rise to the tendency to focus thought and emotion on oneself. Selfish or grasping behaviors aim to preserve the individual: "I" want food, safety, and resources necessary for "my" survival. "I" grasp at power, esteem, and privilege over other "I's." Unchecked, the *ahamkara* is the source of the impulses to overcome or deny limits. It is also the part that clings to the notion of an individual self that endures beyond the limited span of life.

The third principle of inner awareness is cognate with the English word "mind," but one should avoid filling this term with familiar associations. Jaideva Singh defines *manas* as "the internal sense; the empirical mind."[15] As a sense, this part of the subjective body plays a crucial role in perception. It is, as it were, the sense of the senses. It perceives the data gleaned through seeing, hearing, smelling, tasting, and touching. From these external sensations, it constructs understanding.[16]

Because it processes the other senses, *manas* is the seat of thought, but the privilege one might like to accord to this faculty is tempered by its inseparability from things that are often treated as its opposite: matter and emotion. Again, because *manas* and the two faculties that precede it emanate from the material principle (*prakrti*), they are part of the material realm, not distinct from it. (Theories that link the mind to a physical organ, the brain, arrive at the same conclusion about mental faculties.) Second, this faculty includes the capacity to

15. Singh, *Yoga of Delight*, 157.
16. Indeed, "without its co-operation with senses, no sensation of any kind is possible . . . it carves images out of the blocks of sensations" (Pandey, *Abhinavagupta*, 380).

desire, making it the seat of the emotions as well. The translation *mind/heart* captures this range.[17] Christian theological anthropology might consider how the category of *manas* could reframe how we view emotion—no longer as an impediment to cognition but as a principle of awareness that reflects the divine image.

Just as *purusa* mirrors the movement of divine consciousness (*cit*) as it becomes aware of its objects, the inner instrument reflects Siva-Sakti's power of the will (*iccha*) and mirrors the divine power of limited satisfaction discussed in the last chapter. As we observed there, Christians have strong warrant for including the desiring faculty in the *imago Dei*, as love is the primary divine attribute (1 John 4:8). Emotion and desire, so often disparaged as impediments to righteousness, are sites in which to recognize the divine image. And these exist in every created thing. As Dionysius puts it, "All things desire [the good]: Everything with mind and reason seeks to know it, everything sentient yearns to perceive it, everything lacking perception has a living and instinctive longing for it, and everything lifeless and merely existent turns, in its own fashion, for a share of it."[18] Because divinity is "both yearning itself and the object of that yearning," divine desire is reflected in humanity and in every facet of creation's mirror.[19]

The will appears in limited form within individuals, of course. Understood as modifications of divine will, however, even "the very states of anger, delusion, etc., appear only as an expression of the consciousness of the . . . Lord"; and the movements of mind/heart can be discerned as the "wondrous play of the (divine) consciousness" (PTv, 40). Though sometimes misdirected or curved in on the self, they nevertheless participate in a fundamental dimension of the divine life.

In light of the subjective body, reading comparatively can help Christians recall that the range of anthropologies in the Christian theological heritage—from the unified "living creature" of Genesis to the

---

17. Tracy Sayuki Tiemeier explores the overlap of intellectual and affective components in the terminology of Tamil devotional poetry and similarly describes the cognate *manam* as "connected with love and devotion to the Lord . . . making the distinction between heart and mind unclear." Tracy Sayuki Tiemeier, "Engendering the 'Mysticism' of the Alvars," *The Journal of Hindu Studies* 3, no. 3 (2010): 343.

18. Pseudo-Dionysius, "The Divine Names," in *Complete Works*, 75.

19. Ibid., 82.

great multiplicity of faculties enumerated by Thomas Aquinas—has used different cultural and philosophical aids to understand the mystery of the human person. Contemporary sciences offer other theories about the capacities and their interrelationship. In view of this variety of helpful frameworks, Christians need not adopt this particular scheme of five faculties, though it has much to recommend it. A more modest goal for conversation with non-dual Saivism is to help extricate contemporary theological anthropology from dualistic patterns of thinking, as well as to remind us that our shorthand language of the "mind" refers to a complex mystery of subjectivity. Each human person is more than two things, and at the same time, she or he is a unified whole.

UNEXCEPTIONAL

The second point to draw from contemplating the parts of the subjective body is that they are unexceptional: they belong not only to humans but also to other sentient beings.

Coming after the litany of the creation of fish, birds, cattle, creeping things, and wild animals of every kind, the proclamation that humankind ('*adam*) was created in the image of God in Genesis appears to distinguish human beings from the other "living creatures" (*nefesh*). But how? Although the content of this image is "radically underdetermined in biblical texts," theologians and philosophers have exerted themselves to identify the quality that distinguishes the human.[20] Does logic set humans apart? Religion? Justice? Conscience? Language? Self-consciousness? The ability to laugh or mourn? To plan and produce for the future?[21] Each of these proposals centers upon faculties housed in the subjective body.

Theological anthropologies that take humans as exceptional in these ways often assume that humanity is the very purpose of creation. Despite the fact that, on a chronology of life in this galaxy, human beings entered the story at quite a late hour, Christian theologians have generally adhered to Origen's opinion that "God put

20. David L. Clough, *On Animals*, vol. 1, *Systematic Theology* (London: T&T Clark, 2012), 65.
21. See ibid., 71–72.

man and the rational nature in general above all irrational beings," and that "providence has made everything primarily for the sake of the rational nature."[22] This anthropocentrism—placing human beings at the center of reality—continues even as contemporary evolutionary biology and zoology negate many of its presuppositions.[23]

Human beings share much more with other species than we had ever imagined. Chimpanzees, our closest genetic neighbors, are a case in point.[24] Chimpanzees exhibit features of culture, including social learning: young chimps imitate their elders to learn how to groom themselves, use tools to crack nuts, and (incredibly) self-medicate by carefully extracting juices and leaves that prevent infections and parasites. Some have learned American Sign Language and taught it to one another. Studies show an aesthetic sensibility in chimpanzees as well as attributes of sympathy, social harmony, reciprocity, and deceit.[25] Because "these very traits are those used to defend human uniqueness," Nancy Howell argues, theological anthropology should pay close attention.[26]

One initial conclusion for theological anthropology is that there is greater continuity between the species than traditional designations of the rational human soul as the unique *imago Dei* have allowed. Put otherwise, the subjective body and its faculties belong to more than human subjects. Elephants mourn their dead. Crows invent tools to solve problems. Dolphins use language and grammar. Bees construct cooperative social worlds. "Brains are in fact so similar across the board that we study fear in the rat's amygdala to treat human phobias," Frans de Waal points out.[27] Individual centers of consciousness

22. Origen, *Contra Celsum* 4.74, cited in Clough, *On Animals*, 10.
23. For an excellent overview of these issues, as well as alternatives to an anthropocentric worldview, see Anna L. Petersen, *Being Human: Ethics, Environment, and Our Place in the World* (Berkeley: University of California Press, 2001).
24. The percentage of genetic material shared between humans and chimpanzees is upwards of 98 percent. Cf. Nancy R. Howell, "Theological Anthropology," in *Creating Women's Theology: A Movement Engaging Process Thought*, ed. Monica A. Coleman, Nancy R. Howell, and Helene Tallon Russell (Eugene, OR: Pickwick, 2011), 146; and Clough, *On Animals*, 29.
25. Howell, "Theological Anthropology," 147–51.
26. Ibid., 152. Frans de Waal identifies a tendency in the cognitive sciences he calls *anthropodenial*: the charge that observations of continuity are merely anthropomorphic projections of human reality onto other species. Frans de Waal, "What I Learned from Tickling Apes," *The New York Times*, April 8, 2016, http://tinyurl.com/hsul48h.
27. Waal, "What I Learned."

of all kinds reflect divine consciousness: they intuit, think, feel, and exhibit self-consciousness to varying degrees.

We can say more. Note the anthropocentric residue in the language of degrees or continuum, reminiscent of the old model of the "great chain of being." On the rationale that humans most perfectly bridge the intellectual and material worlds, this scheme placed human beings at the top, closest to God and angels, followed in descending order by mammals, birds, fish, insects, plants, and insentient matter.[28] Howell is "uncomfortable even with difference in degree," she says, "not because I want to ignore the differences between humans and chimpanzees, but because difference in degree can still be used to establish value judgments or conclusions inappropriate to scientific or scholarly 'objectivity.'"[29] The designation of particular features as the measure for all creatures is both anthropocentric and arbitrary. Waal questions the notion of a singular standard of cognition for differently adapted animals:

> It makes no sense to compare our cognition with one that is distributed over eight independently moving arms, each with its own neural supply, or one that enables a flying organism to catch mobile prey by picking up the echoes of its own shrieks. . . . Instead of a ladder, we are facing an enormous plurality of cognitions with many peaks of specialization.[30]

Within this plurality, humans invariably begin with a human perspective, but nothing prevents us from imagining other points of view.

The continuum in the Indian model differs significantly from the great chain of being. Each of the *tattvas* is not a particular being but a cosmological principle—indeed, a world. Each is inhabited by various beings. Human beings, together with plants, insects, birds, wild animals, and domestic animals, belong to the densest of the worlds,

---

28. In the twentieth century, Arthur O. Lovejoy's characterization in *The Great Chain of Being: A Study of the History of an Idea* (Cambridge, MA: Harvard University Press, 1942) enjoyed considerable influence.

29. Howell, "Theological Anthropology," 153.

30. Waal, "What I Learned." Communication—another criterion—can be assessed by means other than language use, and language itself need not be held to the standards of human grammar, syntax, and vocal apparatus (ibid.).

the earth-*tattva*.[31] In many of these beings, consciousness extends no further than the gross elements. Gavin Flood explains, "A person's experience or perception of a world depends upon the degree of contraction or revelation of supreme consciousness: the more contracted supreme consciousness is, the more particularized and individualized it becomes and the more limited the world of experience or perception."[32] Creatures in all worlds reflect divine consciousness, and they can recognize it in various ways: different beings have different "means to that self-consciousness whose light is never interrupted, which shines equally even in lower creatures like birds, etc., which do not know perceptual or inferential proof even by name" (PTv, 194).[33] For Earth dwellers, who ordinarily perceive themselves as separate from others, that nature usually remains concealed. To that extent, human and nonhuman animals are in the same boat.

Christian theologians and ethicists have also begun to reverse course on the anthropocentric worldview that excepts humans from the rest of the natural world. David Clough notes that in Scripture, humans and other animals are "thought of together":

> Together they are given life by their creator as fleshly creatures made of dust and inspired by the breath of life, . . . together they are the objects of God's providential care, together they are given consideration under the law of Israel and its Rabbinic interpreters, together they are subject to God's judgment and blessing, together they are called to praise their maker and together they gather around God's throne in the new creation.[34]

While Scripture does not negate differences between species, it does put sharp distinctions between the humans and everyone else on religiously shaky ground.

Human beings reflect the *imago Dei* differently than oak trees, chickadees, protozoa, gorillas, and dolphins. Our "singularity,"

31. Flood, *Body and Cosmology*, 67. For a description of the occupants of the other cosmic realms, see ibid., 162, 183.
32. Ibid., 34.
33. As Flood (ibid., 112) explains, "The higher up the hierarchy the more the . . . means of experiencing a world . . . begins to approximate to the reality perceived. . . . The body becomes more clearly bounded and distinct from its world and person in the lower levels, less distinct in higher."
34. Clough, *On Animals*, 40.

Elizabeth Johnson reminds us, was produced through a long process of bio-cultural evolution. Human existence has come to include many cognitive, aesthetic, ethical, and religious behaviors that are not shared by nonhuman animals—including, she notes, the ability "to massively effect the evolution of other species, for good or ill."[35] Revisiting the doctrines of creation and Christology in relation to this insight can help to locate these differences within a theological anthropology.

The theological principle of participation acknowledges a place for all of creation in the divine image. Thomas Aquinas and many of his peers taught that creatures reflect, share, and participate in primary attributes of the creator such as being, goodness, and beauty. He writes,

> For God brought things into being in order that his goodness might be communicated to creatures, and be represented by them; and because this goodness could not be adequately represented by one creature alone, he produced many and diverse creatures, that what was wanting to one in the representation of the divine goodness might be supplied by another. For goodness, which in God is simple and uniform, in creatures is manifold and divided. Hence the whole universe together participates in the divine goodness more perfectly, and represents it better than any single creature whatever.[36]

Although Aquinas himself places differences between creatures into a chain of being, a hierarchy of image-bearing is not theologically necessary. Because the creatures together manifest more of God's image than any could do alone, the chain might be replaced by a prism: all reflect the creator, but from diverse angles. Abhinavagupta calls upon a similar analogy: "just as a pure and colorless crystal takes up the appearance of different types of hues reflected in it, so does the Lord also take up the forms of gods, human beings, animals, and plants (in the manner of reflection)."[37]

Christology sheds additional light on this prism. Despite the

35. Elizabeth A. Johnson, *Ask the Beasts: Darwin and the God of Love* (London: Bloomsbury, 2014), 240, 241.

36. Aquinas, *Summa Theologiae* 1.46.3, cited in Johnson, *Ask the Beasts*, 149.

37. Abhinavagupta, *Essence of the Exact Reality, or, Paramarthasara of Abhinavagupta*, trans. B. N. Pandit (New Delhi: Munshiram Manoharlal, 1991), 23.

undeniable fact that Jesus, the "image of the invisible God" (Col 1:15), is a human being, a careful reading of the passage that makes this claim does not support the anthropomorphic conclusions that have been drawn from it. The hymn, cosmic in scope, calls him "the first-born of all creation, for in him all things in heaven and on earth were created, things visible and invisible. . . . In him all things hold together" (Col 1:15–17). Such a view of Christ appears again in the prologue to John's Gospel: as the Logos of God, he is the principle of creation. The being of all things participates in Christ.

In the incarnation, the Word is made flesh (John 1:14). Johnson emphasizes that the word for flesh is not human being (*anthropos*) or man (*aner*), but *sarx*, a word that here "simply conveys the finite quality of the material world which is fragile, vulnerable, perishable, transitory, the opposite of divinity clothed in majesty." The incarnation relates humanity to all flesh–not only to "the evolutionary network of life on our planet," but beyond it to the very origins of the cosmos.[38] The entire network of life is implicated in the flesh taking of God. Every being reflects divine glory and care.

The redemptive work of Christ also takes a cosmic sweep. It would be an odd asymmetry if systematic theology suddenly shifted away from the broad scope of the doctrines of creation and incarnation and focused salvation and eschatology on human beings alone.[39] Colossians makes the parallel explicit. Christ, the "firstborn of all creation," is also the "firstborn from the dead" (Col 1:15, 18). Just as Christ is "before all things and in him all things hold together," so too, "through him God was pleased to reconcile to Godself all things, whether on earth or in heaven" (Col 1:17, 20). Beginning, middle, and end concern the whole. Not only human beings but "the all" (*ta panta*) are made new as part of the image of the invisible God. Clough therefore argues against considering humanness, as such, the image of God: "like human beings, other kinds of creatures may become images of God in ways particular to them."[40]

Comparative investigation of the subjective body can nuance these developments in Christian systematic theology, which are coming to

38. Johnson, *Ask the Beasts*, 195–96.
39. Cf. Clough, *On Animals*, 104–5.
40. Ibid., 102.

ascertain that humans share many aspects of conscious bodily existence with other creatures. Take ego-sense (*ahamkara*), for instance. Human survival instincts are no less operative than in our biological kin. Like them, we have much invested in preserving our sense of "I," even at the expense of others. It would seem, though, that only humans employ the "I-making" capacity to label and "other" through language.[41] Waal gives this example in relation to nonhuman animals: "When our ancestors moved from hunting to farming, they lost respect for animals and began to look at themselves as the rulers of nature. In order to justify how they treated other species, they had to play down their intelligence and deny them a soul."[42] Humans employ the same mechanism, of course, to create classes of human others, sometimes through explicit association with animals or beasts. Racist and anti-Semitic tropes thrive on such rhetoric. These associations speak volumes not only about human bigotry toward fellow humans but also about human attitudes toward nonhuman animals.

But human beings can also use the faculties of the subjective body to question such attitudes. We can recognize that the use of tropes that equate "animal" or "beast" with the lack of valued traits says more about the anthropocentric worldview of the people that utter them than about the creatures themselves. Similarly, by imagining ourselves together with the rest of the creaturely world rather than as exceptions to it, we have the ability to reverse course on our destruction of these species and their habitats. For example, "We can see this process underway in the halting of biomedical research on chimpanzees and the opposition to the use of killer whales for entertainment."[43] We can imagine what it is like for creatures to be prey to the out-of-sight, routinized horror of factory farms. We can activate the shared, unexceptional faculties of the subjective body to observe our animal neighbors, to be attentive to their particularity, and to understand their claim to our shared world.

---

41. "Humans make terrible distinctions about one another; other animals do not," Jeffrey Moussaieff Masson claims in *Beasts: What Animals Can Teach Us about the Origins of Good and Evil* (New York: Bloomsbury, 2014), 1.

42. Waal, "What I Learned."

43. Ibid.

LIMITED

The third anthropological claim I wish to stake with respect to the subjective body is that it is limited: it is subject to the limitations—in scope, power, knowledge, satiation, time, and place—that veil consciousness in the created realm. The intellect is located within a particular center of consciousness. The ego is uniquely focused on one person: me. The mind can know only what the contingencies of its location in a particular time and place have allowed it to sense and understand. These limitations lead to desires that are never fully satiated. To these shared features of subjectivity, we may add normal variations in their functioning: from infancy to Alzheimer's, from stress to insomnia, from genetic variation to trauma-induced lapses, from autism to intellectual disabilities, human minds operate within limits.

In part, these limits do pertain to materiality: the mind itself, along with the rest of the subjective capacities (intelligence, ego, and so forth), emerges and operates in the limited material realm. Biology, chemistry, and genetics belong to this realm. In contrast with the dualistic reduction of these conditions, however, a theological view of mental capacities as body parts can acknowledge biological dimensions to the mind's limitations without severing them from social, spiritual, and other facets of thought and emotion.

In the first chapter, one of the openings for cognizing pure consciousness beyond subject and object, absent even of "God," was the void. In the microcosm of the individual, this dimension of absence can register in the subjective body as existential dread, darkness, and despair. Testimonies from the frontier of mental illness open up this desolation for theological reflection. Theologian Monica Coleman's memoir, *Bipolar Faith*, unflinchingly presents her years of lonely sadness, her experience of trauma, and her desperate fear of sleep. Contemplating suicide, she looks at herself in the mirror and hardly recognizes herself. She sees a portrait of self-hatred. Her own memory has betrayed her, blocking all joy and friendship with despair. She witnesses someone on the brink of the void: a "woman who lies on the couch all day wishing she could just disappear into nowhere."[44] This face of the void manifests within the limited subjective body.

After receiving her diagnosis, Coleman begins to recite a mantra of her identities: teacher, writer, poet, minister, church member, dancer, beloved—alive. She explains, "I needed to know that there was more to my life, more to who I was, than the pain. I had to be more than depression. More than bipolar."[45] Part of this "more" is that these limited body parts are also pervaded by and participate in divine consciousness. Coleman reflects on how she began to experience the divine, not in rare moments of radical transcendence or stunning revelation, but in mundane activities:

> God was just there. In the hot cup of tea. In the women who gathered. In our laughter. In the knitting. God was in my uniform rows of stitches. God was also in the dropped stitch that created an imperfection.... This is the radical incarnation.... God is in every cell, every person, and every activity. Whether I know it or not. Whether it feels like it or not. God is creating. With yarn and needles, hiccups, unraveling, do-overs, a rhythm, and individual stitches, God is making something new. Something beautiful.[46]

Much of the spiritual advice Coleman had received over the years—to trust Jesus for deliverance, to have more faith, to fault herself—missed the mark. Instead, she learned to discover divine regard in the disorder itself. She writes, "With therapists, medication, meaningful studies, a small church community, a pastor who cared, friends who understood, and a name for my condition, God was knitting me."[47] In all of these forms of healing that are neither denial nor cure, God's loving attention is present.

With a theological anthropology that includes multiple parts, in all of their possible configurations, Christians can recognize the divine reflection in entire persons, not just in some abstracted version of them. The mind's limits are part of a person's identity. Indeed, it can be difficult for people to imagine who they would be *without* these

---

44. Monica A. Coleman, *Bipolar Faith: A Black Woman's Journey with Depression and Faith* (Minneapolis: Fortress Press, 2016), 266.

45. Ibid., 328, cf. 327.

46. Ibid., 332.

47. Ibid., 333.

limits—without their bipolar condition, their autism, their Down syndrome, or other particular forms of embodied subjectivity. As Coleman reflects, "this is the only me I've ever known. . . . the hard parts of my life are not failure. They are evidence that I'm human."[48] Theologians err to restrict the fullness of the *imago Dei* to any particular mental or intellectual benchmark. Every person mirrors divinity, regardless of whether or how they perceive this to be the case.

This diverse, holistic view of the human condition invites a corresponding view of redemption. Sharon Betcher understands "Spirit not as the power to rescue and repair according to some presupposed original state or ideal form, but as the energy for unleashing multiple forms of corporeal flourishing."[49] It should not surprise us that deep mystery continues to surround the human subject amid our differences in mental, developmental, or intellectual capacity. Those of us with these conditions must be able to tell our stories, and have them heard, without fear of stigma.[50] Those of us who consider ourselves "normal" must listen and become aware of how fear of these differences tempts us to silence and exclude. "Meeting one another well is a work of the Spirit," write Jean Vanier and John Swinton.

> It is in and through the Spirit that we are enabled to meet one another as we are, rather than as we might like one another to be. . . . In this space, neither one nor the other is superior. It is a place where we meet in humility, and love without judgment; just two people, recognizing the other as precious and important; two human beings desiring to be present for one to the other.[51]

The religious community's role neither replaces the medical community nor transfers all responsibility to it. Its responsibility is to recognize whole people as *imago Dei* and to attend with care to the various limits and possibilities of subjectivity.

---

48. Ibid., 340.

49. Sharon V. Betcher, *Spirit and the Politics of Disablement* (Minneapolis: Fortress Press, 2007), 50.

50. Sarah Griffith Lund (*Blessed Are the Crazy: Breaking the Silence about Mental Illness, Family, and Church* [St. Louis: Chalice, 2014]) makes the case for the importance of testimony as a practice of the church in relation to mental illness.

51. Jean Vanier and John Swinton, *Mental Health: The Inclusive Church Resource* (London: Darton, Longman & Todd, 2014), 79–80.

PRACTICES OF NAVIGATING THE "IMPURE PATH"

My argument that the subjective body is multiple, unexceptional, and limited subdues modernity's claims of universality and objectivity, but it does not thereby render the thinking faculties unimportant. From the middle of the thirty-six *tattva*s, facing both inward and outward, the parts of the subjective body can be yoked in practices of paying attention. The word *yoga* is related to the Sanskrit (and English) verb "to yoke." And in another cross-cultural resonance, the Katha Upanisad, like Plato's *Phaedrus*, employs yoking as a metaphor for the relation of the faculties of the subjective body to one another:

> Know the self as a rider in a chariot
>   And the body, as simply the chariot.
> Know the intellect as the charioteer,
>   And the mind, as simply the reins.
> The senses, they say, are the horses.
> —Katha Upanisad 3.3–4[52]

Here we witness the role of the subjective body in spiritual practices. The individual self (*purusa*) rides, observing, in a vehicle made up of material components (*prakrti*). The intellect (*buddhi*) holds the mental reins (*manas*), which are in turn yoked to the senses. Created by consciousness and inseparable from the body, this cluster of mental capacities is the command center from which an individual relates to the whole range of thirty-six body parts—in other words, to all of reality.

Nevertheless, the non-dual Saiva tradition locates the subjective body within the "impure path" of consciousness, and we might call the disciplines that employ its parts practices of the impure path. Impurity is not a moral category in this context. On this side of *maya*, consciousness is impure because our perception of unity is muddied by objects that appear to be solid and separate from the subject. Most of us ordinarily do not experience the pure path, on the other side of *maya*, where "everything is . . . thoroughly pervaded by the form of consciousness" (PTlv, 211). Furthermore, each and every one of the

---

52. Olivelle, *Upanisads*, 238–39.

principles of inner awareness—intelligence, sense of self, and mind/heart—operates within the complicated and enmeshed material realm. None of the faculties stand apart from the body. Each evolves from materiality and is subject to its limits.

It is an important spiritual practice to relinquish purity. Intelligence is not a capacity that can achieve full and universal access to the truth. Instead, because it is a kind of wisdom (*buddhi*), this principle of subjectivity causes a person to be awake and aware. A person so awakened (a Buddha) perceives the workings of the other faculties, not least the ego's self-elevation, the stirring of desire, and the arising of emotion. Encounter with limitations can arouse many of these impulses. The human ego, fancying itself the pinnacle of creation, sets itself apart from the other sentient beings. The plant and animal worlds upon which humanity depends would survive quite well without us, yet our presumed superiority justifies our violent dominion over them. Afraid of the mind's unruliness and its limits, we construct thresholds of normality that stigmatize and exclude people with intellectual disabilities and the mentally ill. The boundaries we erect between pure humanity and everything that might disturb its perimeter are *ahamkara*'s most illusory products.

The contemplative traditions teach that the subjective body can become aware, first and foremost, of itself. The Christian desert monastics exemplify how practices of attention can be directed toward the subjective body. They paid special attention to the habits, called "passions," that they wanted to uproot: gluttony, lust, avarice, sadness, anger, acedia, vainglory, and pride. At the center of the passions was the desiring aspect of the human being, the will. Its movements could be discerned in the stirrings of the mind as well as the rest of the body, and so these spiritual seekers learned "to be adept at recognizing or responding to these shifting and often treacherous *logismoi* or thoughts, which revealed so clearly the competing impulses within the monk's inner life."[53] Through practices of contemplation, they could also observe the untrained, flighty nature of

---

53. Douglas E. Christie, *The Blue Sapphire of the Mind: Notes for a Contemplative Ecology* (New York: Oxford University Press, 2013), 48.

the mind, which can lead to the "habits of inattention and careless-ness" that impede awareness of the whole.[54]

The awareness facilitated by practices of yoking the instruments of cognition differs from assuming a universal point of view: As Douglas Christie describes the early Christian desert mothers and fathers, their practices of paying attention (*prosoche*) meant "to know oneself not as a solitary, autonomous being but as one whose identity can only be conceived of as existing within an intricate web of encompassing relationships."[55] Awareness of the whole includes awareness of one's own particular and limited vantage point.

Michele Saracino puts a contemporary spin on practices of the impure path. Globalization, migration, and religious pluralism are making it increasingly difficult to draw clear borders of the self. She explains, "The more we interact with others from previously disparate worlds, the more the boundaries of our identities overlap and intertwine with one another. Our stories leak onto and sometimes become enmeshed with that of another."[56] When we encounter people across boundaries, we become aware of other stories, other ways of narrating the world. We realize that there is no one true story, at least not as told by any one of us. When multiple stories become part of our very selves, whether through heritage, travel, or friendship, we ourselves become the confluence of multiple identities. Like it or not, we abide on the impure path.

Nevertheless, people will try to "do everything and anything to fix those leaky borders and put an end to the emotional onslaught that their permeability brings."[57] Negotiations of identity provoke strong emotions such as fear and avoidance of people whose existence threatens the borders of the self, entitlement to the maintenance of these borders that masks the full humanity of others, and eventually a numbness that blocks hospitality.[58] These tangled thoughts and emotions are the province of the mind/heart. Addressing only the intellectual dimensions of living together—doing no "more than

54. Ibid., 41.
55. Ibid., 34, cf. 47.
56. Michele Saracino, *Being about Borders: A Christian Anthropology of Difference* (Collegeville, MN: Liturgical, 2011), 6–7.
57. Ibid., 7.
58. Ibid., 21.

accept[ing] the commonsense logic that nobody is perfect"—leaves untouched the powerful logic of the affective dimensions.

Awareness of these movements of the ego and the mind/heart, then, is only one dimension of spiritual practice. For communities coming to grips with conflicted feelings in the face of other stories, Saracino recommends practices of mourning. The impure path gives rise to conflict and loss. There are costs when we decenter the self and give up "the one true story about what it means to be human, that of being safe, untouchable, perfect, and having pristine borders."[59] Mourning gives loss the time and attention it needs. Dupuche comes to a similar conclusion: he applies meditation techniques from Abhinavagupta's tradition to the Christian season of Lent in order to expose the "many areas of need, many wounds, not only in the body but also in the memory and in the heart and in the spirit."[60] The wounds of the incarnate Christ open devotees to recognizing the presence of God within their own wounds, and within the things they must mourn. Mourning opens the way to resurrection. God breathes Spirit into the ashes, inspiring the will, giving the strength to face difficult memories and to observe emotion with equanimity, and attuning each of these faculties.[61]

The special expertise of Indian meditation techniques is to observe the mind and emotions without disparagement.[62] The individual center of consciousness, or *purusa*, rides in the chariot made up of the rest of the subjective body. From this vantage point as the witness, it can view every movement of the intellect, ego, and mind/heart. The witness observes the embodied emotions that arise. It identifies the stories the mind and intellect tell about the circumstances that cause these reactions. It compassionately notes the ego's investment in these stories. Beth Berila applies this capacity to the process of unlearning the oppressive ideologies that imprint themselves within the subjective body. Whether the script is a form of internalized oppression, of privilege, or some combination of the two, "mindfulness teaches

59. Ibid., 52.
60. Dupuche, *Jesus the Mantra*, 62.
61. Ibid., 69.
62. For one guide, see Peter Marchand, *The Yoga of the Nine Emotions: The Tantric Practice of Rasa Sadhana* (Rochester, VT: Destiny, 2006); as well as my analysis of a range of religious practices in relation to emotion in Voss Roberts, *Tastes of the Divine*.

us to Witness that storyline and choose not to indulge it."[63] Because the labels that dehumanize us often operate on an unconscious level, intellectualized responses alone rarely uproot them. Practices of witnessing the movement of the subjective body allow us first to become familiar with how these scripts affect us, to accept our reactions with compassion (which is not the same as accepting the oppressive structures), to develop strategies to handle these reactions, and to interrupt the habitual inner narrative.[64]

Even as we strive for greater clarity and linguistic precision about our identities as *imago Dei*, paradox is also an important "habit of the mind."[65] The limits of language are perhaps nowhere more apparent in theological anthropology than when we try to narrate our complex identities vis-à-vis one another. For this reason, it is worth noticing the paradox of contemporary theological responses to mind-body dualisms, which has been to try to *think* differently about the human person. The multiple, unexceptional, and limited subjective body may not be entirely up to the task. The subjective body also steers its chariot outward, into the empirical world. The mind engages the input gathered through touch, taste, smell, hearing and sight. The next chapter accordingly directs its attention to the engaged body so that we might not only think about these matters but attend to what these faculties have to say.

63. Berila, *Integrating Mindfulness*, 82.
64. Ibid., 84–87.
65. Christie, *Blue Sapphire*, 62.

5.

The Engaged Body

There are few phrases more mobile in Christian theology than *the body of Christ*. It refers to the physical body of Jesus. It is present in the eucharistic meal. "The cup of blessing that we bless, is it not a sharing in the blood of Christ? The bread that we break, is it not a sharing in the body of Christ?" (1 Cor 10:16) The church as a whole is taken to be the body of the risen Christ on Earth: partaking in this meal incorporates each person into Christ's body.

The apostle Paul riffs on this metaphor when he employs the body's organs of sense and action to describe what it means for the church to be the body of Christ. Foot, hand, eye, and ear are all necessary parts of the body, for "if all were a single member, where would the body be? As it is, there are many members, yet one body" (1 Cor 12:19–20). Lest any church member protest that it is better to be a brain than a toe, Paul exhorts that "the members of the body that seem to be weaker are indispensable, and those members of the body that we think less honorable we clothe with greater honor" (1 Cor 12:22–23). The body is a unity: when one part suffers—including a toe—all suffer. So, too, with the community gathered in Christ's name.

Through the development of these related meanings, the body of Christ has become a metaphor. It has become easy to spiritualize this body and to forget its physicality. Even Jesus's own corporeality gets papered over. Who can imagine the cherubic babe in the glowing manger covered in afterbirth, spitting up, or sullying his dear swaddling clothes? And how impious to suggest that Jesus experienced sexual intimacy or desire! Each of these functions would require recognition that the body of Christ includes physical organs—some of them more mentionable than others.

If God is spirit (John 4:24), can a body image divinity? Does the physical resemblance of Jesus's body to ours pertain only to his humanity? Or can it be seen as part of the *imago Dei?* The early Christian theologian Irenaeus ushers us into this exploration. Comparison then frames an inquiry into how even the "less respectable members" of the body, as carnal and limited as they may be, belong to the image of God. Building cumulatively upon earlier chapters, we then consider the implications of these insights for the incarnate, ecclesial, and eucharistic bodies of Christ.

BODY AS *IMAGO DEI*

Few resources exist in the Christian theological tradition for thinking about how the physical body images God. Augustine entertains the idea that humanity's upright posture distinguishes humans from beasts because it enables us to look heavenward.[1] A more robust consideration comes from the second-century Christian bishop Irenaeus.

For Irenaeus, the primary difference between God and humanity is not that we have bodies and God does not but that God is uncreated and we are creatures. God's embodied creatures image God insofar as they show forth God's attributes. Their very existence demonstrates God's power and goodness. Their order and harmony reflect God's wisdom. The fact that humans grow and mature in their reflection of God's glory shows God's kindness.[2] The developmental aspect is the key to understanding Irenaeus's anthropology. The human being grows, gains strength, and recovers from sin, "making progress day by day, and ascending towards the perfect, that is, approximating

---

1. Augustine, *The Trinity* 12.1.

2. Irenaeus, *Against Heresies*, trans. Alexander Roberts and William Rambaut, in *Ante-Nicene Fathers*, vol. 1, ed. Alexander Roberts, James Donaldson, and A. Cleveland Coxe (Buffalo, NY: Christian Literature, 1885), 4.38.3; revised and edited by Kevin Knight (New Advent: n.p., 2009), http://tinyurl.com/2hp4ya.

to the uncreated One." In the end, God glorifies the human being through the vision of God, for "the beholding of God is productive of immortality, but immortality renders one near unto God."[3] Thus, although human beings can never become uncreated, they are destined to "receive a faculty of the Uncreated," namely, immortality: "By this arrangement, therefore, and these harmonies, and a sequence of this nature, [the human] is rendered after the image and likeness of the uncreated God."[4]

The centrality of the body in this divinizing process becomes clear in passages where Irenaeus distinguishes between the image and the likeness of God. Humans grow in the *likeness* of God (glory, immortality), but the body, "that fleshly nature which was molded after the image of God" bears the *image* of God from the moment of its creation until its completion.[5] How remarkable! Unlike the later tradition, which would locate the divine image in the capacities of the soul, Irenaeus locates it firmly in the body. Our very flesh takes the imprint of God's image. This affirmation leads him to proclaim that "the glory of God is a living [human being]."[6] God's glory is humanity fully alive, or, as my teacher Don Saliers delights in rendering it, *humanity at full stretch.*

Irenaeus's reasoning about the body is also christological: if the incarnate Christ displays the visible image of the invisible God, then the image must be manifest in the body. The *image* of God, stamped into the flesh, is never lost, but the incarnation makes it possible to recover the *likeness* of God, lost in the fall, through imitation of Christ. Humanity receives the image of God at creation through the creative power of Christ, the Logos, and is restored to the likeness of God through his redemptive grace.[7]

Irenaeus cannot emphasize the importance of the body enough. After all, the purpose of *Against Heresies* is to refute the gnostic sects of his time, especially their teaching that salvation entails becoming spiritual by escaping the clutches of the body. This is nonsense, he

3. Ibid., 4.38.3.
4. Ibid.
5. Ibid., 5.6.1.
6. Ibid., 4.20.7.
7. Ibid., 5.16.2.

says, because severing body from spirit would make a person something less or other than a complete human being.[8] Christ's resurrection in the flesh, anticipating his promises for the life to come, demonstrates the eternal integrity of embodied humanity. For Irenaeus, God's handiwork in the human being is completed not by tearing it apart but by imitating Christ and being transformed by work of the Holy Spirit in the church.[9] The human being is—and always will be—embodied.

After Irenaeus, Christian theologians generally mitigated this affirmation of the body and shifted focus to the faculties that distinguish humanity from other animals. However, the Hindu inclusion of ten organs of sense and action in the human reflection of divinity invites another look at this tantalizing opening into the *imago Dei*.

THE ENGAGED BODY

The engaged body designates what the phrase "body parts" most readily brings to mind. As the non-dual Saiva tradition describes them, however, these parts are more than physical organs. As parts of the divine body, they encompass the very capacity or power (*indriya*) to sense and act.

Organs of Sense	Organs of Action
Hearing	Speaking
Touching	Grasping
Seeing	Walking
Tasting	Excreting
Smelling	Procreating

On the level of the cosmic body, these "organs" are principles that make sensation and action possible. Embodied beings participate in these principles not only insofar as they possess ears, hands, eyes, tongue, nose, and the like, but also insofar as they apply them to their

8. "If any one take away the image and set aside the handiwork," he writes, one "cannot then understand this as being a [human being]." Irenaeus, *Against Heresies* 5.6.1.
9. Ibid.

respective tasks. I call these capacities *the engaged body* because each is a mode of engaging with people and objects in the external world.

Positioned between the elemental body and the subjective body, the engaged body puts them in contact with one another: the external world becomes an object for thought and feeling through the organs of sense and action. "The sense capacities are . . . manifested as instruments as cognition" (PTlv, 210). Everything one hears, touches, sees, tastes, and smells, as well as everything one does in daily life, becomes data for the cognitive operations to process.

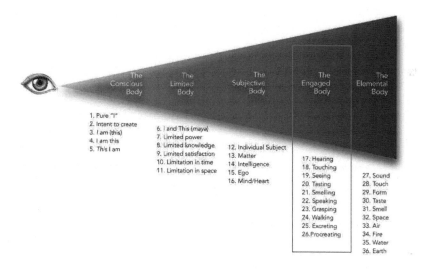

Fig. 5.

The engaged nature of these parts adds a relational twist to the physical body as *imago Dei*. This twist suggests an additional opening for comparison beyond Irenaeus: Christian social Trinitarian thought holds up the relation between self and others as the image of God. According to Catherine LaCugna and John Zizioulas, whose work spurred the retrieval of the social model, human beings in their communities mirror the divine mystery of personhood and relation.[10] The church, the body of Christ empowered by the Spirit, becomes a site to experience this mystery. We will return to the implications of a

10. E.g., Catherine Mowry LaCugna, *God for Us: The Trinity and Christian Life* (San Francisco: HarperSanFrancisco, 1993), 302–3.

relational anthropology for Zizioulas's ecclesiology, but we must first learn the lessons of the engaged body, namely, that the organs of engagement are physical reflections of divine relationality.

Attending to these body parts can also help to articulate the significance of embodied human differences for theological anthropology. We are developing what Elizabeth Johnson calls a "multipolar anthropology" that respects "all persons in their endless combinations of anthropological constants, boundlessly concrete."[11] The organs of sensation and action are among the embodied "constants" that occur in "endless combinations." Through the organs of sensation, human beings are hardwired to attend to our surroundings. Another constant is that, through the organs of action, human beings enact that awareness in community with others. Comparison urges a fine-grained sense of these multiple poles of embodied experience.

THE ORGANS OF SENSATION

Hearing, touching, seeing, tasting, and smelling: in the non-dual Saiva imagination, these processes replicate, in microcosm, the movement of divine consciousness. Creation is perception: as Siva opens his eyes, he gradually perceives the external objects taking form. So, too, as our senses reach out to the things around us, those things become real to us. Each of the sensory functions can be described as "a 'spark,' a 'beam' or a 'ray'" because they "proceed from consciousness like rays of light in order to make contact with their objects."[12] God is present to the world by perceiving its tiniest detail. Scripture states that God watches the sparrow, adorns the lilies, and numbers the hairs on one's head (Luke 12). When we meditate upon and through the senses, we participate in God's attentiveness to creation.

Sensory processes are a wonder to behold. Ten thousand taste buds in the human mouth require only a tenth of a second to identify a flavor. Sound waves pass vibrations through a complex mechanism in the ear: from the eardrum, amplified by miniscule bones, they pass to another membrane and then to the inner ear, where the fluid-filled

11. Johnson, *She Who Is*, 156.
12. Dupuche, *Abhinavagupta*, 54.

cochlea and its twenty-five thousand hairlike receptors translate them to nerve fibers that convey information to the brain.[13] Often disregarded as one of the "lower" senses, the sense of smell and its strong connections to the brain's associative powers can profoundly affect a person's mood. Although these processes do not usually garner much attention, contemplating the inner workings of even one of the physical senses can evoke a sense of awe.

Sensation is so important that the brain is configured to gain sensory information from multiple sources. Lawrence Rosenblum observes, "In some ways, the brain doesn't much care which sense organ provides information."[14] Theories dating back to Aristotle recognize certain "common sensibles," such as "rest, motion, number, size, unity, and shape," which multiple senses can perceive.[15] It is well known that the brain compensates for the loss of one sense through enhancement of the others.[16] This feature, known as neuroplasticity or cross-modal plasticity, is not confined to people who are blind or deaf. Even brief periods of deprivation to one sense result in an increase in activity by the others. Furthermore, processes considered to belong to one sense can be accomplished by others. For example, speech can largely be understood solely by watching faces. Smells, even in isolation from visual stimuli, can communicate attractiveness.

Consider, as well, how the senses work together. The ability to smell food plays an important role in how food tastes: most people have had the experience that food tastes bland when they have a cold.[17] Less well known is that touch stimulates the visual centers of the brain.[18] More than a function solely of skin, the sense of touch

13. Koch and Heil, *Created in God's Image*, 72–73, 93–94.

14. Lawrence D. Rosenblum, *See What I'm Saying: The Extraordinary Powers of Our Five Senses* (New York: W. W. Norton, 2010), xi.

15. Lawrence E. Marks, *The Unity of the Senses: Interrelations among the Modalities* (New York: Academic Press, 1978), 12.

16. Rosenblum (*See What I'm Saying*, chs. 1 and 2) explores the examples of blind mountain bikers who navigate a trail through echolocation (determining the contours of the trail by making clicking sounds) and a league of blindfolded baseball players who play the game with a beeping ball.

17. For how this works, see ibid., 113–15. Less well known is the contribution of sight to the sense of taste. The color of a fruit drink affects the perceived flavor, and the intensity of a food's color influences the perceived intensity of taste. Sound and touch have also been shown to influence perceived freshness, crispness, and other qualities. See ibid., 105–13.

18. Marks, *Unity of the Senses*, 131.

engages tendons and muscles to generate a mental picture of an object's properties. A person can determine an object's size and shape with surprising accuracy simply by picking it up with one finger and a thumb.[19] Even more astonishing is that this kind of estimation can be done with no direct bodily contact. Touching one object with another can determine its qualities, as when one perceives thickness by stirring soup with a spoon, when one determines the texture of a writing surface through a pencil, or when an experienced angler can ascertain the weight and type of fish through the fishing rod.[20] Synesthesia, the phenomenon in which the input of one sense is perceived in terms of another, such as hearing colors or seeing sounds, is an extreme case of these sensory connections.[21]

The complexity and interrelation of the senses are captivating. As microcosms of the divine perception of the world, they image a God who is intrinsically related to others. This embodied relationality becomes even more vivid as we move on to the organs of action: speaking, walking, grasping, excreting, and procreating.

THE ORGANS OF ACTION

Through the organs of action, one engages the embodied beings encountered through the senses. Just as human beings perceive the world through the senses, from infancy we typically begin to make our imprint upon the world through communication and movement, assimilating some things and producing others.

These capacities, too, image the divine. Jesus does all of these things. He speaks. He listens. He moves about with intention. He touches people and attends to their needs. According to social Trinitarian thought, when we witness how God acts, we witness who the three persons truly are. Salvation history discloses the mystery of Trinitarian relation. As Karl Rahner puts it, "The 'economic' Trinity is the 'immanent' Trinity, and the 'immanent' Trinity is the

---

19. Rosenblum, *See What I'm Saying*, 160–64.
20. Ibid., 166.
21. Ibid. For example, brightness has been identified as a feature of both auditory and visual phenomena. This correspondence results in a remarkable degree of similarity in how synesthetes assign color to various pitches (ibid., 90).

'economic Trinity'"; or, in other words, who God is in Godself cannot be separated from who God is for us.[22] God is intrinsically relational, and so are we.

Christ's embodied relation to the world raises scandal. "The Son of Man came eating and drinking," which causes onlookers to say, "'Look, a glutton and a drunkard, a friend of tax collectors and sinners!'" (Matt 11:19). His organs of action include body parts that the apostle Paul euphemistically calls "less respectable members" (1 Cor 12:23), causing further discomfort. God incarnate comes speaking, grasping, walking, eating and drinking—yes—and shitting. Why does excreting merit special mention as a "body part"? Does theology really concern such things?

"LESS RESPECTABLE" MEMBERS?

Indeed, the less respectable members have an important part to play in a holistic theological anthropology. The digestive system is another miracle of the body's design, necessary for every human being, no matter how young, infirm, or divine. Our common embodied lot is present in the nutritive process that is continually expelling waste and toxins through the body's lungs, pores, glands, kidneys, and bowels. Life halts when these cycles fail. Excreting also balances the activity of grasping. We take aspects of the world into ourselves, and we let them go. The organs of excretion merit appreciation and contemplation.

Our list of body parts brings even greater scandal. Although sexual organs certainly belong in a list of parts of the human person, it might seem indecorous to discuss them in the context of theological anthropology (or anywhere other than moral theology, for that matter). There have been very few theological meditations on Christ's genitals, and most crucifixes delicately drape a loincloth where they would be.[23] Epitomized by Augustine's famous angst over his inability to control his erections, the Christian tradition has often treated

22. Karl Rahner, *The Trinity*, trans J. F. Donceel (London: Continuum, 2001), 22. LaCugna (*God for Us*, 243–50) develops this important principle.

23. For a notable exception, see Andy Buechel, *That We Might Become God: The Queerness of Creedal Christianity* (Eugene, OR: Cascade, 2015), 47–56.

sexual activity as something to deny, suppress, and control.[24] Sexual desire is thought to distract from love for God and distort love of neighbor.

By contrast, Abhinavagupta's tantric tradition reserves a special place for sex in its rituals. A few words of contextualization can distinguish this feature of the tradition from whatever the imagination might otherwise wish to supply.

The designation *tantric* means that instead of the texts called the Vedas, which orthodox schools of Hinduism follow, this stream favors another set of scriptures, called Tantras. Tantric traditions define themselves against the Vedic codes of purity and pollution through "a conviction, a universal awareness which inspires confidence that nothing is impure."[25] Divinity, eternally pure, can be found in things usually deemed unclean, such as cremation grounds, funeral ash, and polluting substances like meat, fish, alcohol, and bodily effluvia. One character who embodies this tradition is the dweller in the cremation ground, smeared in ash, who acts offensively to draw the scorn of respectable people; however, the expression chosen by Trika Saivas is that of a householder, externally orthodox but privately practicing tantric forms of meditation.[26]

The sexual rite itself is reserved for very advanced practitioners who have already been initiated into the highest levels of practice. These initiates endeavor to engage in sexual intercourse without attachment: "Rather than seek the fluctuating mental stages of excitement and abatement, the practitioner seeks intimacy with the sexual partner while focusing on their eternal identity as Siva and Sakti, joined together in bliss."[27] This intercourse is hedged by extensive rituals of initiation, preparation, anointing the parts of the body with mantras, and ingesting various taboo substances.[28] In addition to the

---

24. Augustine, *The City of God, Books VIII–XVI*, trans. Gerald G. Walsh and Grace Monahan, Fathers of the Church 14 (Washington, DC: Catholic University Press of America, 2008), 14.16.

25. Dupuche, *Abhinavagupta*, 84–85.

26. According to the "frequently quoted maxim," one would "be privately Kaula, publicly Saiva and Vedic in one's social intercourse." Sanderson, "Saivism," 167.

27. Dupuche, *Abhinavagupta*, 133–34.

28. Dupuche's *Abhinavagupta* provides extensive commentary on the passages in Abhinavagupta's *Tantraloka* that outline these rituals.

length and complexity of these rituals, either desire or disgust would prevent most people from attempting to engage in them.[29]

In order to understand the relation of sex to spiritual realization in this tradition, one must remember that every movement of consciousness replicates Siva's creative expansion and contraction. Perception, desire, understanding, language—all mirror the movement of consciousness toward an object. Different forms of meditation are able to draw attention to the perception and dissolution of duality. Sexual ecstasy is like any other movement of consciousness from self to other and back again. It makes an excellent "token of remembrance of the inherent delight of the Divine Self" because it "is a matter of personal experience to everyone" (PTv, 44).

Contemporary Christian theologians have been working to reverse Christian anti-body and anti-sex rhetoric. Periods of abstinence and the discipline of self-control contribute to spiritual maturity, but sex itself is nothing evil. David Jensen offers counsel that would not be foreign to the Trika tradition: "Sexuality is sacred in its ordinariness, in its everydayness. . . . The journey toward God, sustained by desire, encounters the divine in the midst of the ordinary."[30] Beyond the goal of procreation, sexuality draws humans to seek union and mutual fulfillment with one another. If God encounters humanity in the flesh, then sexuality represents one of many ways to encounter and respond to God through the organs of sense and action.

Because Abhinavagupta's texts discuss rituals of the engaged body from the point of view of male practitioners, we might expand his reflection on the organs of procreation. Astonishingly enough, if procreation results from intercourse, a female body generates an entirely new organ: the placenta. By the end of the first trimester, this fully formed organ supplies antibodies, hormones, oxygen, and nutrients to the fetus. It accomplishes excretory functions by diffusing carbon dioxide, uric acid, and other waste products into the pregnant person's blood. A successful pregnancy results not only in a new organ of action (the placenta) but also the emergence of a novel set of organs of sense and action and a new center of consciousness. Organs

29. Ibid., 85.
30. David H. Jensen, *God, Desire, and a Theology of Human Sexuality* (Louisville: Westminster John Knox, 2013), 28.

generate organs, reflecting the divine activities of creation and providence.

Attention to pregnant embodiment yields further insight into the shared human condition. Not every person will give birth, but each and every human first engages their surroundings through the mediation of a nutrient-rich placenta. As Marcia Mount Shoop muses on the "placenta as a model of relationship" for an embodied theological anthropology, she writes, "Pregnancy shows us what life really is: creative, relational, interconnected, and interdependent. These cellular connections define the nature of our human condition."[31] The organs of procreation are, indeed, microcosms of the relational nature of the *imago Dei*.

None of this should imply the kind of gender essentialism or complementarianism that dogs Christian theological anthropology—the teachings that men and women possess different "natures" that support different, hierarchically ordered roles. Nor must it settle upon the heterosexual spousal pair as the epitome of relation, as influential theologians continue to do.[32] By contrast, in view of the facts that not all people are heterosexual and not all people identify as male or female, Megan DeFranza's exploration of intersex conditions draws out two important points for a Christian teaching of the social *imago Dei*. First, "the binary sex model needs to be expanded to include the intersexed while not being emptied of all notions of difference"; second, "the social *imago* must remain social, resisting contemporary reinterpretation into sexual communion."[33] Sexuality is an important growing edge for expanding theological anthropology in relation to human difference.

The engaged body includes a multiplicity of dimensions that express the relational *imago Dei*. In light of these categories, sexual difference is no more, and no less, important than other differences. The root symbols of Siva-Sakti or Adam-Eve can mask the variety

---

31. Marcia W. Mount Shoop, *Let the Bones Dance: Embodiment and the Body of Christ* (Louisville: Westminster John Knox, 2010), 73.

32. This theme in the relational anthropologies of Karl Barth, John Paul II, and Stanley Grenz is illustrated in Megan K. DeFranza, *Sex Difference in Christian Theology: Male, Female, and Intersex in the Image of God* (Grand Rapids: Eerdmans, 2015), chs. 3 and 4.

33. DeFranza, *Sex Difference*, 152.

of human sexual expressions that develop the image, and theological anthropology is impoverished when it reduces sexual difference to a binary. Even if such symbols stand at the beginning of creation's fecund expansion into diverse forms of community, they need not, for that reason, be treated as the prototype for all relation.[34] Every embodied manner of engaging other people is a microcosm of a relational divinity. Breath, perception, emotion, touch, and listening aptly express the importance of relationship. The self is constituted by relations of all kinds.

BONES AND BRACES

"Our bodies participate in the *imago Dei*," Nancy Eiesland suggests, "not in spite of our impairments and contingencies, but through them."[35] In chapters 2 and 3, we considered the limited body as the divine power to self-limit in order to create. Limitations in power, knowledge, satiation, time, and space reflect this divine power, and each of these limitations apply to the organs of sense and action. It is therefore not the case that only people with perfect hearing can image God through that capacity. The very limits to these modes of sensation and action, whether temporary or permanent, image divinity. As a result, Eiesland observes, "disability does not mean incomplete and difference is not dangerous."[36] If freedom from limit defined the image of God, none would qualify.

This fairly obvious theological point—that the image of God does not rest upon fully functioning body parts—is contradicted when blindness, deafness, and lameness become ableist religious metaphors. Kathy Black illustrates the extent to which metaphors that associate seeing with understanding and hearing with receiving the word of God—and, on the flip side, that associate blindness and deafness with sin—permeate biblical commentaries and sermons on Jesus's healing miracles. These interpretations do not only appear in healing traditions that attribute the persistence of disability to a lack of faith. Mainline preachers are also quite liberal with "metaphorical interpre-

---

34. Ibid., 176.
35. Eiesland, *Disabled God*, 101.
36. Ibid., 47.

tations that identify the disability of a few with the sins of many—for example, 'We are all *deaf* to the word of God.'"[37] Theologians must, therefore, exercise caution when using sensory metaphors, especially when reading them into narratives about actual persons with disabilities.

Theologically, the organs of sensation and action signify the potential for engaging others, and being engaged by others, that marks all sentient beings.[38] Our capacities for engagement are not exhausted by this list of ten organs. For much of the day, my laptop computer is an appendage that allows me to connect with people near and far. Glance around in almost any public place, and one notices that cell phones seem to have sprouted from every hand. The incorporation of machines into our daily and habitual modes of navigating the world heralds a "transhuman" moment: contemporary embodiment and relation are at least part machine.

This situation is no surprise to people for whom prosthetics, wheelchairs, or eyeglasses contribute to their sense of being embodied in the world. From this perspective, Eiesland finds "cultural norms of 'body as natural'" detrimental to recognizing the full humanity of all people:

> My own body composed as it is of metal and plastic, as well as bone and flesh, is my starting point for talking about "bones and braces bodies" as a norm of embodiment. . . . An accessible theological method necessitates that the body be represented as flesh and blood, bones and braces, and not simply the rationalized realm of activity.[39]

---

37. Black, *Healing Homiletic*, 43–44. This association of disability with sin occurs even in recent works that aim to inspire appreciation of the body. Koch and Heil's *Created in God's Image*, for example, describes the intricate workings of the eye and then prompts the following reflection: "'Do I see myself as I really am, or is the me in my mind the product of things about myself to which I am blind?' Seeing is not only a matter of having healthy eyes, but having an open mind and heart as well" (Koch and Heil, *Created in God's Image*, 91). The book also establishes an able-bodied norm for each body part and treats disability as exceptional, as in the statement that "we take our legs and feet for granted until something goes wrong, like breaking a bone in our foot" (ibid., 33).

38. Recall from chapters 2 and 3 that although people with profound physical and intellectual disabilities may not engage their environment in these ways, they *are* embedded within a nexus of engagement.

39. Eiesland, *Disabled God*, 22.

The lure of the "natural" mirrors a romantic preference for things untouched by technology or culture. Food should be straight from the farm. Beauty should look effortless. Health is independence. These mantras succeed in selling us things: processed products in plastic containers with pictures of happy cows, dyes to produce "natural" hair color, and gear to facilitate athletic virtuosity in the rugged wild. The reality is that every aspect of our existence is mediated by culture, and that all of us—not only those of us with visible disabilities—are deeply dependent on the labor and attentions of others, as well as the vehicles, tools, and appliances that facilitate our existence. Human engagement with the world is prosthetic in nature.

Prostheses dissolve customary boundaries in theological anthropology, "questioning the distinctions between humans/machines, human/non-human animals, and humans/nature" and even, perhaps, "deconstructing the boundary between the spiritual and the material, immanence and transcendence."[40] If the engaged body is fundamentally about capacitating connection, then technology is not inherently good or evil. My smart phone impedes my relationships with loved ones if I constantly check my e-mail while we are together, but it can keep us connected when we are apart. It is often the material or technological—a touch, a text message—that mediates the human.

Again, the inclusion of prostheses in the organs of engagement does not negate limitation or impose a compulsory cure for physical or mental impairments. Such an illusion of wholeness was one of the reasons for the development of prosthetics in the United States, Sharon Betcher observes, where they "were cosmetically deployed" in "the young nation of America following the Civil War . . . to project a national image of virility and vitality."[41] Although prosthetics may help to put strangers at ease, a range of factors, including expense and the wearer's own comfort, contribute to a person's choice to accept or reject specific technologies.

Betcher redeploys the idea of prosthesis in a theologically helpful way, not to normalize bodies according to ableist aesthetics, but to

40. With these observations, Elaine Graham challenges Donna Haraway's famous "Cyborg Manifesto" and its dichotomous rejection of the transcendent/sacred in relation to nature. Elaine L. Graham, *Representations of the Post/Human: Monsters, Aliens, and Others in Popular Culture* (New Brunswick, NJ: Rutgers University Press, 2002), 216.

41. Betcher, *Spirit and the Obligation*, 29.

facilitate engagement with the world. "We can think of Spirit, then, as something of a prosthesis," she suggests. "Spirit as prosthesis capacitates our corporeal becoming with the world. As a prosthesis capacitates the body, Spirit capacitates our 'belief in the world,' enables the mutual submission—or entrustment—of flesh one to another."[42] For her, the primary purpose of spirituality is to enable the self to become open to the other.

The Spirit's facilitation does not guarantee that opening to others will be easy and harmonious. Betcher describes donning a prosthesis as a "shuffle," difficult to put on, which applies as well to the work of the Spirit in community: "in other words, the spiritual life feels a bit more like Jacob wrestling the angel than like serene, contemplative placidity."[43] Reaching out to others may very well begin with a divine movement, but it also takes practice. Such engagement may never feel "natural"—because often, it isn't.

If limits permeate every part of the *imago Dei*, then theological anthropology will acknowledge that people engage the world and relate to others in a surprising variety of ways. Human embodiment is fundamentally relational: its senses take in the world, and its activity affects the world in large and small ways. Relation occurs through hands and eyes, or through the help of an attendant or contact lenses. This chapter's comparison suggests that these features of human embodiment, rather than marking an essential difference from divinity, mirror how God relates to the world through the Spirit.

BODIES OF CHRIST

This chapter began by noting the multivalence of the body of Christ: incarnate, eucharistic, churchly. When read in terms of the engaged body, the physicality of the incarnate Christ demonstrates that the capacities to hear, touch, see, taste, smell, speak, grasp, walk, excrete, and procreate belong to embodied divinity, as does the limitation of these capacities and the radical vulnerability of bodies in relation. God dwells in flesh that is receptive to, and received by, others, and so

42. Ibid., 190–91.
43. Ibid., 191.

Jesus calls the bread of the shared meal his body (Matt 26:26, Mark 14:22, Luke 22:19), and the apostle Paul refers to Christians as parts of the body of Christ (1 Cor 12:12, 27).

What happens theologically in the transition from the incarnate body of Christ to its metaphorical senses? If Christians have been tempted to misuse sensory metaphors in ways that marginalize people with disabilities, then it is also worth revisiting the senses in which the "body of Christ" refers to the church and the Eucharist. The question of whom Christian language includes or excludes from full status as *imago Dei*, rather than any denominational litmus test, continues to guide my inquiry.

Theologians have sometimes run too far with the metaphor of the church as the body of Christ, particularly when they have wed it with a christological reading of the *imago Dei*. In this narrow reading, Christ is taken to be the unique and ultimate embodiment of the divine image. The conflation of the image of God with the body of Christ goes something like this:

Christ is "the image of the invisible God" (Col 1:15).

The church is the "body of Christ" (1 Cor 12:27).

Human beings only become the image of God through participation in the church.

This reasoning can be found in the early theologian Irenaeus, who views the body as *imago Dei*, and it appears again in the work of Orthodox theologian John Zizioulas, who contributes a relational interpretation to the image.

Social Trinitarian theology locates the *imago Dei* in relations epitomized by the mutual indwelling of the three persons of the Trinity. For Zizioulas, becoming incorporated into the body of Christ (the church) activates the relational *imago Dei*: "From the fact that a human being is a member of the Church, he becomes an 'image of God,' he exists as God Himself exists, he takes on God's 'way of being'"[44] Before baptism, a person is a "biological hypostasis" oriented toward individualism, but baptism initiates her into the "hypostasis of ecclesial existence,"[45] in which members of the church "mirror the

---

44. John D. Zizioulas, *Being as Communion: Studies in Personhood and the Church* (Crestwood, NY: St. Vladimir's Seminary Press, 1985), 15.

45. Ibid., 52–53.

communion and otherness that exists in the triune God."[46] Like Irenaeus, Zizioulas views the image as a work in progress, a process of divinization that culminates in the eschaton. In the Orthodox tradition, the gathering of the church in worship is a foretaste of the heavenly banquet that "frees [the church] from limitations which are the result of the individualism implied in our natural biological existence."[47] Christian worship makes heaven present on Earth, and with it, a taste of humanity in its full, relational potential.

The underside of this theology is the implication that people who do not name Christ are inferior bearers of the divine image—that those who are unbaptized are, perhaps, less than fully human. These exalted claims about the church as the locus of the *imago Dei* reflect the grace Christians witness in ecclesial community. It is, therefore, the language not only of doctrine but also of doxology, praising God for the life-changing work of the Spirit in the church. As important as these insights are for Christian understandings of church, sacrament, and ultimate destiny, however, they fall short if they restrict humanity's creation in the image of God to the Christian community. This restriction morphs the language of praise and gratitude into religious chauvinism.

The *imago Dei* as relation does not inevitably lead to all of the conclusions Zizioulas reaches. At the root of my disagreement with him lies a differing diagnosis of the human condition. In some versions of the Christian narrative, the created image of God has been lost or attenuated in humanity because of sin. This makes it necessary for special revelation, here mediated by the church, to step in and restore it. Scriptural authors, however, do not seem to draw this inference but maintain the idea that human beings bear the image of God across the canon (see, for just a few examples, Gen 9:6, 1 Cor 11:7, and Jas 3:9).

Comparison intervenes on a phenomenological level: while Zizioulas views the pre-baptismal way of existing as deeply unrelational and individualistic, this meditation on the organs of sensation and action has shown relationship to be a basic dimension of human

---

46. John D. Zizioulas, *Communion and Otherness: Further Studies in Personhood and the Church*, ed. Paul McPartlan (London: T&T Clark, 2006), 4–5.

47. Ibid., 22.

existence. Relation is inescapable. Our bodies are continually taking in sensations from our environment. As soon as we perceive, speak to, move toward, or embrace another person—or are thus engaged by another—we mirror divine relationality. Of course, the quality of our interactions reflects the mutuality of divine relation to differing degrees. If a gesture wounds or robs another, it does not reflect the intent of the God whose name is Love. But in the simple functioning of our senses, in most of our routine and daily movements, the basic fact of interrelation cannot be denied.

Christ need not be named for the deep connection of God with the world to be reflected in human bodies and communities. Baptism does not suddenly bring relationality into being. Relation is the air we breathe. It is the water in which we swim. The image of God is present in the basic sensory and motor functions of the body because these relate self to other. God becomes corporeal in the relational work of the senses, whenever people attend to or are engaged by something external to themselves. This relationship is fundamental. It is intrinsic to the *imago Dei* from the moment of creation. For this reason, Christian theology must disentangle the syllogism in which the church, as the body of Christ, is the only place human beings can be the relational image of God.[48] The image belongs to every human being.

This is not to say that Christ has no role in shaping Christians. On the contrary, Scripture encourages Christians to be "conformed to the image of [Christ]" (Rom 8:29). I suggest that the *imago Christi* marks the particular variation on the theme of the *imago Dei* that Christians are called to play. As Joshua Farris argues, the *imago Christi* is "a distinct category that does not exclude the created/natural image, but builds upon it."[49] The aspiration to resemble Christ does not negate the image of God that belongs to every person. It does not erase the

---

48. With reference to Christ as "the image of the invisible God" in Colossians 1, Joshua Farris argues that it has a unique meaning in this context. There, the image pertains to attributes such as invisibility, preexistence, and being the fullness of deity. Such references to the image of God "are distinctly referring to Christ's divinity," with "a unique title for Christ highlighting his deity, rather than his humanity, as an image." Joshua R. Farris, "A Substantive (Soul) Model of the *Imago Dei*: A Rich Property View," in Farris and Taliaferro, *Ashgate Research Companion*, 174.

49. Ibid., 176.

ways in which all of creation bears the traces of its divine creator. The *telos* of the Christian life is to become like Christ—to be transformed in a way that his particular revelation of divinity and humanity makes possible. The christological image is eschatological in a way that the created image of God is not, since the moral and spiritual qualities entailed in imitating him require a lifetime (and more) of formation and practice. This important distinction between the image of God and the image of Christ indicates that the community that gathers in Christ's name must not denigrate, much less dehumanize, people of other faith traditions. Other paths have different ends; other practices shape and express the image of God in different ways. Amid human diversity, Christians can claim uniquely to be *Christ's* body.

"THIS IS MY BODY"

I have been arguing that the organs of sensation and action—smelling, tasting, seeing, touching, hearing, procreating, excreting, walking, grasping, speaking, and more—reflect divinity because they put humans in fundamental relation to others. In Abhinavagupta's tradition, meditation practices recognize the engaged body as reflecting the divine. Jaideva Singh describes several such methods. In one, "the aspirant contemplates over the body and the nervous system as an epitome of the cosmos."[50] In another, mantras and symbols correlate to different parts of the body for the purpose of worshiping Siva in them.[51] Such practices are easy; they are available to everyone. Through them, "the inner supreme energies of the senses" become "perfect in experiencing the objects" (PTv, 232). Over time, one begins to remember intuitively, even as one moves through one's daily activities, that these capacities image divinity. Christians might similarly benefit from such contemplations on the body.

Christian worship attends primarily to one particular body. Corporeal practices of the ecclesial body—gathering together, celebrating the sacraments, attending to bodies in need—manifest *Christ's* body with particular intensity. Christian encounter with this vulnerable

---

50. Abhinavagupta, *Para-trisika-Vivarana*, 236n9.
51. Ibid., 245–47.

body in worship culminates in the practices that recall his instructions at his last meal, when "he took a loaf of bread, and when he had given thanks, he broke it and gave it to them, saying, 'This is my body, which is given for you. Do this in remembrance of me'" (Luke 22:19). The sacrament of the Eucharist (or Lord's Supper) participates in the body of Jesus, the body of Christ, broken.

The apostle Paul describes the church as the body of Christ in an appeal for unity, but even now fractures within the body of Christ mirror the larger fragmentation patterns in society. Although the existence of denominations has cultivated various charisms, and churches of minoritized populations are spaces of survival and empowerment, the homogeneity of dominant groups that gather around communion tables belies the re-membering of the community celebrated there. By contrast, Marcia Mount Shoop and Mary McClintock Fulkerson draw attention to the relational nature of the body by celebrating the sacrament "face to face," and emphasizing "how it re-members Christ's body by putting broken relationships back together, by gathering in those who are estranged or dis-membered from the community of faith."[52]

Today, the realities of multifaith families, and of people who observe multiple religious and cultural practices, invite reconciliation of an even broader scope. If Christ is "the image of the invisible God" and the one in whom all things (*ta panta*) are created and reconciled, then his body reaches beyond the customary boundaries of the church. If Christians understand Christ as a name for divine wisdom and creativity, then Christians cannot amputate parts of its body.

This chapter's meditation on the organs of sensation and action contributes to an ecclesiology in which diverse parts are indispensable. The senses each have particular modes of perception, but together their functions mingle to convey a single reality. As one scholar puts it, "We do not apprehend the world as a grab-bag of different entities—we do not see one world of sight, hear another of sounds, taste or smell another or yet another."[53] Each part of the

---

52. Mary McClintock Fulkerson and Marcia W. Mount Shoop, *A Body Broken, a Body Betrayed: Race, Memory, and Eucharist in White-Dominant Churches* (Eugene, OR: Cascade, 2015), 136.

53. Marks, *Unity of the Senses*, 185.

body contributes to a person's perception of a single world. Just as the senses are "imperfect instruments . . . not always trustworthy or completely informative, and, indeed, not always in perfect harmony with each other,"[54] the community that gathers in Christ's name can better understand its world and purpose by listening to, and being corrected by, the perceptions of each of its parts. This process of bodily perception as a community should give special honor and attention to the "weaker" and "less respectable" members, so that "the members may have the same care for one another" (1 Cor 12:22–23, 25). Unexpected gifts come from those who perceive in nondominant ways.

The particularity of the sacrament reminds us, however, that practices of the engaged body must attend to suffering bodies. Each of the parts of the engaged body manifests a radiant connection to the divine source of life, but each is also a site where this radical connection with others can be abused or neglected. Each can become the site of profound injury and loss. Their very vulnerability—the very way that they open one to another—exposes them to abuse and violence. To look squarely at this reality, both radiant and tragic, is to perceive "with the eye of incarnation."[55]"If one member suffers, all suffer together with it" (1 Cor 12:26).

The body parts remembered in the Eucharist are, above all, vulnerable, and Christ's vulnerability is the vulnerability shared by all bodies. The crucifixion and resurrection of Christ implicate every organ of sensation and action. Hands and feet pierced and immobilized. Vision clouded by blood trickling from the forehead. Stench of sweat, taste of sour wine. Naked body uncovered. Cessation of all function in death. Lacerations washed, wrapped by the hands of women. Crimson scars and an open wound. This particular body, broken, opens to the other. Jesus Christ represents the divine presence within all vulnerable bodies created in the *imago Dei*.

Attention to suffering in the incarnate, ecclesial, and sacramental bodies of Christ is Christianity's special charism, the particular window it offers into God's fundamental relation with creation. Distinguishing the *imago Dei*—the relational image of God present in all

---

54. Ibid.
55. Gorringe, *Education of Desire*, 29.

people—from the *imago Christi*—the variation on the theme played by Jesus Christ and his followers—frees metaphors surrounding the body of Christ. The church and its sacramental meal make Christ present to the community in order to empower its response to a suffering world. Christians can step forth into the gifts and tasks that are particular to the Christian community, acknowledging the full humanity of people committed to other religious traditions. "How we attend to bodies informs how we are able to enflesh the Body of Christ," writes Mount Shoop.[56] Through compassion and solidarity with suffering bodies, Christians imitate Jesus's way of entering into communion with the world

The engaged body becomes sensitized to the movement of consciousness in each of the senses in order to engage the present moment, one's community, and the wider world with greater attention and care. Becoming attentive to the work of these body parts builds solidarity with the others who share the pleasures, suffering, and limitations of embodiment. And as we attune ourselves to the objects of these senses, awareness of the divine presence extends to the final set of ten body parts: the elemental body.

56. Mount Shoop, *Let the Bones Dance*, 131.

6.

The Elemental Body

These chapters have urged practices of attention that seek divine presence in every part of the God-imaged body. Christianity has never entirely forgotten the radiance of matter, but this recognition sometimes shines only at the fringes of Christendom, such as in the Celtic church's recognition of Christ as King of the Elements.[1] In this stream, George MacLeod, founder of the present-day Iona Community, lamented after the atomic bomb dropped at Hiroshima,

> Suppose the material order, as we have argued, is indeed the garment of Christ, the Temple of the Holy Ghost. Suppose the bread and wine, symbols of creation, are indeed capable of redemption awaiting its Christification. Then what is the atom but the emergent body of Christ? . . . We took His body and we took His blood and we enacted a cosmic Golgotha. We took the key to love and we used it for bloody hell.[2]

Elements as the key to love. Our body. Christ's body. God's own body. Can we perceive the interweaving of heaven and Earth? To hone our attention to the elemental, we must take one more step in our comparative conversation with non-dual Saivism.

The last set of body parts to emerge in the emanation of creation, and in the human reflection of the divine, is *the elemental body.*

1. J. Philip Newell, *Listening for the Heartbeat of God: A Celtic Spirituality* (New York: Paulist, 1997), 48.
2. Quoted in ibid., 88.

Indian traditions enumerate this set of ten parts as the gross and subtle elements. The gross elements—space (ether), air, fire, water, and earth—will be easily recognized as an ancient way to name the fundamental building blocks of the world we experience. The earth principle, which emerges last in this theory of creation, is the densest manifestation of consciousness.[3] The subtle elements—sound, touch, form, taste, and smell—are less familiar. Arising from the principles of engagement in the previous chapter, they give rise to the gross elements and form a zone of interaction between the senses and the physical realm.

Given the dualistic heritage of the Christian West, it can be difficult to imagine what the elements have to do with the *imago Dei*. Is the elemental body the "lowest" part of the image of God? Can it be called the image of God at all? Comparison provides openings to imagine new possibilities. As we have seen, spirit-matter dualism is not the only item on the menu. Scripture offers alternatives, as do many forgotten or suppressed Christian traditions. Philosophers and the scientific community have contributed additional influential worldviews. And, thanks to today's global exchange of ideas, still other options originate from scriptures, philosophies, cultures, and religions that Christians have encountered only relatively recently. Each system provides a map of the world that positions the physical elements in relation to other principles. As we arrive at the end of the line—the elemental body—we consider the ecological and economic implications of this work.

COMPARATIVE WORLDVIEW WORK

Worldviews are imaginative pictures, metaphors for the shape and movement of reality. They configure things in space: above, below, within. A theological worldview evokes the place of God in relation to the world with language of height and depth, proximity and distance, immanence and transcendence.

For some religious thinkers, God is present through general reve-

---

3. Readers should avoid the temptation to call the gross elements the "material" elements, because "matter" encompasses a total of twenty-four body parts, beginning with *prakrti*.

lation within creation, in the human mind, and, as an extension and intensification of this presence, in the sacraments. This immediacy finds voice in the Psalms:

> Where can I go from your spirit?
>> Or where can I flee from your presence?
> If I ascend to heaven, you are there;
>> if I make my bed in Sheol, you are there.
> If I take the wings of the morning
>> and settle at the farthest limits of the sea,
> even there your hand shall lead me,
>> and your right hand shall hold me fast. (Ps 139:7–10)

In contrast to this sense of divine immanence, others apprehend a transcendent deity, a creator of unqualified difference from the creation, whose character cannot be deduced from ordinary ways of being in the world. Again, Scripture supplies visual stimulation. "Thus says the Lord: 'Heaven is my throne and the earth is my footstool'" (Isa 66:1);

> For my thoughts are not your thoughts,
>> nor are your ways my ways, says the Lord.
> For as the heavens are higher than the earth,
>> so are my ways higher than your ways`
>> and my thoughts than your thoughts. (Isa 55:8–9)

Modernity pulled religious thought in the latter direction, as the Enlightenment imbued European common sense with a machine-like world void of sacred mystery. The Protestant Reformation movements played a part, too. Calvinist theologies, with their heavy emphasis on original sin, demarcated the sacred from the secular. The church and the Sabbath were set apart from the rest of life, and an unbridgeable gulf opened between the saved and the damned.[4] If God were to be known—a prospect that even the humanists increasingly doubted—then humanity needed the disruptive word of a special revelation that overturns ordinary ways of knowing. For those influenced by Karl Barth in the twentieth century, the book of nature,

---

4. Newell, *Listening for the Heartbeat*, 52.

previously revered as a source for general revelation about the Creator, is a dead end.

Surveying these developments, Sallie McFague's classic work summarizes four of the basic metaphors for God's relationship to the world that have been prominent in modernity. The deistic model, originating in the seventeenth century, imagines God as a cosmic watchmaker, who winds up the world and steps back to watch it run, machinelike, according to the laws of nature. God is distant and uninvolved. In the dialogic model, grounded in Scripture's depiction of divine speech and human response, God is close at hand in personal relationships with the individuals, while the social and natural worlds fade from view. The monarchical model, which views God as king and humans as subjects, remains popular despite the fading of monarchy as a relevant political structure. Although God is personal, "he" is distant, and "his" rule primarily concerns the social and political realms. Again, the natural world receives little attention. Similarly, the agential model posits God as an actor, whose creative, redemptive, and providential will is realized in history. Its explanatory power has been attenuated by modern science and a reductionistic materialism that now calls this type of causality into question. Although each model has its strengths, McFague observes, their collective effect in modernity is to keep God at a remove from the material world.[5]

It matters religiously whether God is above, within, or surrounding the material world. It matters whether God is near to us. In the spatial configurations of common religious language, one goes *up* to heaven, *down* to hell. One might pray to a God who is *up there* but find divinity *close by* when the beauty of nature strikes a particular chord. God might even be *distant* or altogether *absent* in times of tragedy. Sometimes the human imagination inhabits more than one metaphorical world at a time. The spatial universe that governs one's eternal destiny might differ, for example, from the world one negotiates daily while employed in a laboratory.

McFague is particularly concerned with how a Christian worldview can support a sustainable ecology in light of globalization and

5. Sallie McFague, "Is God in Charge?," in *Essentials of Christian Theology*, ed. William C. Placher (Louisville: Westminster John Knox, 2003), 105–9. See also McFague, *Models of God*, ch. 3.

climate change. Her model of the Earth as God's body makes room in Christian theology to recognize bodies within the image of God.[6] The model of the divine body of consciousness urges us along the same trajectory. In our search for openings within the Christian tradition to recognize the elemental body as *imago Dei*, we will look backward to the millennium preceding modernity for openings to affirm the immanence of God within the physical world. Celtic and other early forms of Christianity could also be pursued, but here we revisit the Christian Neoplatonist metaphysic that was largely abandoned with the Enlightenment and Protestant Reformations.

Because theological metaphors shift as new understandings of the world come and go, this backward glance might seem a strange choice. One criterion for a worldview is how well it makes sense of reality, and contemporary people certainly have a very different conception of the universe than early and medieval Christians. Even modernity's mechanistic, material order appears outdated in light of the pictures of the universe gathered by the Hubble telescope. I suggest, however, that in the broad strokes permitted by the discipline of theology, the metaphor of emanation and return in early Christian metaphysics resonates anew with what contemporary cosmology tells us about the origins of the universe.[7]

The cosmos that originates from the Big Bang is an expanding and contracting world. An infinitesimal, compact mass explodes into scintillatingly hot energy that flings itself outward in all directions. Temperatures cool. Atomic particles begin to coalesce as quarks, gluons, protons, and neutrons materialize. Atoms, then molecules, then clouds, stars, and galaxies gravitate together. Later, life-forms complexify in dynamic profusion, and redshift measurements of galaxies and supernovas reveal an accelerating outward movement. The cosmos expands, evolves, and congeals. It expands and contracts—

6. In addition to the works by McFague discussed here, also see Grace M. Jantzen, *God's World, God's Body* (Philadelphia: Westminster, 1984).

7. The disciplines, of course, differ in scope: "physics and cosmology as sciences are incapable of exploring or directly accounting for the ultimate source of existence and order which philosophy and theology, properly understood, provide. By the same token, philosophy and theology are not equipped to investigate and describe the processes and relationships which contributed to the expansion, cooling, and subsequent structuring of the universe on macroscopic scales." William R. Stoeger, "God, Physics, and the Big Bang," in *The Cambridge Companion to Science and Religion*, ed. Peter Harrison (Cambridge: Cambridge University Press, 2010), 174.

sometimes simultaneously and on different levels.[8] We shall discover that both non-dual Saiva and Neoplatonist metaphysics supply a basic dynamism that can metaphorically house this expanding and contracting cosmos.

A theological model needs only to provide "a basic but unadorned ontological account" that "attempt[s] to render intelligible the ultimate existence and ordering of the dynamisms, relationships, and entities which are the primary concern of the natural sciences."[9] In the two theological models we are considering, emanation is answered by a return. In each, expansion and contraction may happen simultaneously and on different levels. In Christian theology, God is always creating (creatio continua), even as each of God's creatures, held in this sustaining relationship, may be returning to the creator. Abhinavagupta's tradition imagines the dynamic expansion and contraction of the universe occurring within divine consciousness "so rapidly" as to be concurrent, like a vibration or the pulsing of a heart. In Paul Muller-Ortega's description,

> Absolute consciousness is never inert, it is never inactive; it is continuously throbbing, expanding, and contracting with the movement of the Heart. . . . It is this movement which continuously, at every instant, projects manifestation into being. It is this same movement, however, that at every moment resolves this manifestation back into Siva.[10]

This ebb and flow of consciousness offers a helpful metaphorical framework. Just as the scientific story of the universe is not unidirectional but alternates between expansion and contraction, both religious accounts envision a pulsing, dynamic motion occurring within the life of God. Theology's broad strokes might capture the dynamism and motion of the unfolding universe as we know it.

As this chapter takes a second look at the emanation-return structure presumed by so many thinkers in the earlier periods of Christian theology, the criterion for reviving this metaphysic will be its ability not only to make sense of reality but also to engender just and

---

8. For an amplified narration of the Big Bang, in which cooling and reheating, contraction and expansion alternate with one another, see ibid., 176–77.

9. Ibid., 174.

10. Muller-Ortega, Triadic Heart of Siva, 139. For the theme of vibration (spanda), see Dyczkowski, Doctrine of Vibration.

compassionate relations that mirror God's loving intent for creation. Here, we add specificity to McFague's metaphor of planet Earth as God's body by considering earth as an element that, with the other elements, is part of the image of God in humanity. To include these body parts—the neglected and insensate substrate of human experience—in the *imago Dei* is the very antithesis of what many Christians commonly identify as divine. We must, therefore, confront the residue of hierarchy in both emanation traditions.

EMANATION AND HIERARCHY

As we have learned, Abhinavagupta's tradition holds that when the deity Siva opens his eyes, creation unfolds in thirty-six parts, and when he closes his eyes, these parts fold back into pure consciousness. We have seen how the subtle degrees of consciousness gradually differentiate the divine "I" from the created "this," and how the subsequent body parts are increasingly dense, differentiated, and veiled by *maya*. Each principle arises from the last. The structure of this worldview resonates strongly with the emanation-and-return scheme that governed Christian Neoplatonist thought from the first few centuries through the Middle Ages, in which creation emerges from and longs to return to God, the Good Beyond Being. For both traditions, emanation proceeds from the subtle to the material, and spiritual disciplines such as meditation or the sacraments enable the human person to retrace this path and return to the divine source.

Pseudo-Dionysius gives a sense of this ebb and flow when he writes of the Good "that it is the cause of everything, that it is origin, being, and life. To those who fall away it is the voice calling, 'Come back!' and it is the power that raises them up again. It refurbishes and restores the image of God corrupted within them."[11] This language of corruption and restoration signals that, in the Neoplatonist imagination, the closer to the divine source something is, the more it participates in its attributes. A parallel appears in Abhinavagupta's understanding that, as an individual's consciousness folds back into

---

11. Pseudo-Dionysius, "Divine Names," in *Complete Works*, 51; my emphasis.

the unity of divine consciousness through meditation practices, the veils and impurities of *maya* gradually fall away.

As a corollary, the farther a creature is from the original emanation, the more embroiled in matter (and, for Neoplatonists, in nonbeing) it is. Christian theologians used this scheme to rank creatures in a graded hierarchy from being to nonbeing. Thus, as wholly spiritual beings, angels are closest to God. Animals and plants participate in being insofar as they exist, but they are largely confined to the physical realm. Humans straddle the spiritual and material, with a unique ability to participate in God through practices such as the sacraments that enable them to move up the hierarchy of divine goodness, truth, and beauty. Note the inherent ambiguity regarding the physical realm: do the elements in the sacraments mediate the divine, or do they weigh down consciousness and prevent it from returning to its source?

Gavin Flood notices a parallel tension that results, at least in part, from the way in which Abhinavagupta and other thinkers overlay their non-dual interpretation upon earlier dualistic texts.[12] These texts use both emanation language and pervasion language for creation, with differing implications.[13] In an emanation schema, beings further along the chain participate progressively less in the divine source. By contrast, pervasion language signals that all things are infused with divinity. When thinkers use the former terminology, they sometimes devalue the material realm in a manner similar to many Christian Neoplatonists, for whom the goal is to leave behind the "lower" levels of reality and to ascend to the "higher."[14]

In each, however, the problem with the material world is not that it is evil; it is simply not ultimate. When teachers in the non-dual Saiva tradition refer to *maya* as "illusion," they negate neither the fact

12. These dualistic underpinnings include both the Agama literature, which is shared between non-dual Saivism and the Saiva Siddhanta tradition, and the organization of the *tattva*s in Samkhya philosophy. Cf. Flood, *Tantric Body*, 19, 29, 68–69.

13. Flood, *Body and Cosmology*, 89–94.

14. Take, for example, the interpretation from the foreword of Flood's book that "the hierarchical nature of [non-dual Saiva] cosmology is an integral part of it and needs to be understood." Andrew Rawlinson, foreword to *Body and Cosmology*, xi. John Dupuche (*Abhinavagupta*, 84) also observes a teleology in practices of mapping the *tattva*s onto the body: "the aim is to progress rapidly through all levels so as to arrive at the highest level of consciousness which confers all powers."

of the empirical world nor its value as a reflection of Siva-Sakti. The divine body of consciousness nevertheless differs from human experience of it in the cosmos and within themselves. The divine body is real in the ultimate sense, whereas its reflections materialize and fade away with each pulsation of consciousness. Similarly, when the early Christian author of the *Treatise on the Resurrection* asserts the body's material existence is illusory, he reflects the Platonic formal principle that it is "not 'real' in the ultimate sense."[15] The limitations of mortality put the earthly human body in hierarchical (but not dualistic) relation to the resurrected body, in which the imperishable form will shine forth.[16]

Because of these relatively negative implications for the material realm, some postmodern thinkers would rather leave the emanation pattern in the dustbin of history. They problematize any view of God as a Being in relation to created beings (i.e., ontotheology, ousiology). One problem occurs when ontotheology puts transcendent mystery in the same category as other things, a being like other beings.[17] Furthermore, if all of reality is oriented toward the One True Being, then multiplicity, materiality, and difference must be something to overcome.[18] Such ideals smack of a totalitarian authority that would eliminate otherness and silence dissent.[19] To rectify this oppressive order, postmodern theologians call for a fleshy, sacramental order of being. Put succinctly, "The Christian God wants nothing to do with a vertical relation of subordination."[20]

A metaphysic of emanation and return has thus fallen out of favor in contemporary theology. However, the playful, imaginative,

15. Petrey, *Resurrecting Parts*, 36.

16. Ibid., 38–42.

17. Cf. John D. Caputo, *The Weakness of God: A Theology of the Event* (Bloomington: Indiana University Press, 2006), 111–12.

18. See, for instance, Jean-Luc Marion, "The Crossing of Being," in *God Without Being*, trans. Thomas A. Carlson (Chicago: University of Chicago Press, 1991), ch. 3.

19. Cf. John D. Caputo, *The Insistence of God: A Theology of Perhaps* (Bloomington: Indiana University Press, 2013), ix and ch. 1. Anything lying beyond the end of the emanation—prime matter, the abyss, the Platonic *khora*—is feared and abhorred in this light. For a reading of how *khora* figures in postmodern critiques of ontotheology, see Tina Beattie, *Theology after Postmodernity: Divining the Void—A Lacanian Reading of Thomas Aquinas* (Oxford: Oxford University Press, 2013), ch. 17.

20. Richard Kearney, *Anatheism: Returning to God after God* (New York: Columbia University Press, 2010), 91.

postmodern work of reimagining inherited worldviews can find new possibilities in comparative study. How might the gross and subtle elements, as body parts, reopen this pattern of ebb and flow for Christian theology?

A HORIZONTAL TURN

Like the Neoplatonist worldview, the Indian emanation pattern is usually depicted vertically, with the subtlest parts on top and the gross elements at the bottom.[21] Such diagrams convey value. *Up* is not only *higher* but also *better* than *down*. *Lofty* ideals contrast with our *baser* instincts. Feeling *high* is preferable to feeling *low*. In the Christian imagination, God, heaven, and the angels are above the Earth. The visual rhetoric reinforces the hierarchies associated with emanation cosmologies.

In non-dual Saiva theology, beings that are at home in the earth principle experience greater levels of separation than beings in other levels of creation, but it is not the case that the creator actually *is* more distant from them. The tradition employs pervasion terminology to counteract the implication of hierarchy in the emanation of the cosmos. With religious realization, "there occurs a firmness, an increasing fullness of the form of consciousness; a union with its light, a vibration which is characterized by the attainment of supreme freedom. *Everything is then thoroughly pervaded by the form of consciousness*" (PTlv, 211, my emphasis). The liberating insight is that every degree of consciousness is part of the divine and human body. Once one realizes that Siva-Sakti pervades each part, the hierarchy of value dissolves. Meditation on the subtle degrees of creation can reorient one's view of the whole.

For this reason, the illustration that has accompanied each chapter in this book flips the emanation pattern on its side. Flowing side to side, rather than high to low, this arrangement better conveys the liberating crux of the teaching that every dimension of creation shares the nature of divine consciousness. In a horizontal spectrum of embodiment, every part reflects divine consciousness. They vary only

21. For example, Flood, *Body and Cosmology*, 178.

in degrees of subtlety, not in degrees of pervasion by divine presence. Christianity might repurpose the emanation-and-return worldview, which held sway for a millennium in Christian thought, in this shifted form.

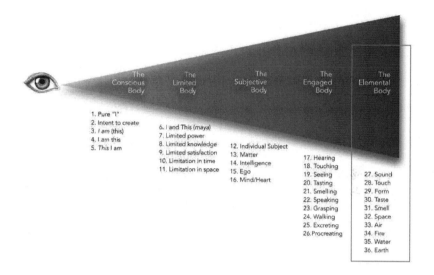

Fig. 6.

Tina Beattie is among the postmodern theologians who have not abandoned an emanation metaphysic. As she reads Thomas Aquinas for his creative synthesis between Neoplatonist and Aristotelian categories, she finds that "Thomas has great difficulty in keeping the two apart, so that his theology shifts between the affirmation of God as form, and the denial that God is form."[22] In passages that show Pseudo-Dionysian influence, he affirms creation's participation in its divine cause; yet on the whole, his theology "has been profoundly unbalanced in privileging form over matter, the one over the many, so that the Trinity and the incarnate God have continuously been erased and overwritten by the drive towards the One of metaphysics and ontotheology."[23] Beattie seeks to right the balance.

First, she loosens the ties between divinity and form. Beattie observes that in Aquinas's defense of divine simplicity, although God

22. Beattie, *Theology after Postmodernity*, 94.
23. Ibid., 327.

cannot be composed of matter, God also cannot be composed of form. If God is simple (one), then there is no composition in God. God creates both form and matter. Both form and matter express God's goodness.

Second, she pulls on the threads of materiality, bodies, and desire in Aquinas's thought. In addition to his language of participation, he affirms the goodness of matter in his interpretation of the incarnation. He wants to avoid the docetist heresy that Christ's humanity is only apparent, and he affirms the truth of the resurrection. He must therefore conclude that the incarnation both deifies the human body and brings matter into God.[24] Salvation history thus turns the hierarchy of creation on its side:

> In this reading, the idea of creation as hierarchical emanation from the divine being yields to a more *horizontal celebration of diversity as a good in itself*, a diversity in which God is revealed and worshipped. Our capacity to understand something of God is enriched by our ability to see something unique of God in every species and individual that we encounter.[25]

Beattie finds a basis for this horizontal orientation in Aquinas himself:

> Not only does Thomas argue that "God is in all things," he also argues that "as the soul is whole in every part of the body, so is God whole in all things and in each one." This is an astonishing insight that opens into a mystical sense of being beyond all human comprehension.[26]

A horizontal worldview holds great potential for affirming the value of the elemental body. A comparative approach adds additional dimensions insofar as it links the emanation pattern to the image of God.

In an interpretation of emanation as the reflection of divinity, diversity and embodiment are not the exception to divine simplicity but its unfolding. Diversity is the very purpose of creation. Without it, divine consciousness would have nothing to be conscious *of*. It would have no object. Everything that exists—elements, sense

24. Ibid., 321–24.
25. Ibid., 316; my emphasis.
26. Ibid., 316, citing Aquinas, *Summa Theologiae* 1.8.1–2.

organs, mental faculties, limitations, individual experiences of consciousness—is the body and the splendor of the divine. For Christians,
these openings appear at the first inkling of creation as an opening in
the Trinity as well as in the maternal body of Mary and the wounds
of the incarnate Christ.[27]

The "image of God" entails a reflection metaphor that accounts for
why the worth of the emanated material realm might be easy to miss.
The divine image in the world is obscured, not because of a "fall" that
obliterates the image, but because of the very nature of mirrors. Mirrors reverse the image of the original. As the mirror analogy functions
in Abhinavagupta's thought, when the thirty-six body parts are projected outward from Siva-Sakti, they appear inverted in the mirror
of the world.[28] A face and its reflection are not different, except they
appear in reverse order. The first principle appears as the last, the second as the second-to-last, and so on. The result is a "non-difference
in difference according to the principle of reflection" (PTv, 120).
Creation is the means by which the high appears as low. Divinity
manifests as the gross elements, and vice versa. This worldview thus
acknowledges that the earth principle will seem far removed from the
divine source from which it emanated. At the same time, non-dual
teaching endeavors to reverse this impression. The basic elements of
worldly experience are no less permeated by divinity than the states
of consciousness one might experience as transcendent.

ELEMENTAL FOUNDATIONS

The emanation-return pattern paints in broad strokes, but it also
engages in detailed brushwork to depict the ordering and relationships between the parts of the divine image. The principles are laid
out in a particular sequence. What can this mean? An anthropocentric interpretation, which ranks certain distinctively human faculties
as superior to the elements, is prone to position the earth, water, and
air as materials to be manipulated and resources to consume.

27. Ibid., 327.
28. Singh maps this inversion vertically with the original and reverse orders of emanation
placed side by side, and lines crossing in the middle to demonstrate how the low principles are
reflected in the high, and vice versa. Abhinavagupta, *Para-trisika-Vivarana*, 107 (chart 2B).

The Indian sources provide a variety of other rationales for ordering the body parts. The senses, for example, can be ranked in terms of how many sentient beings possess them, or in terms of the "richness" of the element to which they correspond.[29] For this reason, James McHugh chooses "the term 'order' as opposed to 'hierarchy,'" cautioning that "we should not from the outset assume that the senses are being ranked by these systems as progressively superior to each other in a general manner. Rather they differ only according to one chosen principle."[30] Our chart ranks the body parts in the order of creation, from subtle to gross. This pattern does not denote a hierarchy of intrinsic worth but signals layers of connection and interdependence (homologies) between them in which the elements are both foundational and religiously significant.

The maxim, "Everything is related to everything else" (*sarvam sarvatmakam*), resonates across India's ancient ritual traditions.[31] The logic of Vedic sacrifice relies on cosmic links (*bandhu*s) between things, such as the eye and the sun, or the breath and the wind. The Upanisads and later philosophical schools develop their teachings of non-dualism from these essential connections. Tantric ritual traditions similarly thrive on mapping the principles of the cosmos onto everything from the alphabet to the human body (cf. PTlv, 210–12).

Homologies among the body parts feature prominently in Abhinavagupta's theology. Take, for example, this passage from the long commentary, which links the elements to the phonemes in the Sanskrit alphabet, to ritual mantras, to Siva-Sakti, and to the senses:

All mantras are of the nature of phonemes and all phonemes are the nature of Siva. All that is considered as drinkable or non-drinkable is (after all) simply water; all that is considered eatable or not eatable is (after all) simply what comes from the element earth. Whether beautiful or ugly, everything is (after all) the product of the element fire. Touch-

29. This is the approach of the Nyaya-Vaisesika school of Indian philosophy. James McHugh, *Sandalwood and Carrion: Smell in Indian Religion and Culture* (Oxford: Oxford University Press, 2012), 46.

30. The scale of "richness" proceeds as follows: "Odor is a special quality of earth, the element that is most rich in sensory properties. The other elements are ordered according to a decrease in sensory potential: water has no odor, but you may taste, see, touch, and hear it; fire can be seen, touched, and heard but not tasted or smelled; wind may be touched and heard; and finally, the element . . . 'space' (*akasa*) is only associated with sound." Ibid., 46.

31. See Bäumer, *Abhinavagupta's Hermeneutics*, 84–85.

able and untouchable are considered to be only a matter of the element air. The hole (whether of the male organ or the female organ) is only a matter of space. . . . There is nothing which is not a product of the five elements. (PTv, 222–23)

We have already observed one pattern of repetition, in which the thirty-six parts replicate on the divine, cosmic, and human levels. Now, their internal pattern of repetition connects them to one another.

A fivefold pattern based on the elements plays out in each of the subsections of the body. The gross and subtle elements parallel one another due to special associations: sound resonates in space, air's contact with the skin mediates touch, fire illuminates form for sight, water is the most basic carrier of taste, and earth is full of rich odors to smell.[32] Each of the organs of sense and action apprehends and acts upon its designated gross element, through the mediation of the corresponding subtle element:

Gross Elements	Subtle Elements	Sense Capacities	Action Capacities
Space	Sound	Hearing	Speaking
Air	Touch	Touching	Grasping
Fire	Form	Seeing	Walking
Water	Taste	Tasting	Excreting
Earth	Smell	Smelling	Procreating

The homologies do not stop with these twenty principles, which belong to the "knowable objects" (PTlv, 211). The principles on the side of the "knower" also relate to one another according to this pattern. These connections become more explicit by inserting five powers of consciousness—consciousness, bliss, intentionality, knowledge,

32. These elemental associations shift in the textual records. For example, the passage from PTv cited above links space not with hearing but with the organs of procreation. It also pairs taste (what can be eaten) with earth, but it does not explicitly name smell. Additionally, smell is associated not only with earth but also with air, or wind, which is "an element so vital to the diffusion of odors"; "one synonym for 'wind' is 'odor carrier' (*gandharvaha*)." McHugh, *Sandalwood and Carrion*, 6, 25.

and action—that link the conscious body to the limited and subjective body:[33]

Conscious Body	Power	Limited Body	Subjective Body[34]
Siva	Consciousness	Limitation in space	Individual subject
Sakti	Bliss	Limitation in time	Materiality
Sadasiva	Intentionality	Limited satisfaction	Intellect, Ego, Mind/Heart
Isvara	Knowledge	Limited knowledge	Organs of sensation
Suddhavidya	Action	Limited power	Organs of action

An inner logic governs these associations. If Siva's power is consciousness, then it is manifest through limitation in space as individual subjects. Sakti's power of bliss, limited in time, manifests as the material principle. The third degree of consciousness is associated with will or intentionality. When unable to satiate itself, it appears in the form of the inner instrument: intellect, ego, and mind/heart. Knowledge, the special power of the fourth principle, is manifest in the limited knowledge gathered by the organs of sensation. Similarly, action, the power of the fifth principle, correlates to the limited powers of the organs of action.

The short commentary closes the loop by tying the elemental body directly to the first degrees of consciousness, writing that the five parts of the conscious body are "formed" of the subtle elements, and their powers "are made of the five 'elemental' powers" (PTlv, 212).[35] The gross elements thus provide the foundation for the rest of the cosmic body, and these connections facilitate recognition of the divine presence in it.

33. Abhinavagupta and Yogaraja articulate these connections between the body parts and the powers in Abhinavagupta, *Introduction to Tantric Philosophy*, 118–21.

34. Cf. Flood, *Body and Cosmology*, 58–61, 65. The perceptive reader will notice that the limitations appear in reverse order. This is intentional on Abhinavagupta's part because the principles of pure consciousness appear as their "reflections or inversions" in the realm of *maya*. Ibid., 60.

35. So, too, for the limitations: "[limited power], formed of air, is that which impels and consists of a limited capacity for action; impure knowledge, formed of fire, which illuminates and consists of a limited capacity for knowing; *maya*: formed of water, is that which satiates; the power of attachment, . . . formed of earth, and consisting of intense affection, is by nature a stopping, an immersion" (PTlv, 211).

This comparative encounter yields intriguing possibilities within an emanation-return pattern. Hierarchy between spirit and matter is not an inevitable byproduct of such a scheme. According to the principle of reflection, the divine image appears, inverted, in the gross elements. Homological reasoning keeps the elemental body operative at all levels of the cosmos. From opposite ends of the spectrum, divine consciousness and the elements are both foundational to everything that exists. This horizontal, fluid, and relational pattern in one emanation worldview opens up new ethical possibilities for its counterpart in the Christian heritage. Let us return, then, to the question of the ecological and economic relationships it might support.

ECOLOGICAL-ECONOMIC BODIES

The elements are, indeed, foundational. We human beings rely utterly upon the topsoil of the Earth, fresh water, energy (fire), and clean air. The elements are also our body parts, quite literally. Upward of 60 percent of the adult human body is water. Our energy depends on calories grown from the Earth's soil. We cannot survive for more than few moments without a breath. Pollutants contained in these basic elements are incorporated into the body. Toxins sicken us through the insidious accumulation of carcinogens or the immediacy of an asthma attack.

As it turns out, the elements also rely utterly upon us. Larry Rasmussen explains that the Earth can no longer replace the resources humans are consuming:

> The resources of the ecosphere were produced in geologic time but humans use them in agricultural and urban time. The fundamental mismatch here might not matter so long as human populations are low and supply (fertile topsoil, good oil, clean air, and fresh water) is seemingly infinite relative to demand. But when soil loss exceeds soil regeneration and oceans acidify and energy resources are on the downside of the bell curve, then nature's natural recharge is history—at least until humans change their ways or dramatically decrease their numbers.[36]

36. Larry R. Rasmussen, *Earth-Honoring Faith: Religious Ethics in a New Key* (Oxford: Oxford University Press, 2013), 52.

In the second decade of the twenty-first century, unseasonable temperatures are perhaps the most tangible effects of the unsustainable lifestyle of the industrialized age. As individuals, we feel powerless to reverse trends like climate change. And, indeed, ecology (from the Greek *oikos*, household) requires far more than individual efforts to recycle and use energy efficiently. It requires a reordering of the house rules—the economy.

Christian ecotheologies have been working hard to change the house rules at the level of thought. Abhinavagupta's positioning of the gross and subtle elements within the body of divine consciousness also encourages us to view earth, water, air, fire, and space as part of the divine body, as objects of divine attention, and as foundational to everything that exists. Should a metaphor like this take hold in society, it might make a difference for climate change, ground water pollution, or any number of ecological concerns.

Other mechanisms, both theological and economic, circumvent a one-to-one correlation between the Earth as divine and healthy ecological practices.[37] The theological mechanisms can be illustrated by posters marketed to Christian youth. In one, a picture of Earth shines blue, green, and white against the black background of outer space with the caption, "This world is not my home." In a Christian two-worlds theology, what happens on this planet is inconsequential because heaven is the more enduring reality. In an even more jarring image, another poster features a rustic scene of a campsite nestled next to a mountain lake, complete with an eight-point buck looking on from the hill. This illustration bears the caption, "Droughts, floods, ecological disaster are signs of Jesus' return. *Praise God!*" This apocalyptic theology anticipates a clean break, leading to a brand-new heaven and Earth. The byproducts of global warming are celebrated as hastening the end. Such teachings rely on anthropologies that ignore and reject the deep relation and mutual constitution of the human being and the *oikos*.

---

37. For a summary of some of the literature on this theme, see Michelle Voss Roberts, "Worldly Advaita? Limits and Possibilities for an Ecofriendly Nondualism," *Religious Studies Review* 34, no. 3 (2008): 137–43.

Fortunately, the theological interventions are beginning to make a difference, and many individuals and congregations are reevaluating their relationship to creation. The ideas will make their full impact for ecology only when entire communities reorder their households—in other words, when the economy can meet the needs of all of its members. Yet significant obstacles block a living wage, clean air, and sustainable farming. One obstacle, of course, is the middle-class devotion to the cult of consumerism. The necessary level of asceticism—of respectful, limited use of material goods—seems nothing short of heroic, certainly not for mere mortals. Another obstacle is addiction to fossil fuels. In many parts of North America, the automobile and the airplane set the pace for patterns of work, travel, and leisure. And let us not forget the problem of scale: governments, large-scale farms, and corporations contribute to pollution, consumption, and depletion at much higher rates than private households. It is difficult for individuals to imagine how actions at the polls or in the marketplace can make a dent in these systemic problems.

Perhaps the largest obstacle for middle-class North Americans is our relative insulation from the consequences of our lifestyles. Our privilege shields us from the human toll that our ecological-economic practices are taking. Disposal sites for toxic waste are located far from the people and corporations responsible for producing them, usually among impoverished, predominantly African American and Latinx communities. Women and children of these communities bear the disproportionate burden of health consequences from exposure to these materials.[38] The ecological and health costs of energy consumption fueled by mountain-top removal, hydraulic fracturing, broken oil pipelines, and incessant wars over oil supply also remain hidden from the affluent. Such costs are not factored into our monthly gas and electric bills, and most of us do not directly become ill from their ecological aftershocks.

The privileges of gender, race, and class ensure that many of us do not feel, in our flesh and bones, the imperative to change the house rules. The highly publicized case of lead-polluted water in Flint, Michigan, has brought environmental racism to the public eye.

---

38. Rasmussen, *Earth-Honoring Faith*, 207.

"Environmental racism" names the "disproportionate exposure" of people of color "to polluted air, water, and soil" that results from the "poverty and segregation that has relegated many blacks and other racial minorities to some of the most industrialized or dilapidated environments."[39] In April 2014, the Flint city government made a calculated decision to save money by switching the city's water source from Lake Huron to the Flint River. The city minimized test results showing high levels of chemicals in the water. The corrosive river water caused lead from pipes to enter the drinking water—and into Flint's children, for whom "the long-term health effects of that poisoning may not be fully understood for years."[40] As residents are left with the financial burden of purchasing bottled water and the constant worry about exposure to the turgid water flowing from the tap, the story has cycled out of the news. Out of sight, out of mind.

On a global scale, not only earth and water but human beings themselves have become "resources" to consume. Theologian Nancy Pineda-Madrid exposes the violent changes that have occurred in her hometown of Juárez, Mexico, since the passage of the North American Free Trade Agreement (NAFTA) in 1993. The rapid expansion of manufacturing in this border city resulted in some 180,000 low-paying jobs, filled primarily by girls and women. At the same time, the murder rate spiked, including what she calls "feminicide," the widespread killing of women and girls, aided by a variety of interlocking economic, state, and religious or ideological interests.[41] As a result of an unrelenting demand for excessive profits and cheap consumer goods, "the female workers came to be known as *mujeres desechables* ('disposable women')."[42] Human resources, indeed.

It matters how we view the elements—both human and nonhuman —upon which human existence is founded. Current consumption patterns in the United States suggest that we view them not at all. They are invisible. Systemic racism, environmental catastrophe, class exploitation, and gender violence have become parts of our collective

---

39. John Eligon, "A Question of Environmental Racism in Flint," *New York Times*, January 21, 2016. http://tinyurl.com/yayt6w89.
   40. Ibid.
   41. Pineda-Madrid, *Suffering and Salvation*, 2.
   42. Ibid., 29.

bodies. These structural sins are, both literally and figuratively, the air that we breathe.

The thought experiment of imagining Christian teaching about the *imago Dei* through the prism of thirty-six body parts has the potential to welcome elemental foundations more fully into the doctrine. These interpretive choices render the doctrine less anthropocentric by incorporating the material elements into the image of God. They also expand the definition of the human. "Human embodiment cannot be relegated to secondary status in any theological anthropology," Amos Yong argues, "The human person must be understood to be *at least embodied*."[43] Elemental embodiment is constitutive of the human. Beyond this, every human existence is rooted, at an elemental level, in provisions by other people near and far. From the mother's milk, to the hands that baked this morning's bread, to the factory workers who stitched one's shirt, we become each other's bodies.

On a horizontal plane, the emanation pattern conveys a visual metaphor of mutuality and equality: human beings exist side-by-side with the natural world in relationships of interdependence and responsibility. Homological connections take this a step further with the claim that human beings are non-different from the natural world. By positioning the elements in a horizontal, homological relationship to everything else, Christians can place a high ethical and religious value on physicality, embodied difference, and interdependence with human and nonhuman nature. Anthropocentric habits, which exploit the elements as nothing more than resources to consume, controvert the fleshy, dusty truth of the incarnation that "starts with the big bang and explodes in the incarnated limits of God to include all matter, humanity, and all beings, to the limits of the universe."[44] These are powerful ideas. But how can we reverse the habits? How can we learn, at the cellular level, to reverence the divine body in all bodies and in the impoverished body of our planetary neighborhood?

43. Yong, *Theology and Down Syndrome*, 171.
44. Robert E. Shore-Goss, "Grace Is Green: Green Incarnational Inclusivities," in *Queering Christianity: Finding a Place at the Table for LGBTQI Christians*, ed. Robert E. Shore Goss, Thomas Bohache, Patrick S. Cheng, and Mona West (Santa Barbara, CA: Praeger, 2013), 72.

McFague, realistic about the difficulties of consumer restraint and radically material forms of neighbor love, is nevertheless optimistic. She points to studies on the brain's plasticity that show that "we might in fact be hard-wired for such self-development, given sufficient practice, training, and attention."[45] Congruent with her attention epistemology, she advocates practices of "attention to the other's material needs" as the means for spiritual and ecological transformation.[46] Our comparative framework adds another layer: practices that attend to the elemental body. To attend to material needs, we must tend the elements.

PRACTICES OF THE ELEMENTAL BODY

The Christian sacramental system already incorporates the elemental body. The waters flow in baptism. The soil produces the bread and wine of the Eucharist. These provide energy (fire) to the bodies of participants. In traditions that practice insufflation, the act of blowing air upon a candidate for baptism exorcises, purifies, and consecrates them with the Holy Spirit.

In the sacramental thought of Thomas Aquinas, the water, bread, wine, and breath are not merely external signs of an internal reality, as some later Protestants would have it. For him, God has designated such signs because "the condition of human nature . . . is such that it has to be led by things corporeal and sensible to things spiritual and intelligible."[47] They possess an instrumental power to "remedy" against sin and perfect the soul, and they imbue the faithful with "a certain spiritual character."[48] Once again, however, note the hierarchical dimension of his worldview. The material character of the sacraments, though essential, is also teleological. The purpose is *to lead* to the spiritual and intelligible.

Contemporary developments of Logos theology go further, affirming that it was Wisdom's good judgment to form the earth

45. Sallie McFague, *Blessed Are the Consumers: Climate Change and the Practice of Restraint* (Minneapolis: Fortress Press, 2013), 123.
46. Ibid., 96.
47. Thomas Aquinas, *Summa Theologiae*, trans. Fathers of the English Dominican Province, vol. 4 (New York: Benziger Brothers, 1948), 3.61.1.
48. Ibid., 3.63.1.

creature from the dust of the ground and breathe into its nostrils the breath of life (Gen 2:7). Niels Gregersen calls God's act of creation *deep incarnation*: "the divine *logos* . . . has assumed not only humanity, but the whole malleable matrix of materiality. By becoming 'flesh' in Jesus, God's eternal *logos* entered into all dimensions of God's world of creation."[49] Andy Buechel similarly reflects that "the fullness of the Divine in Christ does not imply that it is somehow 'lessened' anywhere else."[50] Elizabeth Johnson writes that a metaphysic of creation's participation in divine being means that, icon-like, "the world itself is a revelation and a sacrament . . . because the mystery of divine, self-giving presence is really mediated through the richness of the heavens and the earth."[51] These theologians do not direct the attention away from creation, as if materiality were a mere stepping stone. The heavens truly are telling the glory of God (Ps 19:1).

Like these contemporary ecological theologies, Western philosophy has begun to return to the elements it has neglected. Luce Irigaray observes in her reading of Heidegger that fire and earth, elements associated with Logos, war, and the father, have predominated in Western philosophy. She retrieves the fluid and ambiguous connection first shared with the mother through water and breath.[52] Taking a comparative perspective, ethicist Lenart Škof observes how this "forgetting of air" resembles the veil of *maya*: Western collective amnesia blocks "a spiritual and ethical exchange of air between the subjects themselves, as well as between the subjects and nature. Breath and air became mere biological (and anthropological) phenomena."[53] Life's elemental foundations in water and breath are essential for interpersonal and ecological ethics.

Škof wants to reweave the ties between microcosm and macrocosm, central to the Indian homologies, which modernity severed.

49. Niels Henrik Gregersen, "Deep Incarnation: The Logos Became Flesh," in *Transformative Theological Perspectives*, ed. Karen L. Bloomquist (Minneapolis: Lutheran University Press, 2009), 168–69.

50. Buechel, *That We Might Become God*, 73.

51. Elizabeth A. Johnson, *Abounding in Kindness: Writings for the People of God* (Maryknoll, NY: Orbis, 2015), 46–47.

52. Luce Irigaray, *The Forgetting of Air in Martin Heidegger*, trans. Mary Beth Mader (Austin: University of Texas Press, 1999).

53. Lenart Škof, *Breath of Proximity: Intersubjectivity, Ethics, and Peace* (Dordrecht: Springer, 2015), 153.

In the Vedic world, ritual forms a layer of the homology. He therefore proposes new rituals—"intersubjective rituals such as listening,
touch, caress, compassion, and loving-kindness"—to rekindle a sense
of common humanity and contribute to peace.[54] Most importantly,
these practices should involve sharing breath: "We keep protecting
ourselves while piling up more things around us than we actually
need (things we take from others, from nature), causing others to
suffocate, as they do not get enough of the elemental ingredients of
life—*breath* and peace."[55] Breath (*prana*) is the vital force that moves
through all parts of the body. Because the body is a microcosm,
breath touches every part of the cosmic and divine body: "Breathing
means staying alive and sensing everything and everyone that is alive
around us."[56] A practice as simple as tracing the path of the air as it
moves between interior and shared spaces can make us "more receptive to breath and the life of the other."[57]

Beyond the foundational Christian sacraments of earth (bread and
wine) and water (baptism), ecological attentiveness may require new
practices related to the elements of space and air, and to the breath
that connects all body parts. Space (*akasa*) pervades the cosmos. More
subtle than air, it is still a gross element. Associated with sound and
the capacities to hear and to speak, space connotes the openness of the
sky. If Christians claimed the space element for theological anthropology, could we hear the parts of creation that cry without words?
Air is related to the subtle element of touch, to the skin as the organ
of touch, and to the capacity to reach out and engage with others. It
resonates with our (limited) powers to act, which reflect the unlim-
ited divine capacity for action. These connect us to all aspects of
creation as worthy of attention. Breathing is perhaps the most immediate, most constant embodiment of these connections. If poor air
quality prevents deep breathing, we understand through impoverish-
ment just how vital fresh air is. But when lungs can stretch into a
full in-breath and out-breath, as many meditation practices recommend, the entire emanation and return of the cosmos is replicated in

54. Ibid., 191–92.
55. Ibid., 6; original emphasis.
56. Ibid., 8.
57. Ibid., 6.

the body.[58] The most basic spiritual practice of attention to reclaim, then, is simply to observe the rising and falling of the breath in the body.

Though not named as a body part, breath images God by connecting all parts—a holistic affirmation that returns Christians to our closest religious neighbors. In the early Hebrew Scriptures, the *nefesh chayah*—the living being—is a combination of the elements with divine breath. Rabbi Rachel Timoner explains that, for many Jews, this breath constitutes the image of the imageless God: "Breath is God's intimate gift to us—not only the first breath of the first human being, not only our first breath at the moment of our birth, but all breath, every breath, a moment-by-moment touch from God. . . . With the life breath, God gives us a sensibility, an awareness, a consciousness that makes us in God's image."[59] The most basic, elemental feature of every living moment is an object for attention and reverence. It permeates the image of God.

Breath is intimately related to attentiveness through our capacity for wonder. In awe, in dread, in astonishment, and in curiosity—we draw sudden breath, and we behold. Breathing, we make space within ourselves for others. Our senses come alive. Constricted spaces transform. Breathing together, there is room for all. The Earth begins to speak. Bodies unfold. Breath carries the voices of the exploited and oppressed. Wonderstruck, the privileged pay attention. Fully alive, humanity stretches out into the glory of God.

We share this breath for a limited span. The elements that compose our body are already passing out of us to be recycled into other bodies. The Christian tradition has always anchored its teachings of the goodness of the body in the hope for a resurrected body in the life to come. Our last stop on this itinerary, then, is to wonder how our comparative frame might hold space for eschatological bodies.

---

58. See Nancy L. Roth, *The Breath of God* (New York: Seabury, 2006); and, for a Hindu example, Swami Satchidananda, *The Breath of Life: Integral Yoga Pranayama Level I and Level II* (Buckingham, VA: Integral Yoga, 1993).

59. Rachel Timoner, *Breath of Life: God as Spirit in Judaism* (Brewster, MA: Paraclete, 2011), 14–15.

Epilogue: The Eschatological Body

O Lord, what are human beings that you regard them,
    or mortals that you think of them?
They are like a breath;
    their days are like a passing shadow.
—Psalm 144:3–4

In the Christian theological tradition, reflection on the body entails saying something about an afterlife. Like the resurrected Christ, the individual survives death in some fashion. The mechanism through which this occurs has usually been the soul. The soul's separability from the body promises that the individual will achieve likeness to God: immortality. Variations on this theme abound. Sometimes the soul rests dormant until the last days. Sometimes it lingers in purgatory or goes directly to heaven.

Still, the body must return. The resurrection of the body is one of the pillars of the Nicene Creed. Some of the most creative Christian minds have bent themselves toward working out the details of this teaching. Early on, they were prompted by the case of martyrs, who were torn apart in the arena, burned, or fed to fish. Despite leaving this life in pieces, martyrs would receive an eternal and unblemished body that would nonetheless be "their" body. Early Christian art depicts the beasts of the Earth rendering up the body parts of the martyrs on resurrection day.[1] Some theologians imagined that the resurrection body, regardless of age at death, will be thirty-three

---

1. See Carolyn Walker Bynum, *The Resurrection of the Body in Western Christianity, 200–1336* (New York: Columbia University Press, 1995), ch. 3 and plates 6, 7, 14, and 16.

years old: the age of the resurrected Christ and an age representing maturity and vigor. This body would be without sickness, and memories of one's sojourn on Earth would be merely notional, unable to cause pain. However, the resurrected body would also bear marks of these trials, with the saints and martyrs carrying their scars like badges of honor.[2]

Many Christians thus take eternal life to entail the removal of not only finitude but also the other limits we experience in the here and now. Augustine imagines that everyone will appear with beautiful, symmetrical features, in the "flower of youth." For him, the key to the resurrected body is that "there be no deformity, no infirmity, no languor, no corruption—nothing of any kind which would ill become that kingdom in which the children of the resurrection and of the promise shall be equal to the angels of God."[3] The imagined future holds no place for disability, no place for mortality.

This comparative exercise has encouraged Christians to consider an anthropology in which divinity reflects from at least thirty-six different surfaces in the human being. "If you ever looked at a diamond," Steven Greenebaum observes, "you know that it has many sides, many facets. Each facet is just a little different. Each facet reflects light just a bit differently. Yet would you ever say, 'This facet is right, but that facet is wrong'?"[4] If the *imago Dei* is imagined as a multifaceted jewel rather than a single reflective surface, it cannot support the traditional projections of a single age, ability, or appearance as the telos of the divine image. The brightness of God rebounds from humanity in scintillating shards of colored light.

The promise of blemish-free immortality comforts many people who long for a cure; but in our engagement with disability studies, we have also noted how the eschatological future has been translated into modern narratives of progress and "deployed in the service of compulsory able-bodiedness and able-mindedness."[5] The telos of perfection makes anything other than treatment and progress toward

2. In Mechthild of Magdeburg's vision of heaven, each Christian awaits crowns and riches proportionate to his or her virtue. See Mechthild, *Flowing Light*, 101–7.

3. Augustine, *City of God* 22.20.

4. Steven Greenebaum, *The Interfaith Alternative: Embracing Spiritual Diversity* (Gabriola Island, BC: New Society, 2012), 93–94.

5. Kafer, *Feminist, Queer, Crip*, 27.

a cure unimaginable. *How long will you need that wheelchair? Have you found the right medication to control your depression?* These common questions make normalization compulsory and disability a failure. When campaigns for a cure neglect the real needs of people in the present, the rhetoric of a future without disability communicates a desire that people with disabilities should not exist. Worse, eugenic movements, sterilization programs, and health care inequalities have curtailed the futures of people of color, poor people, and people with disabilities, who have been deemed defective.[6]

Furthermore, the longing for perfected, youthful, and symmetrical resurrection bodies resembles the prelapsarian fantasy that is often embedded in a curative orientation toward disability. Kafer observes that because "the nondisabled body/mind is the default position" whether a person has contracted a condition or has been disabled since birth, "we are expected to take up nostalgic positions toward our former selves, mourning what we have lost and what can now never be."[7] Christian theories about the resurrection of the body have insisted on the continuity of identity from this life to the next. The range of conditions that are considered disabilities, and the variety of ways that people relate to them, complicate this teaching. For people for whom congenital or other conditions have accompanied them throughout their lives, what former self would be restored in the resurrection? For persons who have become who they are through experiences of impairment, what would ensure their continuity of identity in an impairment-free afterlife? Although Augustine is confident that God can correct "all that is wrong" and supply "all that is defective . . . without destroying the integrity of the substance,"[8] it is difficult to imagine ourselves in an eschaton where key components of our identities, creativity, and relationships are eliminated.

The resurrected body of Jesus bears not glorious scars but open wounds (John 20:24–29). If Christ's resurrection entails new and ongoing life in the community that remembers him, then his resurrection body, the ecclesial body of Christ, must not omit all reference to his disability. Similarly, what sense would it make for a person with

6. Ibid., 29–33.
7. Ibid., 43.
8. Augustine, *City of God* 22.19.

Down syndrome to live on in the memories of his family somehow "purified" of that condition? How strange it would be to remember everything about my grandmother, except for how she managed life with multiple sclerosis. We would not be remembering her, but replacing her. The person who "lived on" would be someone who never existed. In closing the wounds of Christ, we close the very vulnerability and relationality that marks us as the image of God. In closing off the embodied diversity we know now, we shade the brilliant multiplicity of the divine reflection.

COMPARATIVE COMPLICATIONS

A comparative approach to eschatological bodies further complicates that question of what survives after death. Abhinavagupta has given us an array of categories to consider. Which of the thirty-six body parts advance to the afterlife? All of them? Perhaps only the parts essential to individuality, such as the *purusa*? Indian traditions allow for an individual person to experience multiple lives, but usually not with the same name and form. If Christian eschatology requires a fully identical self, then must we posit an entirely new cycle of creation/emanation, in which every being emerges and evolves in precisely the same manner as before?

Contemporary science poses a similar set of questions: If something—a mind or center of consciousness—somehow survives apart from the brain and the rest of its body, what guarantees its identity over time? Can its physical body be reconstituted after its decomposition and journey through the bodies of innumerable plants and animals, and somehow remain the same person? Philosophers, too, imagine scenarios in which individual selfhood might persist for eternity, but most will admit that any such scheme "is at best a 'likely tale.'"[9]

In this book, we have attempted to uncouple the essence of the creature from the mind, the rational soul, or any such faculty, so that Christian theological anthropology might better recognize the importance of entire persons and their many body parts. We have

9. Hasker, *Emergent Self*, 235.

also considered the central role of limitation, including limitation in time, in each reflection of the divine. This thought experiment might help to disentangle some of the assumptions and desires behind the desire for immortality. Could the hope for eternal individuality and the obsession with individual salvation be a feature of *ahamkara*, the part of the subjective body that develops—and clings to—a sense of being a particular "I"? Could releasing the grasp on individual immortality mark a return to some of the holistic wisdom of pre-Hellenic biblical views of the human person as *nefesh*—a unified, living, and mortal being?

But how disquieting to release our attachment to individual immortality! As a painkiller, it is powerful. Even so, releasing it might allow us to do theology starting from the limited and graced bodies we actually have. "All flesh is grass" (Isa 40:6). Grass flourishes for a short time, returns to the earth, and is repurposed for new life. Perhaps we have been wrong to assume that our individuality, or our mind, is the part of the *imago Dei* that survives. It has escaped our notice that the elements are the only parts of us that certainly continue beyond this life. At bottom, all life is elemental. Resurrection: new life arises out of the ashes, the corpses, and the compost. Matter lives on, reconstituted, in God.

Indeed, nothing is lost to God. Just as our loved ones live on in our memories—just as parents, authors, and architects leave their mark on the people, documents, and places that survive—divinity holds everything that has ever existed. Not only do our elemental selves live on in others who will flourish, like a breath, on this planet, but we life-loving humans might also accept that every one of our fragile deaths is held within divine consciousness. As Elizabeth Johnson promises in light of Christ's solidarity with creation, none of God's creatures dies alone.[10] Every life is worthy of divine attention and regard.

10. Johnson, *Ask the Beasts*, 201–6.

NON-DUALISM AND THE ESCHATON

In truth, we cannot know with absolute certainty what resurrection means, but the divine presence in all things offers a taste of this reality. Just as the brain or the rational capacity is not the sum total of a person, so too, faith cannot be reduced to cognitive belief. Eschatology—the doctrine of final things—expresses not only the hopes of the living but also the grace we already know within our existence. The coming of the kin-dom of God is both *already* and *not yet*. As we long for its fullness, we glimpse its inbreaking: when the dividing wall of hostility breaks down (Eph 2:14), we realize the vulnerable, luminous, relational image of God in ourselves and in one another.

A monstrous week in July 2016 left the United States reeling and in threat of permanent fracture along ancient lines of racial tension and gun violence. On Tuesday, July 4, the tally of people shot by guns over the holiday weekend stood at eighty-four in the city of Chicago alone, fourteen of whom died. On Wednesday came video footage of Alton Sterling, a black man, being shot and killed by white police officers. On Thursday, we witnessed Philando Castile, who had been pulled over for a broken taillight, being shot by a police officer as he reached for his wallet. His girlfriend and her four-year-old daughter sat inches away in the car. On Friday, a sniper opened fire on police at a Black Lives Matter rally, killing five officers. And on Sunday, the people mourned openly in the pews.[11] We sang,

O Savior, from the mountain side,
Make haste to heal these hearts of pain;
Among these restless throngs abide,
O tread the city's streets again:

Till all shall learn compassion's might
And follow where your feet have trod,
Till glorious from your realm of light,
Shall come the city of our God.[12]

11. Anna Fleig, "A Green & Growing Faith: Faithful Questioning," sermon, Congregational United Church of Christ, July 10, 2016, mp3 audio, 18:01, http://tinyurl.com/ydxsjpll.

12. Frank Mason North, "Where Cross the Crowded Ways of Life," in *The New Century Hymnal* (Cleveland, OH: Pilgrim, 1995), hymn 543, http://tinyurl.com/ydy7qqe8.

If only we would "learn compassion's might"—that would be heaven. Heaven: to have no doubt that one's life matters. Heaven: to register the mattering of others in the depths of the amygdala, in the reflexes of the trigger finger. To recoil from the grim habits of violence, exclusion, and self-loathing that hold us captive. This afterlife is not a static condition of wholeness but, as theologian Shelly Rambo describes it, a fragile and ongoing condition of *after-living*—living after the collective trauma—that opens us to peace.[13]

Worship unveils the divine presence and attention that is present in every moment and every place, and worship transcends the walls and rites of the church. Analyzing the sacramental sensitivities of Marcella Althaus-Reid, Andy Buechel calls attention to three characteristics of worship: "1) enact a communal relationship to the Divine, 2) demonstrate radical inclusivity, and 3) offer resistance to hegemonic forces in church, state, and society."[14] Certainly, the deep, holy, and firm affirmation of the *imago Dei* has manifested itself with these qualities in the rites of the gay bar, the protest, the sit-in, and the festival. And certainly, Christian worship often fails on these criteria, undergirded by theologies that trim the edges off the image of God. The church's sacraments should not, for that reason, be abandoned. They participate in the already-and-not-yet dimensions of the eschaton. The church, after all, is "made up of people who are themselves in the process of being divinized, and not yet there."[15] The heavenly banquet—communal, inclusive, and countercultural—is still breaking in.

Living into the fullness of the divine image means becoming fully transparent to divine attention and love. Jesus, as the image of God, is an icon into this reality. Christ personifies, in his own delimited way, what each of us might become through grace. As Thomas Reynolds puts it, "The power of God is unseemly and strange, disclosing itself paradoxically not in autonomy but in relational vulnerability. . . . Hence, far from vindicating the conventional and normal, Christ's

13. Shelly Rambo, "Salvation in the After-Living: Reflections on Salvation with Joshua Ralston and Sharon Betcher," in *Comparing Faithfully: Insights for Systematic Theological Reflection*, ed. Michelle Voss Roberts (New York: Fordham University Press, 2016), 302–8.

14. Buechel, *That We Might Become God*, 80.

15. Ibid., 92.

work actually subverts it by pointing to the palpable and life-giving presence of the divine in human vulnerability."[16] What would lead us to believe that this "unseemly and strange" way of loving would reverse course in the afterlife, fulfilling human fantasies of limitlessness and autonomy, but abrogating the way of Jesus? His way was never the way of isolation or sameness. Through this icon, "in his fleshy body," the letter to the Colossians avers, "God was pleased to reconcile to Godself all things" (Col 1:22, 20). Difference, multiplicity, and limited bodies endure as the sites of the divine, reconciling presence.

Despite a vastly different conception of what happens after an individual's earthly life, Abhinavagupta's non-dual tradition teaches something remarkably similar about the present. As Bettina Bäumer explains, "in the highest non-dualism, even the duality of bondage and liberation is absent."[17] The ideal of liberation while living (*jivanmukti*) affirms that one need not wait until death to experience union with the Absolute. Non-dualism applies to the relation between this life and what comes next. Christians can similarly affirm that the "end" is the recognition of what is really real—that divinity permeates every cell. In this sense at least, these body parts *are* the eschatological body, and the eschaton is already here.

The disciples on the road to Emmaus finally recognize Christ in their midst through the breaking of the bread. The contemplative practices described in each chapter aim to develop exactly this kind of awareness—a full-bodied, engaged attentiveness to the embodiment of the divine image in one another. Resurrection life lifts the veils of separation. We recognize God, all in all. In every facet of God's diverse reflections, the divine image shines.

16. Reynolds, *Vulnerable Communion*, 197.
17. Bäumer, *Abhinavagupta's Hermeneutics*, 70, cf. 21.

Bibliography

Abhinavagupta. *Abhinavagupta's Philosophy of Revelation: An Edition and Annotated Translation of* Malinislokavarttika I, *1–399*. Translated by Jürgen Hanneder. Groningen: Egbert Forsten, 1998.

―――. *Essence of the Exact Reality, or, Paramarthasara of Abhinavagupta*. Translated by B. N. Pandit. New Delhi: Munshiram Manoharlal, 1991.

―――. *An Introduction to Tantric Philosophy: The Paramarthasara of Abhinavagupta and Its Commentary of Yogaraja*. Translated by Lyne Bansat-Boudon and Kamalesha Datta Tripathi, 59–316. London: Routledge, 2011.

―――. *Paratrisikalaghuvrttih*. In *The Triadic Heart of Siva: Kaula Tantricism of Abhinavagupta in the Non-Dual Shaivism of Kashmir*, by Paul Eduardo Muller-Ortega, 203–32. Albany: State University of New York Press, 1989.

―――. *Para-trisika-Vivarana: The Secret of Tantric Mysticism*. Edited by Bettina Bäumer. Translated by Jaideva Singh. Delhi: Motilal Banarsidass, 1988.

Angell, Marcia. "The Epidemic of Mental Illness: Why?" *The New York Review of Books*, June 23, 2011. http://tinyurl.com/y9g4nbez.

Anselm. *Proslogion: With the Replies of Gaunilo and Anselm*. Translated by Thomas Williams. Indianapolis: Hackett, 2011.

Aquinas, Thomas. *Summa Theologiae*. Translated by the Fathers of the English Dominican Province. 5 vols. New York: Benziger Brothers, 1948.

Augustine. *The City of God, Books VIII–XVI*. Translated by Gerald G.

Walsh and Grace Monahan. Fathers of the Church 14. Washington, DC: Catholic University Press of America, 2008.

_____. *The City of God, Books XVII–XXII.* Translated by Gerald G. Walsh and Daniel J. Honan. Fathers of the Church 24. Washington, DC: Catholic University Press of America, 2008.

_____. *Confessions.* Translated by Henry Chadwick. Oxford: Oxford University Press, 1991.

_____. *Tractates on the Gospel of John, 11–27.* Translated by John W. Rettig. Fathers of the Church 79. Washington, DC: Catholic University of America Press, 1988.

_____. *The Trinity.* Edited by John E. Rotelle. Translated by Edmund Hill. Brooklyn, NY: New City, 1991.

Bamford, Nicholas. *Converging Theologies: Comparing and Converging Terms within the Byzantine and Pratyabhijña (Kashmir Saivite) Traditions within a Space for Convergence.* Delhi: ISPCK, 2011.

Bäumer, Bettina. *Abhinavagupta's Hermeneutics of the Absolute Anuttaraprakriya: An Interpretation of his Paratrisika Vivarana.* Shimla: Indian Institute of Advanced Study, 2011.

_____. Bettina Sharada Bäumer. http://tinyurl.com/y722fzjx.

Beattie, Tina. *Theology after Postmodernity: Divining the Void—A Lacanian Reading of Thomas Aquinas.* Oxford: Oxford University Press, 2013.

Berila, Beth. *Integrating Mindfulness into Anti-Oppression Pedagogy: Social Justice in Higher Education.* London: Routledge, 2016.

Betcher, Sharon V. "Revisiting *Midnight's Children*: Critical Disability and Postcolonial Studies Interventions in Christology." *Postscripts: The Journal of Sacred Texts and Contemporary Worlds* 7, no. 3 (2016): 311–34.

_____. *Spirit and the Obligation of Social Flesh: A Secular Theology for the Global City.* New York: Fordham University Press, 2014.

_____. *Spirit and the Politics of Disablement.* Minneapolis: Fortress Press, 2007.

Bidlack, Bede Benjamin. "What Child Is This? Jesus, Lord Lao, and Divine Identity." In *Comparing Faithfully: Insights for Systematic Theological Reflection*, edited by Michelle Voss Roberts, 195–215. New York: Fordham University Press, 2016.

Black, Kathy. *A Healing Homiletic: Preaching and Disability*. Nashville: Abingdon, 1996.

Block, Jennie Weiss. *Copious Hosting: A Theology of Access for People with Disabilities*. New York: Continuum, 2002.

Bourgeault, Cynthia. *The Heart of Centering Prayer: Nondual Christianity in Theory and Practice*. Boulder: Shambhala, 2016.

Briggs, Sheila. "Can an Enslaved God Liberate? Hermeneutical Reflections on Philippians 2:6–11." *Semeia* 47 (1989): 137–53.

Buechel, Andy. *That We Might Become God: The Queerness of Creedal Christianity*. Eugene, OR: Cascade, 2015.

Bynum, Carolyn Walker. *The Resurrection of the Body in Western Christianity, 200–1336*. New York: Columbia University Press, 1995.

Caputo, John D. *The Insistence of God: A Theology of Perhaps*. Bloomington: Indiana University Press, 2013.

_____. *The Weakness of God: A Theology of the Event*. Bloomington: Indiana University Press, 2006.

Carey, Benedict. "Most Will Be Mentally Ill at Some Point, Study Says." *New York Times*, June 7, 2005. http://tinyurl.com/y8v72gzd.

Cassidy, Laurie. "Picturing Suffering: The Moral Dilemmas in Gazing at Photographs of Human Anguish." In *She Who Imagines: Feminist Theological Aesthetics*, edited by Laurie Cassidy and Maureen H. O'Connell, 103–24. Collegeville, MN: Liturgical, 2012.

Cassidy, Laurie, and Maureen H. O'Connell, eds. *She Who Imagines: Feminist Theological Aesthetics*. Collegeville, MN: Liturgical, 2012.

Christie, Douglas E. *The Blue Sapphire of the Mind: Notes for a Contemplative Ecology*. New York: Oxford University Press, 2013.

Clooney, Francis X. *Comparative Theology: Deep Learning Across Religious Borders*. Chichester: Wiley-Blackwell, 2010.

Clough, David L. *On Animals*. Vol. 1, *Systematic Theology*. London: T&T Clark, 2012.

Cobb, John B., Jr., and David Ray Griffin. *Process Theology: An Introductory Exposition*. Philadelphia: Westminster, 1976.

Coleman, Monica A. *Bipolar Faith: A Black Woman's Journey with Depression and Faith*. Minneapolis: Fortress Press, 2016.

Cone, James H. *The Cross and the Lynching Tree*. Maryknoll, NY: Orbis, 2013.

Copeland, M. Shawn. "The Critical Aesthetics of Race." In *She Who Imagines: Feminist Theological Aesthetics*, edited by Laurie Cassidy and Maureen H. O'Connell, 73–86. Collegeville, MN: Liturgical, 2012.

———. *Enfleshing Freedom: Body, Race, and Being*. Minneapolis: Fortress Press, 2010.

Creamer, Deborah Beth. *Disability and Christian Theology: Embodied Limits and Constructive Possibilities*. Oxford: Oxford University Press, 2009.

DeFranza, Megan K. *Sex Difference in Christian Theology: Male, Female, and Intersex in the Image of God*. Grand Rapids: Eerdmans, 2015.

Division of Clinical Psychology. "Division of Clinical Psychology Position Statement on the Classification of Behaviour and Experience in Relation to Functional Psychiatric Diagnoses: Time for a Paradigm Shift." May 2013. PDF. http://tinyurl.com/ycc9kypg.

Doniger O'Flaherty, Wendy, trans. *The Rig Veda: An Anthology*. New York: Penguin, 1981.

Douglas, Kelly Brown. *Sexuality and the Black Church: A Womanist Perspective*. Maryknoll, NY: Orbis, 1999.

Dupuche, John. *Abhinavagupta: The Kula Ritual, as Elaborated in Chapter 29 of the Tantraloka*. Delhi: Motilal Banarsidass, 2003.

———. *Jesus the Mantra of God: An Exploration of Mantra Meditation*. Melbourne: David Lovell, 2005.

Dyczkowski, Mark. *The Doctrine of Vibration: An Analysis of the Doctrines and Practices of Kashmir Shaivism*. Albany: State University of New York Press, 1987.

———. The Trika Shaivism of Kashmir: Lectures, Writings, Music by Mark Dyczkowski. http://www.anuttaratrikakula.org/.

Eckhart, Meister. *Meister Eckhart: The Essential Sermons, Commentaries, Treatises, and Defense*. Translated by Edmund Colledge and Bernard McGinn. New York: Paulist, 1981.

———. *Meister Eckhart: Teacher and Preacher*. Edited by Bernard McGinn. New York: Paulist, 1986.

Eiesland, Nancy L. *The Disabled God: Toward a Liberatory Theology of Disability*. Nashville: Abingdon, 1994.

Eligon, John. "A Question of Environmental Racism in Flint." *New York Times*. January 21, 2016. http://tinyurl.com/yayt6w89.

Farris, Joshua R. "A Substantive (Soul) Model of the *Imago Dei*: A Rich Property View." In *The Ashgate Research Companion to Theological Anthropology*, edited by Joshua R. Farris and Charles Taliaferro, 165–78. Burlington, VT: Ashgate, 2015.

Farris, Joshua R., and Charles Taliaferro, eds. *The Ashgate Research Companion to Theological Anthropology*. Burlington, VT: Ashgate, 2015.

Fleig, Anna. "A Green and Growing Faith: Faithful Questioning." Sermon, Congregational United Church of Christ, July 10, 2016. Mp3 audio. 18:01. http://tinyurl.com/ydxsjpll.

Flood, Gavin. *Body and Cosmology in Kashmir Saivism*. San Francisco: Mellen Research University Press, 1993.

―――. *The Tantric Body: The Secret Tradition of Hindu Religion*. London: I. B. Tauris, 2005.

Fulkerson, Mary McClintock, and Marcia W. Mount Shoop. *A Body Broken, a Body Betrayed: Race, Memory, and Eucharist in White-Dominant Churches*. Eugene, OR: Cascade, 2015.

Gandolfo, Elizabeth O'Donnell. *The Power and Vulnerability of Love: A Theological Anthropology*. Minneapolis: Fortress Press, 2015.

Gonzalez, Michelle A. *Created in God's Image: An Introduction to Feminist Theological Anthropology*. Maryknoll, NY: Orbis, 2007.

Gorringe, Timothy. *The Education of Desire: Towards a Theology of the Senses*. Harrisburg, PA: Trinity International, 2002.

Graham, Elaine L. *Representations of the Post/Human: Monsters, Aliens, and Others in Popular Culture*. New Brunswick, NJ: Rutgers University Press, 2002.

Green, Joel B. "Why the *Imago Dei* Should Not Be Identified with the Soul." In *The Ashgate Research Companion to Theological Anthropology*, edited by Joshua R. Farris and Charles Taliaferro, 179–90. Burlington, VT: Ashgate, 2015.

Greenebaum, Steven. *The Interfaith Alternative: Embracing Spiritual Diversity*. Gabriola Island, BC: New Society, 2012.

Gregersen, Niels Henrik. "Deep Incarnation: The Logos Became Flesh." In *Transformative Theological Perspectives*, edited by Karen L. Bloomquist, 167–82. Minneapolis: Lutheran University Press, 2009.

Hagen, Chris. "Rancho Los Amigos—Revised." Centre for Neuro Skills. 1997. http://tinyurl.com/ybwqhlmu.

Halloran, Nathan. "*Maya, Anava Mala* and Original Sin: A Comparative Study." *Journal of Hindu-Christian Studies* 26, no. 1 (2013): 67–79.

Harshaw, Jill. *God Beyond Words: Christian Theology and the Spiritual Experiences of People with Profound Intellectual Disabilities.* London: Jessica Kingsley, 2016.

Hartshorne, Charles. *Omnipotence and Other Theological Mistakes.* Albany: State University of New York Press, 1984.

Hasker, William. *The Emergent Self.* Ithaca, NY: Cornell University Press, 1999.

———. "Why Emergence?" In *The Ashgate Research Companion to Theological Anthropology*, edited by Joshua R. Farris and Charles Taliaferro, 151–61. Burlington, VT: Ashgate, 2015.

Haslam, Molly Claire. *A Constructive Theology of Intellectual Disability: Human Being as Mutuality and Response.* New York: Fordham University Press, 2012.

Hicks, Derek S. *Reclaiming Spirit in the Black Faith Tradition.* New York: Palgrave Macmillan, 2012.

Hill Fletcher, Jeannine. *Motherhood as Metaphor: Engendering Interreligious Dialogue.* New York: Fordham University Press, 2013.

Howell, Nancy R. "Theological Anthropology." In *Creating Women's Theology: A Movement Engaging Process Thought*, edited by Monica A. Coleman, Nancy R. Howell, and Helene Tallon Russell, 145–57. Eugene, OR: Pickwick, 2011.

Hyman, Steven E. "The Diagnosis of Mental Disorders: The Problem of Reification." *Annual Review of Clinical Psychology* 6, no. 1 (2010): 155–79.

Irenaeus. *Against Heresies.* Translated by Alexander Roberts and William Rambaut. In *Ante-Nicene Fathers*, vol. 1. Edited by Alexander Roberts, James Donaldson, and A. Cleveland Coxe. Buffalo, NY: Christian Literature, 1885. Revised and edited by Kevin Knight. New Advent: n.p., 2009. http://tinyurl.com/2hp4ya.

Irigaray, Luce. *The Forgetting of Air in Martin Heidegger.* Translated by Mary Beth Mader. Austin: University of Texas Press, 1999.

Jabès, Edmond. *From the Book to the Book: An Edmond Jabès Reader.* Translated by Rosmarie Waldrop. Hanover, NH: University Press of New England, 1991.

Jantzen, Grace M. *God's World, God's Body.* Philadelphia: Westminster, 1984.

Jensen, David H. *God, Desire, and a Theology of Human Sexuality.* Louisville: Westminster John Knox, 2013.

Johnson, Elizabeth A. *Abounding in Kindness: Writings for the People of God.* Maryknoll, NY: Orbis, 2015.

_____. *Ask the Beasts: Darwin and the God of Love.* London: Bloomsbury, 2014.

_____. *She Who Is: The Mystery of God in Feminist Theological Discourse.* New York: Crossroad, 1992.

Kafer, Alison. *Feminist, Queer, Crip.* Bloomington: Indiana University Press, 2013.

Kaufman, Gordon D. *In Face of Mystery: A Constructive Theology.* Cambridge, MA: Harvard University Press, 1993.

Kearney, Richard. *Anatheism: Returning to God after God.* New York: Columbia University Press, 2010.

Keller, Catherine. *The Face of the Deep: A Theology of Becoming.* London: Routledge, 2003.

Knight, Jennie S. *Feminist Mysticism and Images of God: A Practical Theology.* St. Louis: Chalice, 2011.

Koch, Carl, and Joyce Heil. *Created in God's Image: Meditating on Our Body.* Winona, MN: Saint Mary's Press, 1991.

LaCugna, Catherine Mowry. *God for Us: The Trinity and Christian Life.* San Francisco: HarperSanFrancisco, 1993.

Lakshmanjoo, Swami. *Kashmir Shaivism: The Secret Supreme.* Albany: State University of New York Press, 1988.

Lawrence, David Peter. *Rediscovering God with Transcendental Argument: A Contemporary Interpretation of Monistic Kashmiri Saiva Philosophy.* Albany: State University of New York Press, 1999.

_____. "Remarks on Abhinavagupta's Use of the Analogy of Reflection." *Journal of Indian Philosophy* 33, no. 5–6 (2005): 583–99.

Lindbeck, George A. *The Nature of Doctrine: Religion and Theology in a Postliberal Age.* Philadelphia: Westminster, 1984.

Lott, Eric J. *God and the Universe in the Vedantic Theology of Ramanuja: A Study in His Use of the Self-Body Analogy.* Madras: Ramanuja Research Society, 1976.

Lovejoy, Arthur O. *The Great Chain of Being: A Study of the History of an Idea.* Cambridge, MA: Harvard University Press, 1942.

Lukin, Josh. "Disability and Blackness." In *The Disability Studies Reader*, edited by Lennard J. Davis, 308–15. London: Taylor & Francis, 2013.

Lund, Sarah Griffith. *Blessed Are the Crazy: Breaking the Silence about Mental Illness, Family, and Church.* St. Louis: Chalice, 2014.

Marchand, Peter. *The Yoga of the Nine Emotions: The Tantric Practice of Rasa Sadhana.* Rochester, VT: Destiny, 2006.

Marion, Jean-Luc. *God without Being.* Translated by Thomas A. Carlson. Chicago: University of Chicago Press, 1991.

Marks, Lawrence E. *The Unity of the Senses: Interrelations among the Modalities.* New York: Academic Press, 1978.

Masson, Jeffrey Moussaieff. *Beasts: What Animals Can Teach Us about the Origins of Good and Evil.* New York: Bloomsbury, 2014.

McFague, Sallie. *Blessed Are the Consumers: Climate Change and the Practice of Restraint.* Minneapolis: Fortress Press, 2013.

_____. *The Body of God: An Ecological Theology.* Minneapolis: Fortress Press, 1993.

_____. "Is God in Charge?" In *Essentials of Christian Theology*, edited by William C. Placher, 101–16. Louisville: Westminster John Knox, 2003.

_____. *Models of God: Theology for an Ecological, Nuclear Age.* Philadelphia: Fortress Press, 1987.

McGinn, Bernard. *The Flowering of Mysticism: Men and Women in the New Mysticism—1200–1350.* New York: Crossroad, 1998.

_____, ed. *Meister Eckhart and the Beguine Mystics: Hadewijch of Brabant, Mechthild of Magdeburg, and Marguerite Porete.* New York: Continuum, 1994.

_____. "Theological Summary." In *Meister Eckhart: The Essential Sermons, Commentaries, Treatises, and Defense*, 24–61. Translated by Edmund Colledge and Bernard McGinn. New York: Paulist, 1981.

McGrath, Alister E. *Christian Theology: An Introduction.* 5th ed. Oxford: Wiley-Blackwell, 2011.

McHugh, James. *Sandalwood and Carrion: Smell in Indian Religion and Culture.* Oxford: Oxford University Press, 2012.

Mechthild of Magdeburg. *The Flowing Light of the Godhead.* Translated by Frank Tobin. New York: Paulist, 1998.

Mesle, C. Robert. *Process Theology: A Basic Introduction.* St. Louis: Chalice, 1993.

Miller, Barbara Stoler, trans. *The Bhagavad-Gita: Krishna's Counsel in Time of War.* New York: Bantam, 1986.

Moltmann, Jürgen. *The Crucified God: The Cross of Christ as the Foundation and Criticism of Christian Theology.* Minneapolis: Fortress Press, 1993.

Mount Shoop, Marcia W. *Let the Bones Dance: Embodiment and the Body of Christ.* Louisville: Westminster John Knox, 2010.

Muller-Ortega, Paul Eduardo. *The Triadic Heart of Siva: Kaula Tantricism of Abhinavagupta in the Non-Dual Shaivism of Kashmir.* Albany: State University of New York Press, 1989.

Nemec, John. *The Ubiquitous Siva: Somananda's Sivadrsti and His Tantric Interlocutors.* Oxford: Oxford University Press, 2011.

Newell, J. Philip. *Listening for the Heartbeat of God: A Celtic Spirituality.* New York: Paulist, 1997.

Niebuhr, Reinhold. *The Nature and Destiny of Man: A Christian Interpretation.* Vol. 1, *Human Nature.* New York: Charles Scribner's Sons, 1964.

North, Frank Mason. "Where Cross the Crowded Ways of Life." In *The New Century Hymnal,* hymn 543. Cleveland, OH: Pilgrim, 1995. http://tinyurl.com/ydy7qqe8.

Nussbaum, Martha C. *The Fragility of Goodness: Luck and Ethics in Greek Tragedy and Philosophy.* Cambridge: Cambridge University Press, 1986.

Olivelle, Patrick, trans. *Upanisads.* Oxford: Oxford University Press, 1996.

Padoux, André. *Vac: The Concept of the Word in Selected Hindu Tantras.* Translated by Jacques Gontier. Albany: State University of New York Press, 1990.

Pandey, Kanti Chandra. *Abhinavagupta: An Historical and Philosophical Study.* 2nd ed. Varanasi: Chowkhamba Sanskrit Series, 1963.

Paulsell, Stephanie. *Honoring the Body: Meditations on a Christian Practice.* San Francisco: Jossey-Bass, 2002.

Peterson, Anna L. *Being Human: Ethics, Environment, and Our Place in the World.* Berkeley: University of California Press, 2001.

Petrey, Taylor G. *Resurrecting Parts: Early Christians on Desire, Reproduction, and Sexual Difference.* London: Routledge, 2016.

Pineda-Madrid, Nancy. *Suffering and Salvation in Ciudad Juárez.* Minneapolis: Fortress Press, 2011.

Placher, William C., ed. *Essentials of Christian Theology.* Louisville: Westminster John Knox, 2003.

Porete, Marguerite. *The Mirror of Simple Souls.* Translated by Ellen Babinsky. New York: Paulist, 1993.

Pseudo-Dionysius. *The Complete Works.* Translated by Colm Luibheid. New York: Paulist, 1987.

Rahner, Karl. *The Trinity.* Translated by J. F. Donceel. London: Continuum, 2001.

Rambachan, Anantanand. *The Advaita Worldview: God, World, and Humanity.* Albany: State University of New York Press, 2006.

Rambo, Shelly. "Salvation in the After-Living: Reflections on Salvation with Joshua Ralston and Sharon Betcher." In *Comparing Faithfully: Insights for Systematic Theological Reflection,* edited by Michelle Voss Roberts, 296–316. New York: Fordham University Press, 2016.

Rasmussen, Larry L. *Earth-Honoring Faith: Religious Ethics in a New Key.* Oxford: Oxford University Press, 2013.

Ratié, Isabelle. *Le Soi et l'autre: Identité, Différence et Altérité dans la Philosophie de la Pratyabhijña.* Leiden: Brill, 2011.

Rawlinson, Andrew. Foreword to *Body and Cosmology in Kashmir Saivism,* by Gavin D. Flood, ix–xii. San Francisco: Mellen Research University Press, 1993.

Reynolds, Thomas E. *Vulnerable Communion: A Theology of Disability and Hospitality.* Grand Rapids: Brazos, 2008.

Rosenblum, Lawrence D. *See What I'm Saying: The Extraordinary Powers of Our Five Senses.* New York: W. W. Norton, 2010.

Roth, Nancy L. *The Breath of God: An Approach to Prayer.* New York: Seabury, 2006.

Ruether, Rosemary Radford. *Sexism and God-Talk: Toward a Feminist Theology.* Boston: Beacon, 1993.

Ryan, Thomas, ed. *Reclaiming the Body in Christian Spirituality*. New York: Paulist, 2004.

Sacks, Jonathan. *The Dignity of Difference: How to Avoid the Clash of Civilizations*. New York: Continuum, 2002.

Sahi, Jyoti. *Holy Ground: A New Approach to the Mission of the Church of India*. Auckland, NZL: Pace, 1998.

Saiving, Valerie. "The Human Situation: A Feminine View." In *Womanspirit Rising: A Feminist Reader in Religion*, edited by Carol P. Christ and Judith Plaskow, 25–42. New York: Harper & Row, 1979.

Saliers, Don E. *Worship Come to Its Senses*. Nashville: Abingdon, 1996.

Samuel, Geoffrey. "The Subtle Body in India and Beyond." In *Religion and the Subtle Body in Asia and the West: Between Mind and Body*, edited by Geoffrey Samuel and Jay Johnston, 33–47. London: Routledge, 2013.

Samuel, Geoffrey, and Jay Johnston, eds. *Religion and the Subtle Body in Asia and the West: Between Mind and Body*. London: Routledge, 2013.

Sanderson, Alexis. "Saivism and the Tantric Traditions." In *The World's Religions: The Religions of Asia*, edited by Friedhelm Hardy, 128–72. London: Routledge, 1988.

Sanford, Matthew. *Waking: A Memoir of Trauma and Transcendence*. Emmaus, PA: Rodale, 2006.

Saracino, Michele. *Being about Borders: A Christian Anthropology of Difference*. Collegeville, MN: Liturgical, 2011.

Satchidananda, Swami. *The Breath of Life: Integral Yoga Pranayama Level I and Level II*. Buckingham, VA: Integral Yoga, 1993.

Scull, Andrew. *Madness: A Very Short Introduction*. Oxford: Oxford University Press, 2011.

SenSharma, Deba Brata. *The Philosophy of Sadhana: With Special Reference to the Trika Philosophy of Kashmir*. Albany: State University of New York Press, 1990.

Shore-Goss, Robert E. "Grace Is Green: Green Incarnational Inclusivities." In *Queering Christianity: Finding a Place at the Table for LGBTQI Christians*, ed. Robert E. Shore-Goss, Thomas Bohache, Patrick S. Cheng, and Mona West, 65–81. Santa Barbara, CA: Praeger, 2013.

Silburn, Lilian. *Kundalini: The Energy of the Depths*. Albany: State University of New York Press, 1988.

Singh, Jaideva. Introduction to *Pratyabhijñahrdayam: The Secret of Self-Recognition*, 1–33. Translated by Jaideva Singh. 4th rev. ed. Delhi: Motilal Banarsidass, 2003.

———, trans. *Vijñanabhairava or Divine Consciousness: A Treasury of 112 Types of Yoga*. Delhi: Motilal Banarsidass, 1979.

———, trans. *The Yoga of Delight, Wonder, and Astonishment: A Translation of the Vijñana-Bhairava*. Albany: State University of New York Press, 1991.

Škof, Lenart. *Breath of Proximity: Intersubjectivity, Ethics, and Peace*. Dordrecht: Springer, 2015.

Stiker, Henri-Jacques. *A History of Disability*. Translated by William Sayers. Ann Arbor: University of Michigan Press, 1999.

Stoeger, William R. "God, Physics, and the Big Bang." In *The Cambridge Companion to Science and Religion*, edited by Peter Harrison, 173–89. Cambridge: Cambridge University Press, 2010.

Stuart, Elizabeth. "Disruptive Bodies: Disability, Embodiment and Sexuality." In *Good News of the Body: Sexual Theology and Feminism*, edited by Lisa Isherwood, 166–84. New York: New York University Press, 2000.

Suchocki, Marjorie Hewitt. *Divinity and Diversity: A Christian Affirmation of Religious Pluralism*. Nashville: Abingdon, 2003.

Teel, Karen. *Racism and the Image of God*. New York: Palgrave Macmillan, 2010.

Thunberg, Lars. *Microcosm and Mediator: The Theological Anthropology of Maximus the Confessor*. 2nd ed. Chicago: Open Court, 1995.

Tiemeier, Tracy Sayuki. "Engendering the 'Mysticism' of the Alvars." *The Journal of Hindu Studies* 3, no. 3 (2010): 337–53.

Timoner, Rachel. *Breath of Life: God as Spirit in Judaism*. Brewster, MA: Paraclete, 2011.

Tracy, David. *Blessed Rage for Order: The New Pluralism in Theology*. New York: Seabury, 1975.

Vanier, Jean. *Becoming Human*. New York: Paulist, 1998.

Vanier, Jean, and John Swinton. *Mental Health: The Inclusive Church Resource*. London: Darton, Longman & Todd, 2014.

Voss Roberts, Michelle, ed. *Comparing Faithfully: Insights for Systematic Theological Reflection*. New York: Fordham University Press, 2016.

———. "Embodiment, Anthropology, and Comparison: Thinking-Feeling with Abhinavagupta." In *How to Do Comparative Theology*, edited by Francis X. Clooney and Klaus von Stosch. New York: Fordham University Press, 2017.

_____. *Tastes of the Divine: Hindu and Christian Theologies of Emotion*. New York: Fordham University Press, 2014.

_____. "Worldly Advaita? Limits and Possibilities for an Ecofriendly Nondualism." *Religious Studies Review* 34, no. 3 (2008): 137–43.

_____. Practicing the Image of God. https://www.michellevossroberts.com/practices.html.

Waal, Frans de. "What I Learned from Tickling Apes." *New York Times*, April 8, 2016. http://tinyurl.com/hsul48h.

Weil, Simone. *Waiting for God*. Translated by Emma Craufurd. New York: Putnam, 1951.

Welch, Sharon D. *Sweet Dreams in America: Making Ethics and Spirituality Work*. New York: Routledge, 1999.

Whitehead, Alfred North. *Process and Reality: An Essay in Cosmology*. Edited by David Ray Griffin and Donald W. Sherburne. Corrected edition. Gifford Lectures. New York: Free Press, 1978.

Wiesel, Elie. *Night*. Translated by Marion Wiesel. New York: Macmillan, 2012.

Williams, Delores S. *Sisters in the Wilderness: The Challenge of Womanist God-Talk*. Maryknoll, NY: Orbis, 1993.

Winkler, Patricia A. "Traumatic Brain Injury." In *Umphred's Neurological Rehabilitation*, edited by Darcy A. Umphred, Rolando T. Lazaro, Margaret L. Roller, and Gordon Burton, 753–90. 6th ed. St. Louis: Mosby, 2013.

Yong, Amos. *Theology and Down Syndrome: Reimagining Disability in Late Modernity*. Waco, TX: Baylor University Press, 2007.

Zizioulas, John D. *Being as Communion: Studies in Personhood and the Church*. Crestwood, NY: St. Vladimir's Seminary Press, 1985.

_____. *Communion and Otherness: Further Studies in Personhood and the Church*. Edited by Paul McPartlan. London: T&T Clark, 2006.

Index

Abhinavagupta, xxx, xxxiii–xl,
  8n19, 26, 35–37, 58, 62, 90,
  99, 110–11, 120, 131–32, 137,
  140n34, 142, 154, 158
ableism, 32, 38, 42, 49–51, 115,
  152–53
absence, divine, 20–21, 22, 93
afterlife, xviii, 151, 153–55,
  157–58
Altizer, Thomas, 21n42
Americans with Disabilities Act of
  1990, 82
Anselm, 55, 71
anthropocentrism, 87–88, 89, 92,
  145
anthropomorphism, 55, 87n26, 91
anxiety, 31, 40, 43, 46, 73
apatheia, 54–55, 70
apophatic theology, 14–16, 21, 22,
  56
Aquinas, Thomas, xx, xxiii, xxv,
  14, 55, 85, 90, 135–36, 146
Aristotle, xxv, 48, 107
asceticism, xlvi, 143
attention, 10, 146, 149, 157; epistemology, xxxviii, xlv, 146.
  See also practices of attention
Augustine, xxiv, 10, 25–26, 29, 31,
  65, 102, 109, 152, 153

Bamford, Nicholas, 13n25, 82
baptism, 117–19, 146, 148
Bäumer, Bettina, xxxvn26, 158
Beattie, Tina, 133n19, 135–36
being, 15, 17–19, 21–22, 24,
  61–62, 88–90, 114, 127,
  131–36, 155
Berila, Beth, xliii–xliv, 99–100
Betcher, Sharon V., 45, 46n44, 47,
  95, 115–16
Bhagavad Gita, 38n18, 80, 81n7
biological reductionism, 78–79
Black, Kathy, 51, 113
Black Lives Matter, xix, 156
blindness, xxix, 29–30, 107, 113,
  114n37
body, 74, 102–4, 106, 108–16,
  117, 123, 134; of Christ,
  101–2, 103, 105, 116–19,
  120–23, 125, 152–54; of consciousness, xxxvi, xxxix, 7–9,
  58, 129, 133; subtle, xxxvii;
  world as God's, 56–58, 59,
  129, 131
body parts. See *tattvas*
boundaries, 25, 36, 50, 98, 115,
  121
brain injury, 1–2
breath, xvii, 26, 89, 113, 138,
  146–49

Buber, Martin, 23–24
Buechel, Andy, 147, 157

Caputo, John D., 133n19
Cassidy, Laurie, 75–76
cerebral palsy, 4–5
Christ, 11, 27, 48–49, 55, 62, 63,
    70, 73, 82n9, 91, 103, 104;
    image of, xxviii, 53, 119–23.
    See also Jesus
Christie, Douglas E., 98
Christology, xxiv, xxviii–xxix, 82,
    90, 103, 117, 120. See also
    Logos
church, xix, 94, 101, 104–5,
    116–23, 157
classical theism, 54–56, 60, 67
clergy, xlii, 47–48
climate change, 57, 129, 142
Clooney, Francis X., xxxiin18
Clough, David L., 89, 91
Cobb, John B., Jr., 40, 60n15
Coleman, Monica A., 93–95
Colossians, 119n48, 158
coma, xxvii–xxix, 1–2, 27–28
comparative theology,
    xxxii–xxxiil, xxxv–xxxvi,
    xxxix, 54
Cone, James H., 73–74
consciousness: divine, xxxv,
    xxxvii–xxxvix, xlvi, 7, 12–13,
    37, 64, 70, 81, 84–89, 130,
    134, 136, 141–42, 155; self-,
    3, 6, 10, 24, 31, 86–89,
    131–32. See also under limita-
    tion

constructive theology, xx, xxxii,
    xxxv
consumerism, 49, 143–44, 146
contemplation. See meditation
Copeland, M. Shawn, 74–75
cosmology, xxxviii, 35–36, 80,
    129–30, 132n14
Creamer, Deborah Beth, xli,
    32–35, 38, 57, 63n25, 68
creation, xxxvii–xxxix, 8–9,
    11–12, 20, 31, 35–36, 44, 52,
    54, 57–61, 63–64, 67, 68–72,
    90–91, 97; emanation, xxxix,
    12, 21, 129–37, 141, 145, 148;
    ex nihilo, 12, 71n48; in Scrip-
    ture, xviii, xxiii–xxiv, 86
creativity, xxvi–xxvii, 3, 26, 38,
    44, 60, 67, 153
cross, 48–49, 73–74
crucifixion, 55, 73, 122
culture, xxxii, 46, 66, 87, 115
cure, 47–48, 50–51, 94, 115,
    152–53

death, xviii, xxvn7, 29, 31, 44, 57,
    153–55
Descartes, 77
desert monastics, 97–98
desire, 37, 42–44, 54, 70–72,
    84–85, 110–11
Diagnostic and Statistical Manual
    of Mental Disorders, 78–79
difference, xxv, xxiv, xxxviii,
    9n20, 57n9, 58n13, 59, 63,
    74, 88, 112–13, 116, 133, 137,
    158

disability: Christian theologians of, xix–xx, xxvii, 33–35, 51–52, 63n25; developmental, xxvii, xli, 4–6, 93, 95; and discrimination, 33–35; limits model of, xli, 33–35, 49, 68, 80; medical model of, 33–35, 50; minority model of, 34; profound intellectual, xxviii, xli, 4–6, 9, 23–26, 32

diversity, 36, 47, 52, 59, 66, 136, 154

docetism, xxiv, 136

dominion, xxvi–xxvii, 60, 97

dualism, 77, 78n1, 69n43, 81; Platonic, xxiv–xxv; spirit–matter, xxiv, 100, 126, 141

Dupuche, John, xxxviii, 26–28, 99, 132n14

early Christianity, xviii, xx, xxviii, 11, 44, 70–71, 98, 129, 133

Earth, xxiii–xxiv, xxvi, 57, 62, 66, 89, 125–31, 141; as element, 126, 131, 137–38, 142, 147

Eckhart, Meister, 15, 16–20, 22

ecology, 30, 41, 47, 57n8, 147, 148

economy, 30, 46, 49, 51, 126, 141–44

ego, 39, 46; ego-sense (ahamkara), 80, 82–84, 92, 93–97, 99, 140, 155

Eiesland, Nancy L., 49, 53, 62–63, 113, 114

elements, 89, 125, 132, 134, 135–42, 144–49, 155

emanation-return. See creation

embodiment, xxiv, xliii–xlvi, 3–4, 33, 36, 57, 63. See also body

emergentism, 2–4, 7, 9, 23

emotion, 25–26, 84–85, 97–99

Enlightenment, 30, 127, 129

epistemology. See under attention

equality, 10, 17–19, 48, 145

eschatology, xxix, 91, 118, 120, 151–58

Eucharist, 101–2, 116–18, 121–23, 146

Farris, Joshua R., 119

feminicide, 144

feminist theology, xix, xxiii, xliii, 40, 60–61, 67–68, 78

finitude, 31, 44, 53, 68, 81, 152

Flint, Michigan, 143–44

Flood, Gavin, xxxix, 89, 132

freedom, 31, 37, 43, 44, 60–61, 113

Gandolfo, Elizabeth O'Donnell, 48n50, 61–62, 69, 74–75

gender, xxix, 31, 112, 143, 144

Genesis, xviii, xxv, xxvi, 45, 85–86

genitals, 109, 111–12, 139

Glasgow Coma Scale, 1–2, 4, 7

globalization, 39, 41, 47, 49, 51, 98, 126, 128, 144

Gnosticism, xxiv, xxxi, 103–4

God: as Absolute, 22, 43, 158; as Father, 10, 17–19, 43; as

Good Beyond Being, 131–36; image of (see *imago Dei*); kindom of, 156; as Lady Love, 16; likeness of, 75, 82n10, 103, 151; knowledge of, 12–13, 27–28; models of, xxxi, 54–57, 128

goddesses, xxxiv–xxxvi, 42

goodness, xxiv, 3, 21, 31, 48, 71, 90, 102, 132, 136, 149

Green, Joel B., xviii

Griffin, David Ray, 40

gross elements, 89, 126, 134, 137–42, 148

Hadewijch of Antwerp, 16

Halloran, Nathan, 69

Hartshorne, Charles, 58, 64

Haslam, Molly Claire, xxviii, 4–6, 23–24

healing, 30, 44, 51, 94, 113–14

heaven. *See* afterlife

hierarchy, xix–xx, xxvii, xxxix, xlii, 21–22, 89n33, 90, 112, 131–38, 141

Hill Fletcher, Jeannine, 43

Holy Spirit, 11, 13, 17–19, 104, 146

homology, 138–41, 145, 147–48

Howell, Nancy R., 87, 88

human nature, xxiii, 30–32, 55, 112, 145–46

I-It, 23

I-This. *See* subject-object

I-Thou, 23–24

identity, xxvii–xxxviii, xxxiii, 35, 40, 46, 74, 94, 98, 100, 153–54

image, original (*bimba*), xxxvii–xxxl, xlvn43. See also *imago Dei*, reflection

imagination, xxv, 72–76, 83

imago Dei, xxvii–xxx, xxxv–xxxvi, xxxix, xliv–xlvi, 6, 9, 13, 22–28, 79–85, 87, 89, 95, 100, 102–5, 112–13, 126, 129, 131, 145, 152, 155, 157; and *imago Christi*, 116–23; and limitation, 31–32, 35, 39, 53–54, 59, 62, 67–68, 70–71

immanence, 20, 58, 115, 126–29

immutability, 40, 54, 57n9, 64

impairment, 2, 34, 50–51, 79–80, 113–15, 153

imperialism, xxxi–xxxii, 46

impurity, 69n43, 96–100, 110, 132

incarnation, 12n23, 38, 53, 55, 62, 65–67, 82n9, 91, 99, 102–3, 109, 116–22, 135–37, 145; deep, 147; radical, 66, 94

individual subject (*purusa*), 80–83, 85, 96–99, 140, 154

individuality, xli, 84, 117–18, 154–55

industrialization, 142–44

intellect, xxiii, xxv, xxvi, 13, 41–42, 83n13, 93, 95–100, 140. *See also under* disability

interdependence, xxvii–xxviii, 47, 112, 145

interreligious dialogue, xxxi–xxxiii

Irenaeus of Lyons, 102–5, 117
Irigaray, Luce, 147

Jabès, Edmond, 22
Jensen, David H., 111
Jesus, xxiv, xxvi, xxix, xxx, 27–30,
    55, 65, 68, 91, 94, 101–2, 108,
    113, 117–22. *See also* Christ
John (book of), 11, 17, 18, 27, 28,
    30, 44, 91, 102, 153
Johnson, Elizabeth A., 60–61, 90,
    91, 106, 147, 155
Judaism, xxx, 35, 44, 149

Kafer, Alison, 41, 45, 50–51,
    75n62, 153
Katha Upanisad, 81n7, 96
Kaufman, Gordon D., 5
Keller, Catherine, 71n48
kenosis, 48–49
Knight, Jennie S., xliii–xliv
knowledge, xli, 8n19, 12–13,
    27–28, 37, 41–42, 44, 50, 54,
    63–64, 67, 73, 83, 93, 113,
    139–40. *See also* limitation

lament, 51, 56, 74, 76, 86–87, 99,
    156
Lawrence, David Peter, 12
Lent, 99
liberation theology, xix, xxiii, xliii
likeness, xxv–xxvi, 48, 75, 82n10,
    103, 151
limitation, xli–xlii, 28, 30, 48–52,
    54, 59–67, 93–95, 140; of
    consciousness (*see* maya); of

knowledge, 37, 41–42, 50,
    54, 63–67; of power, 37,
    39–41, 50, 54, 59–63; of satis-
    faction, 37, 42–44, 54, 70–72;
    in space, 37, 46–47, 54,
    63–67; in time, 37, 44–45, 50,
    54, 63–67
Lindbeck, George A., 5
liturgy, xiv, xliii
Logos, xxxi, xli, 11–13, 91, 103,
    146–47; and Sophia, 11–13.
    See also Christology
Lonergan, Bernard, 12
Lord's Supper. *See* Eucharist
love, xxvii–xxviii, 13, 38, 43–44,
    110, 125, 146; divine, 52,
    55–56, 60–64, 71–71, 75, 85,
    119, 157; toward God, xxvi,
    16, 38, 55
lynching, 73–74

maleness, xix, xxix, xliii, 25
manas. See mind/heart
manifestation, xxxvii–xxxix, xliii,
    27, 83, 130
mantra, 26–28, 120, 138
marginalization, 49, 64, 117
material nature (*prakrti*), 80–84,
    93, 96–97, 126n3
maya, 18, 20, 28, 36–38, 59, 69,
    96, 131–32, 140n35, 147
McFague, Sallie, xxxin17, xlv,
    56–57, 64, 128–29, 131, 146
McGinn, Bernard, 15
McHugh, James, 138, 139n32
Mechthild of Magdeburg, 16

meditation, xxxvii, xli, xliv, 14, 20, 21–22, 26–27, 72–74, 97, 99, 106, 111, 120, 131, 148, 158

memory, xxv, 10, 83, 98

mental illness, xli, 20, 77–81, 93–94

metaphysics, xviii, 20–22, 35, 77, 129–30, 133, 135, 147

method, xix, xx, 26, 54, 114

microcosm, xxxvii, 9, 24, 82n8, 93, 106, 108, 112–13, 147–48

mind, xvii, xx, xxv, xxx, xxxi, 10, 13, 17, 77–78, 80, 83–86, 93, 97–100, 127, 154–55

mind/heart, xli, 13n26, 80, 82–85, 96–99, 140

mirror, xxxii, xxxvi–xxxviii, 7, 9, 25, 27–28, 58n13, 64, 67, 83, 85, 95, 105, 111, 116, 119, 137

modernity, 30, 43, 73, 77, 96, 127–29, 147, 152

Moltmann, Jürgen, 55

monism, xxxiv, xxxvi, 19

morality, xx, xxv, xxvii, 3, 48, 74, 78, 109

motherhood, 8, 43, 61–62, 72, 145, 147

Mount Shoop, Marcia W., 112, 121, 123

mourning. *See* lament

Muller-Ortega, Paul Eduardo, 130

mutuality, xxvii, 41, 72, 111, 116, 117, 119, 145

natural theology, 12n23

nefesh, xviii, xx, 86, 149, 155

Neoplatonism, 31, 129–32, 134–35

New Testament, xviii, xxx, 11

Nicene Creed, 151

Niebuhr, Reinhold, 30–32, 38–47, 53, 67–68, 73

non-dualism, xxxix, 15–20, 138, 156–58

normativity, xix, 45, 74

omnibenevolence, 54

omnipotence, 21, 35, 37, 39, 48, 49, 52–54, 60, 63–64

omnipresence, 35, 54, 66

omniscience, 35, 37, 52–54, 63

ontotheology, 13, 18, 21n42, 130, 133, 135

organs, 101, 102, 104–6, 111–21, 139, 140; of action, 108–11, 140; of sense, 106–8, 137, 140

Origen, 86

othering, xvii, xix

panentheism, xxxvi, 57–58

pantheism, xxxvi, 57

Paratrisika-laghuvrtti, xxxv, 36n14, 38n16, 42, 82n8, 83n11, 96, 105, 134, 138–40

Paratrisika-Vivarana, xxxv–xxxviii, 8n18, 36n14, 58, 83, 85, 89, 111, 120, 137, 139

paternalism, 46

patriarchy, xxiii, xliii

Paul, apostle, xxviii, 31, 48, 101, 109, 117, 121

peace, 148, 157

perception, 8, 9n20, 10, 13–15, 26, 84, 89, 106

pervasion, 132, 134, 135

phenomenology, 3, 118

Pineda-Madrid, Nancy, xxxiii, 144

placenta, 111–12

pleasure, 9, 26, 58, 123

pluralism, xix–xx, 98

pollution, xxxv, 110, 142, 143

Porete, Marguerite, 16

postcolonial theology, xix, xxxii, 46–47

postmodernism, 133–35

power, 11, 37, 49, 56, 58, 68, 69n43, 70–72, 74, 83–85, 104, 113, 140. See also under limitation

practices of attention, xliii–xlvii, 25–28, 47–52, 72–76, 96–100, 120–23, 146–49, 158

pride, 31, 39–43, 46–47, 50, 68, 73, 97

process theology, 40, 54, 60–61, 64–65, 67

procreation, 111–13, 139n32

prostheses, 34, 50, 114–16

Protestant Reformation, 127, 129

Pseudo-Dionysius, 15n28, 70, 85, 131, 135

queer theology, xix

race, 32, 143; environmental

racism, 143–45; –ism, xxiv, 73–75, 156

Rahner, Karl, 108–9

Rambo, Shelly, 157

Ranchos Los Amigos Scale, 1–2, 4, 7

Rasmussen, Larry L., 141

rationalism, xxv–xxviii, 10–13, 25, 77, 81, 86–87, 114, 156. See also soul

recognition, 4, 7, 12–13, 24–26, 82

redemption, 55, 60, 65, 69, 71, 73, 91, 95, 103, 125, 128

reflection, xxx, xxxii, 6, 9, 13, 19, 25, 35, 58, 65–66, 102, 104, 106, 125, 133, 136–37, 141, 154; *pratibimba*, xxxv–xxxviii, xlv

relationality, 43, 59, 72, 103, 106, 108, 119, 154

resurrection, xviii, 3, 63, 99, 122, 133, 136, 149, 151–55

Reynolds, Thomas E., 5–6, 51–52, 157–58

Rosenblum, Lawrence D., 107–8

sacrament, 120–23, 127, 131–32, 147–48, 157

Sakti, xxxiv–xxxviii, 8, 11, 14, 19, 61, 81, 110, 140. See also Siva–Sakti

Saiva Siddhanta, xxxiv, 69n43, 132

Saivism, non-dual, xx, xxx–xxxv, 6, 12, 24, 26–27, 58n13, 61, 69n43, 80, 83, 132n12

Saliers, Don E., xlviin45, 103
salvation, xviii, 17, 30, 55, 65, 82,
    91, 103, 108, 127, 136, 155
Samkhya, 80, 81n7, 82, 132n12
Sanford, Matthew, xvii, xx
Saracino, Michele, 98–99
sarx, xviii, 91
satisfaction, limited. *See* desire
science, 1–3, 41, 79, 86–87, 128,
    129n7, 130, 154; Big Bang,
    129, 145; evolution, 52, 65,
    87, 90–91
Scull, Andrew, 77–78
self: -consciousness, 3, 10, 24, 31,
    86–89, 131–32; -hood, 81, 84
senses, xlii, xlvi–xlvii, 83–84, 96,
    106–8, 116–23, 138
sex, 16, 26, 31, 102, 109–13
sexuality, 32, 69, 110–13
sin, xxix, 29–31, 33, 38–41, 44,
    46–47, 59, 67–69, 102, 118,
    146; and disability, xxix,
    29–31, 33, 53, 68, 113–14;
    original, 68–69, 127
Singh, Jaideva, 8n18, 26n52,
    83n13, 84, 120, 137n28
Siva, xxxiv, xxxvii–xxxix, 7–8, 11,
    13–15, 37–39, 61, 72, 81, 83,
    106, 110–12, 120, 130–31,
    138, 140. *See also* Siva–Sakti
Siva–Sakti, xxxiv–xxxvi, 8–9, 11,
    13, 24, 37–38, 61, 81, 85, 112,
    133–34, 137–38
Škof, Lenart, 147–48
slaves, 46, 48–49, 57, 69n43

solidarity, 40, 48, 51, 61–62, 72,
    74, 123, 155
Sophia. *See under* Logos
soteriology, xxxviii, 82
soul, xxiv–xxv, 3–4, 16–20, 22–23,
    79, 92; immortal, 77–78, 151;
    rational, xviii, 31, 81, 87, 154
sound, 27, 106, 108, 126, 139, 148;
    primordial, 12, 27
space: as element, 126, 139–40,
    142, 148. *See also* imitation
Stuart, Elizabeth, 33
subject-object, xxxix, 4, 8–9,
    15–20, 25, 26, 37, 59, 69n43
subtle elements, 126, 134, 138–40,
    142, 148
Suchocki, Marjorie Hewitt, 66
suffering, 45, 50, 53, 55–56, 57n9,
    61–63, 69–71, 73–76, 122–23
Swinton, John, 95
synesthesia, 108
systematic theology, 91

Tantra, xxxv, xxxvii, 26, 110–11,
    138
*tattva*s, xxxvii–xl, xliv, xlvii, 154; as
    conscious body, 8–9, 13–15,
    25, 26; as elemental body,
    125, 131, 132n14, 134,
    137–41, 145, 148; as engaged
    body, 104–6, 122–23; as sub-
    jective body, 80–81, 88–89,
    96
theological anthropology: func-
    tional, xxvi; multipolar, 106;

relational, xxvii–xxviii, 65;
    substance, xxvi, 6
Timoner, Rachel, 149
tower of Babel, 29, 44
tragedy, 44–45, 56, 63, 67, 70, 73,
    128
transcendence, 3, 20, 25, 26, 42,
    57–58, 94, 115, 126; self-,
    6n14, 31–32
transformation, 28, 56, 62, 75,
    104, 120, 146
trauma, 1–2, 20–21, 45, 93, 157
Trika, xxx, xxxiv–xxxv, 80n6,
    110–11
Trinity, xxvi, xli, 10–13, 16–19,
    22, 55, 59, 61–62, 135, 137;
    social, 105, 108–9, 117–18
Trump, Donald J., xix

union, 15–20, 28, 82, 158; in dif-
    ference, 11, 17, 26

Vanier, Jean, 95
Vedas, xxxv, 110

void, 7, 11, 20–22, 25, 28, 93–94
vulnerability, xxviii, 47, 48n50, 52,
    55, 61–62, 75–76, 91, 116,
    121–22, 156–58

Waal, Frans de, 87–88, 92
wholeness, 51, 63, 115, 157
will: buddhi, 83; free, 29, 64, 68;
    iccha, 61, 85; as moral capac-
    ity, xix, xxv–xxvi, 10, 31, 85,
    97, 99, 130, 140
Williams, Delores S., xxviin11
women, xxiii–xxv, xxix, xliii, 15,
    25, 40, 43, 57, 60, 94, 112,
    122, 143–44
worldview, 126–29, 134, 141;
    horizontal, 134, 136, 137,
    141, 145

yearning. See desire
Yong, Amos, 2–7, 23, 145

Zizioulas, John D., 105–6, 117–18